The Lyrics of Richard de Semilli:

A Critical Edition and Musical Transcription

medieval & renaissance texts & studies

VOLUME 81

The Lyrics of Richard de Semilli:

A Critical Edition and Musical Transcription

Susan M. Johnson

Medieval & Renaissance texts & studies
Binghamton, New York
1992

Library of Congress Cataloging-in-Publication Data

Johnson, Susan M., 1951–
    The lyrics of Richard de Semilli : a critical edition and musical
transcription / Susan M. Johnson.
        p. cm. — (Medieval & Renaissance texts & studies ; v. 81)
    Includes bibliographical references and index.
    ISBN 0–86698–092–X
        1. Trouvères. 2. Trouvère songs. 3. Songs, Old French—Texts.
4. Music—France—500–1400—History and criticism. 5. French poetry—
To 1500—History and criticism. I. Semilli, Richard de. II. Title.
III. Series.
ML182.J6 1992
782.4'3—dc20   91–31586
                                                                       CIP
                                                                        MN

This book is made to last.
It is set in Palatino, smythe-sewn
and printed on acid-free paper
to library specifications

Printed in the United States of America

Contents

Acknowledgments

I would like to express my appreciation to a number of people who have helped with this project. First, to Vincent Corrigan who reviewed the musical transcriptions. The commentary on the music was reviewed by Hendrik van der Werf whose comments and suggestions proved most valuable. I would also like to thank Margaret Switten and the National Endowment for the Humanities who brought the three of us together at an institute on the Medieval Lyric.

Special thanks goes to Donald Freund and David Turnbow who prepared the photo-ready copies of the music using Finale software.

Finally, for his constant encouragement and support, I am especially grateful to Samuel N. Rosenberg who introduced me to Old French lyric and the art of editing.

Bibliography and List of Abbreviations

Aubry, Pierre. *Trouvères et Troubadours*. Paris: Alcan, 1909.

[Aubry, *T et T*]

———. *Trouvères and Troubadours: A Popular Treatise*. Translated by Claude Aveling. New York: Cooper Square, 1969.

[Aubry, *T and T*]

———, and Alfred Jeanroy. *Le Chansonnier de l'Arsenal (trouvères du XII*e*–XIII*e* siècle). Reproduction phototypique du manuscrit 5198 de la Bibliothèque de l'Arsenal*. 2 vols. Paris: P. Geuthner, 1909–12.

[Aubry, *Arsenal*]

Bartsch, Karl. *Altfranzösische Romanzen und Pastourellen*. Leipzig, 1870. Reprint. Darmstadt: Wissenschaftliche Buchgesellschaft, 1967.

[Bartsch]

Baumgartner, Emmanuèle, and Françoise Ferrand. *Poèmes d'amour des XII*e* et XIII*e* siècles*. Bibliothèque médiévale 10/18, 1581. Paris: Union Générale d'Editions, 1983. [Baumgartner]

Bec, Pierre. *La Lyrique française au moyen âge (XII*e* et XIII*e* siècles). Contribution à une typologie des genres poétiques médiévaux*. Vol. 1, *Etudes*; Vol. 2, *Textes*. Paris: A. & J. Picard, 1978–79. [Bec]

Burger, Michel. *Recherches sur la structure et l'origine des vers romans*. Geneva: Droz; Paris: Minard, 1957. [Burger]

Chambers, Frank M. *An Introduction to Old Provençal Versification*. Philadelphia: American Philosophical Society, 1985. [Chambers]

Cluzel, I. M., and L. Pressouyre. *Les Origines de la poésie lyrique d'oïl et les premiers trouvères*. 2d ed. Paris: A. G. Nizet, 1969. [Cluzel]

Cremonesi, Carla. *Lirica francese del medio evo*. Milan: Istituto editoriale cisalpino, 1955. [Cremonesi]

Dragonetti, Roger. *La Technique poétique des trouvères dans la chanson courtoise*. Bruges, 1960. Reprint. Geneva: Slatkine Reprints, 1979.

[Dragonetti]

Foulet, Alfred, and Mary Blakely Speer. *On Editing Old French Texts*. Lawrence, KS: Regents Press of Kansas, 1979.

Foulet, Lucien. *Petite syntaxe de l'ancien français*. 3d ed. Paris: Champion, 1977. [Foulet, *Petite syntaxe*]

Frappier, Jean. *La Poésie lyrique en France aux XIIe et XIIIe siècles.* Paris: Centre de Documentation Universitaire, [1963].   [Frappier]

Gennrich, Friedrich. *Die altfranzösische Rotrouenge.* Halle: Max Niemeyer, 1925.   [Gennrich, *Rotrouenge*]

———. *Grundriss einer Formenlehre des mittelalterlichen Liedes als Grundlage einer musikalischen Formenlehre des Liedes.* Halle: Max Niemeyer, 1932.   [Gennrich, *Grundriss*]

———. "Grundsätzliches zu den Troubadour- und Trouvèreweisen." *Zeitschrift für romanische Philologie* 57 (1937): 31–56.
                                                                    [Gennrich, *ZfrP*]

———. *Troubadours, Trouvères, Minne- und Meistergesang.* Cologne: Arno Volk, 1951.   [Gennrich, *TTMM*]

———. *Troubadours, Trouvères, Minne- und Meistergesang.* Translated by Rodney E. Dennis. Cologne: Arno Volk, 1960.
                                                              [Gennrich, *TTMM trans.*]

———. *Übertragungsmaterial zur Rhythmik der Ars Antiqua.* Darmstadt, 1954.   [Gennrich, *Rhythmik*]

———. "Zu den altfranzösischen Rotrouengen." *Zeitschrift für romanische Philologie* 46 (1926): 335–41.

Gérold, Théodore. *La Musique au moyen âge.* Classiques français du moyen âge 73. Paris: Champion, 1932.   [Gérold I]

———. *Histoire de la musique des origines à la fin du XIVe siècle.* Paris: Librairie Renouard, 1936.   [Gérold II]

Godefroy, Frédéric. *Dictionnaire de l'ancienne langue française et de tous ses dialectes du IXe au XVe siècle.* 10 vols. Paris: Champion, 1880–1938. Reprint. New York: Kraus, 1961.

Gossen, Charles Théodore. *Grammaire de l'ancien picard.* 2d ed. Paris: Klincksieck, 1970.   [Gossen]

Greimas, A. J. *Dictionnaire de l'ancien français jusqu'au milieu du XIVe siècle.* Paris: Larousse, 1968.

Gröber, Gustav. *Grundriss der romanischen Philologie.* 2 vols. Strasbourg, 1880–1902.   [Gröber]

Jeanroy, Alfred. *Bibliographie sommaire des chansonniers français du moyen âge.* Classiques français du moyen âge 18. Paris: Champion, 1974.

———. "G. Steffens. Der kritische Text der Gedichte von Richart de Semilli." Review of Steffens's edition. *Romania* 31 (1902): 440–43.
                                                                    [Jeanroy, *Review*]

———. *Les Origines de la poésie lyrique en France au moyen âge.* 4th ed. Paris: Champion, 1969.   [Jeanroy, *Origines*]

———. "Notes sur le tournoiement des dames." *Romania* 28 (1899): 232–44.   [Jeanroy, *Notes*]

Johnson, Susan M. "The Role of the Refrain in the Pastourelles à refrain." In *Literary and Historical Perspectives of the Middle Ages.*

Proceedings of the 1981 SEMA Meeting, edited by Patricia W. Cummins et al., 78–92. Morgantown, WV: West Virginia University Press, 1982.   [Johnson, *Pastourelles*]

————. "The Role of the Refrain in Old French Lyric Poetry." Ph.D. diss., Indiana University, 1983.   [Johnson, *Refrain*]

Karp, Theodore. "The Trouvère Manuscript Tradition." In *Twenty-Fifth Anniversary Festschrift (1937–1962). (Dept. of Music, Queen's College of the City University of New York),* edited by Albert Mell, 25–52. New York: Queen's College Press, 1964.   [Karp]

La Borde, J.-B. de. *Essai sur la musique ancienne et moderne.* Vol. 2. Paris: P.-D. Pierres, 1780.   [La Borde II]

Langlois, Ernest. "Remarques sur les chansonniers français." *Romania* 45 (1918–19): 321–50.

Le Gentil, Pierre. *Le Virelai et le villancico: le problème des origines arabes.* Paris: Les Belles Lettres, 1954.   [Le Gentil]

Linker, Robert White. *A Bibliography of Old French Lyrics.* University, MS: Romance Monographs, 1979.   [L]

Lote, Georges. *Histoire du vers français.* Vols. 1–3, *Le moyen âge.* Paris: Boivin, 1949–55.   [Lote]

Ménard, Philippe. *Syntaxe de l'ancien français.* Bordeaux: SOBODI, 1973.   [Ménard]

Meyer, Paul. "Des rapports de la poésie des trouvères avec celle des troubadours." *Romania* 19 (1890): 1–62.

Moignet, Gérard. *Grammaire de l'ancien français.* Paris: Klincksieck, 1976.   [Moignet]

Mölk, U., and F. Wolfzettel. *Répertoire métrique de la poésie lyrique française des origines à 1350.* Munich: W. Fink, 1972.   [MW]

Monmerqué, N., and Fr. Michel. *Théâtre français au moyen âge.* Paris, 1839.   [Monmerqué-Michel]

Noack, Fritz. "Der Strophenausgang in seinem Verhältnis zum Refrain und Strophengrundstock in der refrainhaltigen altfranzösischen Lyrik." *Ausgaben und Abhandlungen aus dem Gebiete der romanischen Philologie* 98 (1899): 1–152.   [Noack]

Paris, Paulin. "Chansonniers." In *Histoire littéraire de la France.* Vol. 23, pp. 512–831. Paris, 1856.   [Paris, *Chansonniers*]

Petersen Dyggve, Holger. "Les dames du 'Tournoiement' de Huon d'Oisi." *Neuphilologische Mitteilungen* 36 (1935): 65–84.

————. "Deux dames du 'Tournoiement' de Huon d'Oisi." *Neuphilologische Mitteilungen* 41 (1940): 157–80.

————. *Onomastique des trouvères.* Annales Academiae Scientiarum Fennicae, ser. B, vol. 30. Helsinki: Suomalaisen Tiedeakatemain Toimituksiam, 1934. Reprint. New York: Lenox Hill, 1973.

[Petersen Dyggve, *Onomastique*]

————. "Les personnages du 'Tournoiement aus dames.'" *Neuphilologische Mitteilungen* 36 (1935): 145–92.
[Petersen Dyggve, *Personnages*]

Pope, Mildred K. *From Latin to Modern French with Especial Consideration of Anglo-Norman: Phonology and Morphology.* Manchester: Manchester University Press, 1934. [Pope]

Prunières, H. *Nouvelle histoire de la musique.* 2 vols. Paris: Rieder, 1934–36. [Prunières]

Rosenberg, Samuel N., and Hans Tischler. *Chanter m'estuet. Songs of the Trouvères.* Bloomington, IN: Indiana University Press, 1981.
[Rosenberg]

Schläger, G. "Über Musik und Strophenbau der altfranzösischen Romanzen." In *Forschungen zur romanischen Philologie. Festgabe für Hermann Suchier*, 115–60, Anhang I–XXVII. Halle: Max Niemeyer, 1900. Reprint. Geneva: Slatkine, 1978. [Schläger]

Schwan, E. *Die altfranzösischen Liederhandschriften, ihr Verhältniss, ihre Entstehung und ihre Bestimmung.* Berlin: Weidmann, 1886.

Spanke, Hans. *Eine altfranzösische Liedersammlung.* Halle: Max Niemeyer, 1925. [Spanke]

————. *G. Raynauds Bibliographie des altfranzösischen Liedes.* Leiden: E. J. Brill, 1955. [RS]

Steffens, Georg. "Der kritische Text der Gedichte von Richart de Semilli." In *Beiträge zur romanischen und englischen Philologie. Festgabe für Wendelin Foerster*, 331–62. Halle: Max Niemeyer, 1902.
[Steffens]

Tobler, Adolphe, and Erhard Lommatsch. *Altfranzösisches Wörterbuch.* 10 vols. Berlin: Weidmann, 1925–43; Wiesbaden: Steiner, 1951–.

Toja, Gianluigi. *Lirica cortese d'oïl, sec. XII–XIII.* Bologna: Patron, 1966.
[Toja]

Van den Boogaard, Nico H. J. *Rondeaux et refrains du XIIᵉ siècle au début du XIVᵉ.* Paris: Klincksieck, 1969. [VB]

Van der Werf, Hendrik. *The Chansons of the Troubadours and Trouvères. A Study of the Melodies and their Relation to the Poems.* Utrecht: Oosthoek, 1972.

————. "Rotrouenge." In *New Grove Dictionary of Music and Musicians*, edited by Stanley Sadie, vol. 16, pp. 259–60. London: MacMillan Publishers Limited, 1980. [Van der Werf, *Rotrouenge*]

Verrier, Paul. *Le Vers français.* 3 vols. Paris: H. Didier, 1931–32.

Zumthor, Paul. *Essai de poétique médiévale.* Paris: Seuil, 1972.
[Zumthor, *Essai*]

————. *Langue et techniques poétiques à l'époque romane (XIᵉ–XIIIᵉ siècles).* Paris: Klincksieck, 1963.

Introduction

Previous Editions

"Le charmant poète que Richard de Semilli!" This is how Alfred Jeanroy described our poet.[1] Richard is charming, and often original and inventive. Complete editions of both his poems and music were published around the turn of the century. But these editions, and most of the editions of individual poems that have been published since that time, do not present these works as they were known in the Middle Ages, that is, as songs in which the words and melody united to form a single, indivisible entity. This edition seeks to restore the *songs*, in a form that will be of use to literary scholars, musicologists, and performers, so that they can be enjoyed as they were so many centuries ago.

Editions of the Texts

Steffens, Georg. "Der kritische Text der Gedichte von Richart de Semilli."

Jeanroy, Alfred. "Notes sur le tournoiement des dames."

The only edition that includes most of Richard de Semilli's poems was done by Georg Steffens. This edition presents the ten poems attributed to Richard in the manuscripts, and it includes a long discussion of the filiation of the five manuscripts (*KNPVX*). The transcription of each of the songs is based on one manuscript, with the exception of RS 868, where Steffens combined the rather different versions of two manuscripts. Unfortunately, one finds a fair number of errors in these texts, either in transcription, punctuation, or typography: A. Jeanroy mentions some forty such errors in his review of the edition,[2] and there are about thirty more in the variants. Although many of these errors do not impede one's understanding of the text, others are rather disconcerting: *amenee* for *ame nee* (RS 22, line 23), *mout* for *mont* (RS 538, line 2), *greve* for *gieue* (RS 533, line 27), *ja* for *j'ai* (RS 538, line 32),

---

[1] Jeanroy, *Review* 440.
[2] Jeanroy, *Review* 440–43.

among others. Jeanroy also criticized this edition for its lack of notes and commentary on the texts, the language, and versification. One might add that there is neither a glossary nor any reference at all to the music.

Steffens's edition does not include an eleventh poem, RS 1044a, that had been published a few years earlier by Jeanroy[3] and that in all probability should be attributed to Richard as well (see the section below on attribution). This poem, one of the rare examples of the genre called the "Tournoiement des dames," is found only in MS X. Jeanroy's edition of this piece is quite good in general; he made only a few emendations to re-establish the proper meter. The only questionable correction is the regular substitution of *els* for *il* (a dialectal form of the feminine pronoun), a correction that Jeanroy made no doubt to facilitate our understanding of the text (he notes this change in the rejected readings).

Edition of the Music
Aubry, Pierre, and Alfred Jeanroy. *Le Chansonnier de l'Arsenal (trouvères du XIIᵉ–XIIIᵉ siècle). Reproduction phototypique du manuscrit 5198 de la Bibliothèque de l'Arsenal.*

The only complete edition of the music was published by Pierre Aubry in the first volume of the facsimile edition of MS K. The melodies are transcribed as they are found in MS K in modal rhythm. It does not appear that Aubry consulted the other manuscripts (although there is no statement of editorial policy), but he does occasionally emend the pitches. As is often the case with early musical editions of the trouvères, only the first stanza of the poem accompanies the melody, and, consequently, one must seek the other stanzas in Steffens's edition or elsewhere.

These three editions, all published early in this century, are now quite difficult to find. Because of this and because of the limitations already noted, it seems appropriate to present a new edition of Richard de Semilli—an edition that includes the commentary useful to modern scholarship while it preserves the integrity of the song in a way that has not been done since the manuscripts of the Middle Ages.

---

[3] Jeanroy, *Notes* 232–44.

Life and Works

We know almost nothing about the life of our poet, and only a few bits of information can be gleaned from the manuscripts and the poems themselves. In manuscript attributions he is called *Maistre* Richard de Semilli, which leads one to assume that he was a cleric. Three of his poems (RS 868, 1362 and 1583) are set near Paris, and twice (RS 614 and 868) the poet mentions the Seine. These few indications suggest that Richard came from Paris or that he lived there.[4] His literary activity dates to the end of the twelfth century,[5] and thus he belongs to the first generation of lyric poets writing in Old French.

While many poets of this generation, such as Gace Brulé and Blondel de Nesle, devoted themselves to developing the themes and forms of the *chanson courtoise*, Richard's works are much more varied, both in genre and form, and some poems even reveal a reluctance to accept at face value the rituals of courtly love. Ten poems are attributed to him without question, and another piece (RS 1044a) was probably written by him. This small corpus includes five courtly love songs, two non-courtly love songs, one of the rare examples of the genre known as the "Tournoiement des dames," two pastourelles, and a hybrid piece that unites the themes of the pastourelle and the *chanson de malmariée*.

The best known of Richard's poems today are his pastourelles, since they have appeared in some anthologies. All three of these poems, which are some of the earliest examples of the genre in Old French,[6] present interesting variations on the traditional theme. In RS 1583 (song 1) we find an introspective and melancholic knight whose thoughts and reactions to his encounter with a shepherdess and her lover are unusual indeed. Rejected immediately by the girl, who prefers her shepherd, Robin, the knight stays to observe their merriment and love-making. Rather than disdaining these simple pleasures, he sees in them a joy that he himself has never found in love. He considers it unjust that a simple peasant can find joy while he, who has always served Love faithfully, has experienced only pain and suffering. Comparing their idyllic situation to his own leads him to curse Love and reject the ideals of his class. The shepherd's last sally as he sends the knight away probably reflects the knight's feelings as much as his own: his joy and pleasure are so great that he would not give them up for all the wealth in the royal treasury. The knight too would be this

---

[4] Petersen Dyggve, *Onomastique* 216; Frappier 63.
[5] Gröber, II, pt. 1, 671.
[6] Frappier 63–64.

happy if he could find such a love. The irony in this situation is evident, and it implies a criticism of courtly love, which condemns the lover to a life of despair while mere peasants can experience all the pleasures of love.

The second pastourelle (song 6, RS 527) has a more traditional plot: the girl needs little coaxing before she gives in to the knight's demands. But the poem distinguishes itself from the tradition in its use of the refrain. Normally, the refrain of a pastourelle is introduced as the song being sung by the shepherdess when the knight comes upon her, and it reflects her ideas and her state of mind. In the course of the poem the refrain becomes a part of the dialogue between the two characters, and often its meaning is the subject of the discussion. In this poem, the refrain presents the knight's point of view: he addresses the girl and promises her his fidelity. This rather courtly expression of his feelings remains outside of the conversation (except perhaps in stanza 2) and seems to be the knight's private reaction to the sight of the girl.[7] Very few pastourelles attribute the refrain to the knight, but this technique gives us insight once again into his personality and thoughts and leaves us with the impression that this knight is not the unfeeling pleasure-seeker that one usually associates with this genre.

The last pastourelle (song 8, RS 1362) is in fact a hybrid piece that combines the plot of the pastourelle with the theme of the *chanson de malmariée* (song of an unhappily married woman). Instead of a shepherdess, the knight meets a lady ("une dame") who complains bitterly about her husband and who is quite ready and willing to take a lover, provided a certain amount of discretion is observed. The refrain, "Dame qui a mal mari, s'el fet ami, / n'en fet pas a blasmer," is typical of the *chanson de malmariée*. Initially, it attracts the knight's attention and encourages him in his pursuit; later on, when the woman accepts him as her lover, it serves to justify her actions. Although there are other poems where a knight encounters and consoles a *malmariée* (see, for example, RS 607 and RS 88), they do not include all the elements that Richard has succeeded in incorporating. The charm and originality of this piece come from the skillful combination, the complete fusion of these two traditional genres.

Richard's courtly love songs draw on many of the traditional motifs of this genre, but he succeeds in varying and renewing them by using a number of different techniques.

As an opening motif Richard always refers to the composition of his song as a way of praising his lady (songs 2 and 3, RS 22, 1860), expressing his love for her (song 7, RS 614), or venting his pain and

---

[7] Johnson, *Pastourelles*.

sorrow (songs 4 and 5, RS 1820, 538). This motif, of course, is not unusual, but Richard uses it to the exclusion of other common motifs, such as the coming of spring and the joyous songs of the birds (only song 7 hints at this theme). The importance he places on the traditional association between composing songs and loving—the two are nearly synonymous in courtly lyric—is explained by a third less traditional element that he adds in several songs: the lady must also accept the song as a token that she returns his love. What the lover fears is the rejection of his song and, by implication, the rejection of his love. The timid lover of song 2 (RS 22) suggests that his lady can send the song back to him, and it will never be sung again if it does not please her. But it will be sung with joy if she accepts it (2:35–40). The lovers of songs 4 and 7 (RS 1820, 614) express their despair by noting that the lady does not care for their songs (4:1–2, 7:41–42). If his poetry, his only means of expressing his love for her, cannot move her, then his situation is hopeless indeed. Although this connection between accepting the song and accepting the lover is perhaps implicit in the rhetoric of the *chanson courtoise*, few poets express it this explicitly. Unless the lady accepts the song, there is little point in composing it, perhaps little point in loving, were it not for the hope that some day she will respond.

The love songs explore the different emotional states that the lover may experience. In song 2 (RS 22), for example, we find a timid lover who is so overwhelmed by his lady's noble qualities and high rank that he cannot even muster the courage to declare his love. He fears that this irreproachable woman might suffer blame as a result of his audacity and cannot stand the thought of such a stain on her reputation.

In songs 4, 5, and 7 (RS 1820, 538, 614) it is a lover in despair who speaks. He accuses himself of folly for having chosen an inaccessible and indifferent lady who causes him unending suffering. He thinks about ways of escaping. Perhaps he could flee and find relief and a better life in another land (song 4), or perhaps suicide is the solution (song 5). But in the end he realizes that love controls him and that he can do nothing to escape it or to fight it. He knows that this love is impossible (no one can obtain this woman's love) but that he will continue to suffer for her; and he resigns himself to this torment.

Although Richard often uses the abstract vocabulary that typifies the rhetoric of courtly love, he also refers to concrete, everyday things. His lady is, of course, the most beautiful, the most praiseworthy, the most prudent and wise, and she surpasses all others:

> Ne sai de son ator
> N'en chastiau ne en tour
> Nule, si en sui au tor

> De morir s'il li gree.   (5:23–26)

In fact, if she would respond, she could perform miracles:

> Jamés nul mal n'eüst
> Ne morir ne deüst
> Qui entre voz braz geüst
> Jusques a l'ajornee.   (5:33–36)

But this same superiority puts her out of the reach of the lover, inaccessible, it seems, to any lover:

> Melz porroit l'en toute Saigne
> Lancier en un pot dedenz
> Q'i avenisse a nul tens.   (7:35–37)

Many lovers say that they are dying for love of their lady, but Richard finds a novel and graphic way of portraying his death:

> Bien voi, tuer me puis
> Ou noier en un puis.   (5:13–14)

In each of these comparisons a common object (a castle, a pot, a well) or an everday action (sleeping in another's arms) intensifies the effect of the hyperbole and makes the comparison all the more striking. Richard uses a similar technique in one of his *envois*. He sends the song not just to his lady but to the door of her house, where it will be performed (5:41–43). These references give one the impression of a lover who lives and suffers in the real world and are a refreshing change from the abstractions of most courtly lyric.

The most original of Richard's love songs (song 3, RS 1860) takes a rather different approach to the subject. Here the lover is impatient and aggressive. He has served and suffered for his lady for a long time and declares in the refrain of the first stanza that it is time that she return his love. The refrain changes in the following stanzas into a question asking (or demanding) when he will receive the reward for his efforts. In stanzas 1 and 2, the lover makes statements intended to prove that he merits the reward he seeks. Then in stanza 3 he switches tactics and implies that the woman too has a stake in their relationship. He first warns her against arrogance and suggests that she may not always have the opportunity he is offering her. Then in a stanza that foreshadows the theme and technique that Ronsard will use nearly four hundred years later in "Quand vous serez bien vieille," he imagines his lady as an old woman, whom no one cares to love any more, accusing herself of folly for not accepting the offers she received in her youth. The insistent question of the refrain—"Et quant m'iert vostre amor donee?"— returns to complete the lover's argument. While other poets do sometimes reprimand their lady and suggest that she will have regrets some day (usually for having "killed" her lover by her indifference), the argument Richard uses in this poem and his concrete way of presenting it seem truly new and fresh for the poetry of the period.

Richard's two non-courtly (or *popularisant*) love songs have a much lighter and almost playful tone. In both poems the lover takes great pleasure in describing in detail the physical beauty and good qualities of his beloved. He sings the joys of a simple love that lacks the suffering and pretense of the courtly world. This comparison to courtly love is brought out quite nicely in song 9 (RS 533), where the refrain advises women on how they should behave. In public she should be well-mannered and circumspect, as any courtly lady should be, but alone with her lover this facade is no longer necessary, and she should be vivacious, charming, and amorous. In stanzas 5 and 6 it becomes clear that the lover's lady is an example of this ideal woman, and he rejoices in his good fortune.

The lover of song 10 (RS 868) has been smitten by a married woman whom he saw by chance. He is so overwhelmed by her beauty that he almost mentions her name, something a courtly lover would never dare to do. But the suffering and despair of courtly love have nothing to do with this lover. He is happy just to praise this wonderful lady, preferring this pleasure to any physical pleasure he might have with her—he states quite plainly that this is not of interest to him. He expresses the simple joy of loving a beautiful creature without concern or fear about his love being returned.

In these two poems, as in the first pastourelle (song 1, RS 1583), we see that Richard has not been completely taken in by the fashion of courtly love. He expresses a yearning (or is it nostalgia?) for a more straightforward relationship between a man and a woman in which they can both share their love and joy.

The last poem (song 11, RS 1044a), which was probably written by Richard, is one of the three surviving examples of a genre that has been called the "Tournoiement des dames." These poems describe a joust in which all of the combatants are ladies. The two other poems are apparently satiric in intent. Richard's poem, however, merely expresses loving concern for the weaker sex, for these noble ladies who have not been trained to endure such an ordeal. The tone of the poem remains lighthearted as there is not much real danger. The ladies are prudent ("sages") and have decided to fight with blunted lances. The battle ends amicably when the king's messenger arrives and orders them to stop. The poet's prayers to a variety of saints (found in an internal refrain) prove to be unnecessary after all.

As this brief summary of his works shows, Richard handles a variety of themes and genres skillfully, and he has his moments of true originality and innovation. The form of his poems and melodies shows diversity and a willingness to experiment as well. He often uses forms that are of popular origin, and he has a definite liking for refrains, and yet he is also well versed in the techniques of the *grand chant courtois*.

Songs 2, 3, 4, and 7 (RS 22, 1860, 1820, 614) have the structure as well as the themes of this privileged genre. Although his metrical patterns and melodic structures do not stray from well-established forms, he does use a variety of these conventional forms. He also sometimes modifies these structures by adding refrains. Song 3 has a single refrain, and song 4 uses multiple refrains.

Four other songs (nos. 5, 6, 8, and 9; RS 538, 527, 1362, 533) have the structure of what has been called the *rotrouenge*, a genre of popular origin that by definition includes a refrain. It is not surprising that Richard uses this form for pastourelles and one of his non-courtly love songs, but another love song that is completely courtly in both tone and themes also takes this form. This song (no. 5) not only has the structure of a *rotrouenge*; it also shares its metrical structure and melody with one of the pastourelles (song 6). It is as if Richard wrote a counterfact of one of his own pieces. Hearing such different texts sung to the same melody must have had an interesting effect on the audience and created unusual associations and resonances.

Richard's songs show us a skillful poet and songwriter who was interested in a variety of forms and themes and innovative enough to play with and sometimes blend different types. In a lyric tradition known for its conventions, Richard stands as a distinct and inventive figure. And perhaps this is all we need to know about his life.

Manuscripts

The poems of Richard de Semilli are found in five manuscripts:

K — Paris, Bibliothèque de l'Arsenal 5198. Facsimile and partial edition: P. Aubry and A. Jeanroy, *Le Chansonnier de l'Arsenal (trouvères du XIIᵉ–XIIIᵉ siècle). Reproduction phototypique du manuscrit 5198 de la Bibliothèque de l'Arsenal*. 2 vols. (Paris: P. Geuthner, 1909–1912).

N — Paris, Bibliothèque Nationale, français 845.
P — Paris, Bibliothèque Nationale, français 847.
V — Paris, Bibliothèque Nationale, français 24406.
X — Paris, Bibliothèque Nationale, nouv. acq. fr. 1050.

All of the manuscripts belong to the same family. Manuscripts KNX

are closely related while manuscripts *PV* are somewhat less closely
related to this group. In general, the manuscripts divide the poems into
two groups: first a series of poems classified by author, then a series
of anonymous pieces. Manuscripts *KNX* present the poems in approximately the same order (except for some missing poems), and there are
rubrics for the ascribed pieces. In general, MS *V* presents the poems in
an order similar to that of *KNX* but without attributions in the series
arranged by author. MS *P* contains more or less the same poems as the
other manuscripts but it presents them in a different order.

Of the eleven poems that one can attribute to Richard de Semilli, ten
appear in *KP*, nine in *X*, and eight in *NV*. Manuscripts *KNVX* present
the poems in the same order.

Order of the songs in the manuscripts:

RS	K	N	V	X	P
1583	170bis-ter	81r-81v	45r-45v	122r	185v-186v
22	171	81v-82r	45v-46r	122r-122v	183v-184r
1860	171-172	82r-82v	46r-46v	122v-123r	101r-102r
1820	172-173	82v-83r	46v-47r	123r-124r	98v-99v
538	174	83r-83v	47r	124r-124v	97v-98v
527	174-175	83v-84r	47r-47v	124v-125r	97r-97v
614	174-176	84r-84v	47v-48r	125r-125v	96v-97r
1362	176	84v	48r	125v-	172r-172v
533	177				99v-100r
868	177-178				100r-100v
1044a				127r	

Manuscript *X* was probably the most complete for the works of
Richard, but two leaves have now disappeared. The first, fol. 121, no
doubt included the initial stanzas of RS 1583. It was replaced in the
eighteenth century by a copy of the text of *N*. The second leaf, fol. 126,
probably contained the end of RS 1362, the complete texts of RS 533
and RS 868, and the first stanza of RS 1044a.

The manuscripts preserve ten of Richard's melodies. The melody of
RS 1044a (unicum of *X*) has been almost completely lost because of a
missing leaf: notation remains for only the final hemistich.

While the manuscripts form a homogeneous group in so far as the
texts are concerned, the situation is somewhat different for the music.
Manuscripts *KNPX* are still a closely knit family, and they all agree on
the basic structure of the melody. The variants that occur are limited
in general to ornamental notes (for example, plicas or a two-note
ligature instead of a single note), and occasionally one finds a note
transcribed a tone higher or lower. MS *V*, on the other hand, is very

individualistic. This manuscript regularly presents melodies that have nothing in common with the rest of the manuscript tradition, and it shows certain peculiarities that are difficult to explain (no repetitions where one would expect them, many hypo- and hypermetric lines, and so on). This is a characteristic of the whole manuscript,[8] and the notations of Richard's melodies are good examples of its idiosyncrasy. For this reason, I have not included a transcription of the melodies in MS *V*, and it is not noted in the variants. Some remarks on the idiosyncrasies of *V* are found in the critical commentary under *Music*.

Attribution

The attribution of ten poems to Richard de Semilli poses no problems, as can be seen in the following chart (abbreviations: R: Richard de Semilli; AN: anonymous;—: the poem does not appear in the manuscript):

Song	RS	*K*	*N*	*P*	*V*	*X*
1	1583	R	R	AN	AN	AN
2	22	R	R	AN	AN	R
3	1860	R	R	R	AN	R
4	1820	R	R	R	AN	R
5	538	R	R	R	AN	R
6	527	R	R	R	AN	R
7	614	R	R	R	AN	R
8	1362	R	R	AN	AN	R
9	533	R	—	R	—	—
10	868	R	—	R	—	—
11	1044a	—	—	—	—	AN

Manuscripts *KN* attribute all of the poems they contain to Richard. MS *P* ascribes most of the poems to him, but songs 1, 2, and 8 (RS 1583, 22, and 1362) appear in the series of anonymous pieces. In MS *V* none of the poems are attributed to an author so the lack of an attribution to Richard is not significant. All of the poems are attributed to Richard in MS *X* except for songs 1 and 11 (RS 1583 and 1044a), and in both cases the leaf containing the first stanza has disappeared, taking the attribution with it.

The only poem whose attribution is not certain is song 11 (RS 1044a). It has already been noted that MSS *KNVX* present Richard's poems in

---

[8] Karp, especially 26–28.

the same order, and in all of these manuscripts the poems of the Vidame de Chartres follow those of Richard. Song 11 (RS 1044a), which is lacking an attribution because of a missing leaf, is followed by the notation, "Ci comencent les chançons au Visdame de Chartres." Thus it seems probable that this piece belonged to the series of poems attributed to Richard.[9] This song also has certain stylistic traits that suggest that Richard may have written it, although this cannot of course be proven with certainty. The poem includes a refrain, which is normal for Richard (eight out of ten poems have a refrain), and it uses twelve-syllable lines, a meter that is rare in lyric poetry, but that is found in another of Richard's poems, song 9 (RS 533). The attribution of this poem to Richard is probable, and this edition accepts it without hesitation.

Versification

Although detailed notes on versification are found in the commentary after each poem, the following study of Richard's versification will give the reader a more general view of the techniques he uses.

Rhymes
The following list gives all of the masculine and feminine rhymes in alphabetical order. The number of lines containing each rhyme is indicated in parentheses, followed by the number of the poem in this edition and the stanza number.

Masculine rhymes
  -a (8): 3.2, 5.1
  -ai / -oi (5): 3.5
  -aint (6): 5.5, 10b.6 (–aint/-oint)
  -ant (13): 2.5, 3.2, 11.4
  -as (10): 4.5, 11.5
  -aut (10): 4.1, 6.5, 8.4
  -ens (10): 3.4 (–ens/-enz), 6.3, 7.5
  -ent (17): 3.4, 8.3, 10a.5, 11.3
  -er (56): 1.3, 2.1, 3.1, 3.5, 4.3–5, 7.3, 8.1–6, 10.1, 10a.7
  -et (11): 1.2, 10.4
  -eüst (3): 5.4
  -ez (6): 1.1–2
  -i (27): 1.4, 8.1–6, 10.3, 10a.6, 10b.5, 11.2
  -in (3): 8.1

---

[9] Jeanroy, *Notes* 235–36.

-ir (27): 2.4, 4.2, 4.4, 7.1–2, 7.6, 8.6
-is (30): 1.1 (–is/-iz), 3.3 (–is/-iz), 4.2, 6.2, 6.4, 7.4, 8.5
-it (8): 1.5 (–it/-ist/-uit)
-oi (9): 8.2, 11.6
-oir (8): 2.3, 4.1 (–oir/-oier)
-oit (8): 1.4
-on (10): 1.5, 3.1, 4.3
-onc (1): 4.4
-ont (3): 4.1
-or / -our (7): 4.3, 5.3
-ort (2): 4.2
-ueil (3): 3.3
-uer (16): 4.3, 6.1–5
-uis (6): 5.2, 6.1
-uit (3): 10.2
Feminine rhymes
-ace (2): 4.4
-age (8): 2.1–2
-aille (2): 9.5
-aine / -aigne (38): 7.5, 10a.1–7, 10b.1–6
-ance (4): 7.3
-ee (60): 2.3, 2.5, 3.1–5, 5.1–5, 6.1–5, 9.1, 11.1
-eille (2): 9.2
-ele (6): 1.3, 7.1
-ere, -erre (4): 6.2, 9.6
-ete (3): 4.2, 9.3
-ie (15): 4.5, 6.4, 7.2, 7.4, 9.4
-oie (8): 2.4, 6.3, 9.5
-oise (2): 9.6
-ue (24): 9.1–7
-ure (4): 7.6

The majority of the rhymes are masculine: of the 508 rhymes, 326 (64 per cent) are masculine and 182 (36 per cent) are feminine.

Most of the time, Richard uses only simple, sufficient rhymes, although there are a few examples here and there of more complex rhymes, such as paronymic, homonymic, derived, and rich rhymes. Song 5 (RS 538) is remarkable for its systematic use of difficult rhymes in all of the stanzas and in the refrain (see the notes on the poem for a detailed study).

Stanza structure
The following tables give a general view of the length of the stanzas and their metrical structure, and they show that Richard uses many

different combinations without any particular preference. In these tables, an asterisk (*) indicates a multiple-refrain song, nos. 1 or 4 (RS 1583 or 1820). For these poems, the refrain and the transitional line between the stanza proper and the refrain have not been counted since the number and the length of these lines varies from stanza to stanza.

Number of lines in a stanza
    10   Songs 3, 5, 6 (RS 1860, 538, 527)
     8   Songs 1*, 2, 4*, 7, 10a (RS 1583, 22, 1820, 614, 868)
     7   Song 8 (RS 1362)
     6   Songs 10b, 11 (RS 868, 1044a)
     5   Song 9 (RS 533)

Isometric stanzas
    12 syllable lines   Songs 9, 11 (RS 533, 1044a)
    10 syllable lines   Songs 1*, 4* (RS 1583, 1820)
     7 syllable lines   Songs 2, 7 (RS 22, 614)

Heterometric stanzas
    6 and 11 syllable lines   Song 8 (RS 1362)
    7 and 8 syllable lines   Song 3 (RS 1860)
    6, 7, and 10 syllable lines   Songs 5, 6 (RS 538, 527)
    4, 6, 8, and 9 syllable lines Song 10 (RS 868)

Rhyme schemes
The following chart gives all of the rhyme schemes in alphabetical order.

Song	RS									
11	1044a	a	a	a	a	A	a			
1	1583	a	a	a	a	a	a	a	a	v	R
10	868	a	a	a	b'	B'	B'	(B' | B')		
8	1362	a	a	a	b	C	B				
9	533	a'	a'	B'	B'	B'					
5	538	a'	a'	b	b	b	a'	C	C	C	A'
6	527	a'	a'	b	b	b	c'	D	D	D	C'
2	22	a'	b	a'	b	b	a'	a'	b		
7	614	a'	b	a'	b	b	a'	a'	b		
3	1860	a	b	a	b	b	a	a	c'	A	C'
4	1820	a	b	a	b	b	a	b	a	v	R

Richard often uses masculine rhymes, and in songs 1, 4, 8, and 11 (RS 1583, 1820, 1362, 1044a) he uses them exclusively. There is also one piece, song 9 (RS 533), in which all of the rhymes are feminine.

    Richard has a true liking and talent for refrains, and he uses all of the structural types that exist in Old French except for the word-refrain. In his works one finds single-refrain songs (*chansons à refrain*) where the same refrain is repeated after each stanza, songs 3, 5, 6, 8, 9, and 10 (RS 1860, 538, 527, 1362, 533, 868); an internal refrain, song 11 (RS 1044a); variable refrains in which small changes may occur from stanza to stanza (either in the first line of the refrain to facilitate the transition from the stanza or at the rhyme word to accomodate the change to a new set of rhymes) in songs 3 and 11 (RS 1860, 1044a); and multiple-refrain songs (*chansons avec des refrains*), songs 1 and 4 (RS 1583, 1820). In this last form, which is peculiar to the trouvère lyric, a different "refrain" or short ditty, metrically and musically distinct from the stanza and the other "refrains," apppears at the end of each stanza.

It should be noted that songs 2 and 7 (RS 22 and 614) have exactly the same structure and that songs 5 and 6 (RS 538 and 527) have nearly the same structure. This structural similarity is reinforced by the music: each pair also shares the same melody.

Richard uses courtly structures as well as structures of popular origin. Songs 2, 3, 4, and 7 (RS 22, 1860, 1820, 614) all use the tripartite structure that is typical of the *grand chant courtois*. In the *frons* Richard always uses alternating rhymes (*abab*) with or without an alternation of masculine and feminine rhymes. There is more variation in the *cauda*: in songs 2 and 7 (RS 22 and 614) one finds enclosing rhymes, *baab* (*cobla crotz encadenada*), in 4 (RS 1820) alternating rhymes in reversed order, *baba* (a variation of the type *cobla encadenada*), and in 3 (RS 1860) the arrangement *baac* (*cobla cadena caudada* ending with an additional rhyme). The rhyme schemes of songs 2, 4, and 7 (RS 22, 1820, 614) occur frequently in trouvère poetry, while that of song 3 (RS 1860) is rare. It should be noted that Richard adds refrains to two of his courtly songs, nos. 3 and 4 (RS 1860 and 1820).

Four pieces—5, 6, 8, and 9 (RS 538, 527, 1362, 538)—were given the name "rotrouenge" by Friedrich Gennrich. This term existed in the Middle Ages but, as often happens, the poems designated in this way do not give us a very precise idea of what the term meant for the authors.

In his study *Die altfranzösische Rotrouenge*, Gennrich uses this term to designate a formal genre which is defined by the combination of a specific metrical and musical structure. In its simplest form, the *rotrouenge* consists of a series of monorhymed stanzas followed by a refrain that introduces a new rhyme. In the music, one finds a single melodic phrase which is repeated for each of the monorhymed verses, followed by a new melodic phrase for the refrain.

Text: a a . . . B̲ ̲B̲

Music: A A . . .   B

In a more complex form, the stanza ends in a rhyme that introduces one of the rhymes of the refrain, and the melody of the refrain repeats that of the last lines of the stanza:

Text: a   a . . a b AB or BB

Music: A A . .   B   B

This form, as Gennrich has defined it, shares certain characteristics with the *ballette* and the *virelai*, and it can be confused with them, especially if the music has not survived. Two characteristics seem to distinguish the *rotrouenge* from these other genres: there are normally more than three stanzas and more than two monorhymed verses in each stanza.

Scholars do not agree on the origin of this form, and they readily admit that it is difficult to define, although they continue to use the term.[10] In this edition, the term *rotrouenge* is used as a practical way of designating the bipartite structure defined by Gennrich (we have no other term to describe it). But this is done with the knowledge and a caution that this form is not well defined in the Middle Ages and that Gennrich's definition may not correspond to the genre the trouvères had in mind.

Arrangement of the rhymes among the stanzas

Richard has a definite preference for *coblas singulars* in which each stanza introduces a new set of rhyme sounds. *Coblas doblas*, where the rhyme sounds change every two stanzas, occurs only once in the first two stanzas of song 2 (RS 22). But Richard often links the stanzas by using one rhyme sound throughout the poem. In song 5 (RS 538), the a-rhyme remains the same, resulting in *coblas singulars capcaudadas* (a technique by which the last rhyme of one stanza is repeated and becomes the first rhyme of the following stanza). In four single-refrain songs—3, 6, 8, and 10 (RS 1860, 527, 1362, 868)—the stanza proper ends in a rhyme that has no counterpart in the stanza, a *rim estramp*, that links the refrain to the stanza. This *rim estramp* repeats the same sound in all of the stanzas and serves to announce the refrain and to unify the structure of the poem.

---

[10] See for example: Bec, vol. 1, 183–89; Zumthor, *Essai* 263; Frappier 23–24; Le Gentil 184–85; Lote, vol. 2, 203–5; Spanke 294–301; van der Werf, *Rotrouenge*; Chambers 233–34.

Musical Structure

In his melodies, Richard used relatively simple structures that do not depart from the tradition already established by the troubadours and the earliest trouvères. In general his melodies are syllabic and their range rarely exceeds an octave.

In order to facilitate comparisons, I have devised the following chart, which presents structural diagrams of the melodies in alphabetical order:

Song	RS										
9	533	A	A / A′		A	A′					
1	1583	A	A′	A	A′	B	B′	B	B′	v	R
6	527	A	A	B / B							
5	538	A	A	B / B		same melody					
8	1362	A	A	B / B							
2	22	A	B	A	B	C	D	E	F		
7	614	A	B	A	B	C	D	E	F	same melody	
4	1820	A	B	A	B	C	D	E	F	v	R
3	1860	A	B	A	C	D	E	F	G / F	G	
10	868	A	B	C	D / D′	D	D′	D			

Richard uses two basic structures for most of his songs: the tripartite structure AB AB X which is typical of the courtly *chanson*, and a bipartite structure that Gennrich has associated with the *rotrouenge*, AA B/B. Although these structures are traditional, there are a number of interesting variations. Two courtly *chansons*, nos. 3 and 4 (RS 1860 and 1820), include refrains. The addition of a refrain modifies the normal structure and creates repetitions where one does not usually expect them. In the *rotrouenges*, the second musical phrase can extend to two to four lines.

Two songs show somewhat less common structures. In song 10 (RS 868), we find a through-composed melody in the stanza (ABCD) which is a natural consequence of the varying length of the lines in the text. The result is a song that shows great variety, since each line introduces a new melodic phrase. Song 1 (RS 1583), by contrast, has an extremely repetitive melody showing slight variations only in the refrain and the transitional line.

It should be noted that two pairs of songs, nos. 2 and 7 (RS 22, 614) and nos. 5 and 6 (RS 538, 527), have the same or nearly the same metrical structure, and they also share the same melody.

The Language of the Texts

The first part of this section looks at the traits of Richard's language that affect the rhymes he uses. The second section identifies spellings and grammatical forms used by the scribes that differ from Francien forms of the period. References to the manuscripts indicate only the base manuscript. This is followed by the number of the poem in this edition and a reference to the line or stanza.

The Author
A study of the rhymes reveals the following traits of Richard's language.

1. *-aine / -aigne*. The word *Saigne* rhymes with words in *-aine* (K 7, str. 5; P 10a, str. 2). It is probable that the palatalized *n* is only a graphy.[11]
2. *-ai / -oi*. The presence of the rhyme *moi* (K 3, str. 5) in a series in *-ai* (*delai, trai, arrai*) indicates that the diphthong *oi* has been reduced to [wè].[12]
3. *-aint / -oint*. The rhyme *point* (K 10b, str. 6) in a series in *-aint* (*maint, m'aint*) is perhaps a very early example of the reduction of the diphthong *-oin*. Pope notes several examples of this reduction in the south-east in the thirteenth century, but it is normally a late development.[13]
4. *-ens / -enz; -is / -iz*. Occasionally final *-z* and *-s* are found together in rhymes. This is a characteristic trait of Picard where [-ts] was reduced to [-s] at a very early date.[14] One finds rhymes in *-is / -iz*: *Paris / berbiz / m'assis / requis / Denis* (K 1, str. 1) and *assis / pris / petiz / dis / mis* (K 3, str. 3); and rhymes in *-ens / -enz: tens / genz / sens* (K 3, str. 4).
5. *-ens / -enz* vs. *-ent*. Certain rhymes indicate that *-s* (or *-z*) and *-t* were pronounced in word final position. The rhymes *-ens / -enz* are distinct from those in *-ent* in K 3, str. 4.
6. *-ie* for *-iee*. There is one example of a rhyme based on the Picard form of the feminine past participle: *chaucie* (past participle of *chaucier*) rhymes with *chaucie* (n.f., i.e., *la chaussée*) (P 9, str. 4).
7. *o / ou*. The manuscripts do not distinguish between the graphies *o* and *ou* and one finds the series of rhymes *ator / tour / tor* (K 5, str. 3).

---

[11] Gossen § 60.
[12] Pope § 519.
[13] Pope § 474–75.
[14] Pope § 1320 xxi; Gossen § 40.

Imperfect Rhymes

1. Several imperfect rhymes are the result of ascending diphthongs:
   -it / -ist / -uit (K 1, str. 5): *vit / dist / Crist / deduit / delit / cuit / nuit.*
   -ai / -oi (K 3, str. 5): *delai / moi / trai / arrai.*
   -aint / -oint (K 10b, str. 6): *m'aint / point / maint.*
2. In K 4, str. 1, *souloier* rhymes with *valoir / desespoir / avoir.*
3. In the unique manuscript of song 11 (MS X) the last line ends with *pou*, which should rhyme with *roi / desroi / soi / quoi / Eloi.* I have emended the text, substituting the other form of this word, *poi.*

The Scribes

The manuscripts that served as the base for the texts (i.e., *KPX*) all have a limited number of northern and eastern dialectal traits, including a number of Picard grammatical forms and spellings.

Vowels

1. *ai* for *ei*: *paine* for *peine* (K 3:18, 4:26, 7:33, 10b:16; P 10a:20 and refr.), *Saigne* (K 7:35; P 10a:12) and *Sainne* (K 10b:10) for *Seine*, *amaine* for *ameine* (K 7:38), *demaine* for *demeine* (KP 10:refr), *maine* for *meine* (K 10b:4; P 10a:4).
2. *e* for *ai*: *mes* for *mais* (K 6:4, X 11:15), *jamés* for *jamais* (K 4:40), *pes* for *paix* (X 11:14), *meson* for *maison* (P 9:26), *seson* for *saison* (K 3:9, 7:1), *besai* for *baisai* (K 6:42), *besier* for *baisier* (P 10a:51), *fesoit* for *faisoit* (K 1:34), *fere* for *faire* (K 7:6), *fet* for *fait* (K 1:16, 3:5, 4:23, etc.), *lessiez* for *laissiez* (K 8:22), *let* for *lait* (K 8:16), *leroie* for *lairoie* (K 6:refr), *plesir* for *plaisir* (K 4:41), *plera* for *plaira* (K 3:16), *set* for *sait* (K 2:13, 4:42), *tres* for *trais* (K 6:11, 8:7).
3. *eu*, *el* (where *l* represents vocalized *l*) for *ieu*: *melz* for *mieux* (K 1:6, 1:30, 2:27, 4:38), *Dex* for *Dieu* (K 1:10, 4:29, 4:42, 4:54, etc.).
4. *iau* for *eau*: *biau* for *beau* (K 1:5, 2:13, 4:29), *biaus, biax* for *beaux* (K 1:9; P 10a:33), *biaucop* for *beaucoup* (K 7:46), *chastiau* for *chasteau* (K 5:24).
5. *o / ou*. The manuscripts do not distinguish between these two graphies. One finds for example: *tor, tour* (K 5:24–25), *pour* (the normal spelling in K), *por* (K 6:12), *amors* (the normal spelling in K), *jor* (K 4:29), *ajornee* (K 5:36), *renouvelle* (K 7:1), *couvient* (K 4:19), *trouver* (K 4:28).

Consonants

1. *ch* for *c*: *douche* for *douce* (K 10b:21).
2. *-c-*, *-s-* for intervocalic *-ss-*: *richece* for *richesse* (K 1:50), *viellece* for *vieillesse* (K 3:33), *m'asoage* for *m'assoage* (K 2:7).
3. *-g* for *-ng*: *loig* for *loing* (K 1:44), *conpaig* for *conpaing* (P 10a:3).

Morphology
1. *il* for *elles* (*X* 11). This dialectal form of the north and east[15] occurs only in song 11.
2. *mi* for *me* (*K* 1:20), Picard form.[16]
3. *j·os* contraction of *je vous* (*K* 7:19). This is a rare contraction that occurs in texts from the north and east.[17]
4. *-ie* for *-iee*: *chaucie* (*P* 9:16), *fiancies* (*X* 11:13). Picard form of the feminine past participle.[18]
5. *-és* for *-ez*: *gardés* (*X* 11:refr). This is the only example of this second person plural ending in the texts, but this spelling occurs frequently in *X*.[19]
6. *-oiz* for *-ez*: *diroiz* (*K* 3:34). This is the only example of this future ending for the second person plural.[20]
7. *-iom* for *-ions*: *veniom* (*P* 10a:1). This first person plural ending for the imperfect occurs only once in the texts.[21]
8. Future with reduction of *-vr* to *-r*: *arrai* for *avrai* (*K* 3:47). This is the only example of this form in the texts and it appears alongside Francien forms: *avrai* (*K* 5:15), *avras* (*K* 7:31), *avra* (*X* 11:16).[22]

Flexional errors
1. *qui* for *cui* (*K* 1:42, 3:19, 5:refr, 5:31, 6:22, 6:45). This confusion of forms occurs frequently in thirteenth-century manuscripts.[23] *Qui* is always used in place of *cui* in MS *K* in these texts.
2. *cil* for *ceus* (*K* 4:16), *nus* for *nul* (*K* 8:28), *tez* for *tel* (*K* 1:10). All of these cases are examples of attraction. The nominative case is used instead of the oblique simply because the pronoun is the antecedent of the subject relative pronoun *qui*.[24]

Editorial Policy

The Texts
The text of each poem in this edition is transcribed from a single base

---

[15] Moignet 38.
[16] Pope § 832; Moignet 38.
[17] Ménard § 48; Moignet 39.
[18] Gossen § 8; Pope § 1320 v.
[19] Moignet 62.
[20] Pope § 967; Moignet 67.
[21] Pope § 1326 xv; Moignet 61–62.
[22] Pope § 976; Moignet 70.
[23] Ménard § 67.
[24] Moignet 90.

manuscript. In a group of manuscripts as homogeneous as *KNPVX* most of the variants are orthographic or obvious scribal errors. There are, however, a few significant variants that determined the choice of the base manuscript.

For most of the poems—songs 1, 2, 3, 4, 5, 6, 7, 8 (RS 1583, 22, 1860, 1820, 538, 527, 614, 1362)—*K* served as the base manuscript because it is the most complete (it contains ten of Richard's poems and includes stanzas that are missing in other manuscripts) and because it has fewer errors and individual readings.

Poems 9 and 10 (RS 533 and 868) appear only in MSS *KP*, and the two manuscripts present significantly different versions of the texts. For song 9 (RS 533), MS *P* was chosen as the base because it is the most complete (it includes two stanzas that are not found in MS *K*) and because it has fewer erroneous readings. Song 10 (RS 868) poses other problems: the differences between the two versions involve the number of stanzas, the content of the stanzas, and the length of the refrain. Since previous editions have conflated the two versions, I have decided to present both versions of the text as they exist in the manuscripts with the necessary comparisons and commentary.

The question of base manuscript does not arise for poem 11 (RS 1044a) since this text appears only in MS *X*.

Once chosen, the base manuscript was emended only:

(1) to correct a non-grammatical form when the proper form appears in another manuscript;

(2) to re-establish the meter, when this is possible;

(3) to clarify the meaning of a passage when another manuscript has a more logical reading.

Whenever possible, the faulty reading was emended according to a reading from another manuscript. On rare occasions, all of the manuscripts have faulty readings, and in that case the emendation is given in square brackets in the text.

The Music

The musical transcriptions present the notation of the manuscript that served as the base for the text, with the exception of song 9 (RS 533), where a significant variant led to the choice of the one other manuscript as the base. In general, I have not emended the base manuscript, and as a result one sometimes finds small variations when one might expect a literal repetition. Such possible repetitions are mentioned specifically in the *Variants*. In songs 1 and 6 (RS 1583 and 527) emendations have been made for metrical reasons. In both cases the notation for one line is one syllable short but the same melodic phrase is repeated elsewhere with the same tones and the necessary number of syllables. The difference between the two phrases is in the distribution of the notes—one has a two-note neume where the other has two separate neumes. I have emended the transcription, using the phrase with two separate neumes, in order to re-establish the meter.

The fundamental problem in interpreting the melodies of the troubadours and trouvères concerns the rhythm. The notation used in these manuscripts clearly indicates the pitch of the note but gives no indication of its relative duration. Since one manuscript, MS *O*, does sometimes use a semi-mensural notation, some musicologists have proposed theories, based on the rhythmic modes, as to how to interpret the rhythm of all of these songs. The validity of this procedure is a much debated question, but it may be noted that the resulting rhythmic transcriptions have a number of drawbacks. The rhythmic modes impose rigid rhythms on a poetry that does not have regular metrical feet. As a result they often accent syllables that are unstressed in the text, thus distorting its meaning. In addition, the theories proposed do not lead to consistent results: different transcribers often arrive at varying rhythmic interpretations.

Faced with this situation, Hendrik van der Werf has proposed a different approach. Basing his argument on statements in a medieval treatise on music by Grocheio and the variants in the melodies found in the manuscripts, he suggests that these songs were sung in a "declamatory rhythm" in which each note was "more or less" equal in length.[25] The key words are "more or less," for this gives the performer the flexibility to vary the rhythm somewhat according to the natural flow and changing meter of the text (much as one would in a poetry recitation).

Given his conclusions, Van der Werf suggests that the melodies of the troubadours and trouvères be transcribed in a modernized version of the non-mensural notation found in the manuscripts, which will allow the performer, who must make the ultimate decision in these matters, to develop an interpretation unimpeded by another's rhythmic interpretation.

Van der Werf's recommendations have been adopted here as they seem the most reasonable solution given our lack of knowledge as to how these songs were actually performed. The melodies are given in a simplified notation without stemmed notes or bar lines that would indicate the relative duration of the notes.

---

[25] Van der Werf, *The Chansons of the Troubadours and Trouvères* (Utrecht: Oosthoek, 1972), 35–45.

Organization of the Edition

Order of the texts

The songs of Richard de Semilli appear in the same order in four of the five manuscripts, *KNVX*. Since this order is as logical as any other arrangement (by Raynaud-Spanke or Mölk-Wolfzettel number, thematic genre, formal genre, and so on) it has been adopted for this edition; this order also has the advantage of respecting the manuscript tradition. The songs appear as follows:

Song	RS	
1	1583	*pastourelle* (multiple refrains)
2	22	*chanson d'amour courtoise*
3	1860	*chanson d'amour courtoise* (variable single refrain)
4	1820	*chanson d'amour courtoise* (multiple refrains)
5	538	*chanson d'amour courtoise* (single refrain)
6	527	*pastourelle* (single refrain)
7	614	*chanson d'amour courtoise*
8	1362	*pastourelle-chanson de malmariée* (single refrain)
9	533	*chanson d'amour popularisante* (single refrain)
10	868	*chanson d'amour popularisante* (single refrain)
11	1044a	"*Le Tournoiement des dames*" (variable, interior refrain)

Critical apparatus and notes

Each song is preceded by an initial section of notes that provides the following information:

Bibliographies – Lists the poem's number in the standard bibliographies:
  RS – Hans Spanke, *G. Raynauds Bibliographie des altfranzösischen Liedes*.
  L – Robert White Linker, *A Bibliography of Old French Lyrics*.
  M – U. Mölk and F. Wolfzettel, *Répertoire métrique de la poésie lyrique française des origines à 1350*.
Refrain – The number of the refrain (VB) as listed in Nico H. J. van den Boogaard's *Rondeaux et refrains du XII*^e *siècle au début du XIV*^e.
Manuscripts – The conventional sigla are used to indicate the manuscripts in which the poem appears. The first manuscript listed is the one that was used as the base. The sigla are followed by references to the folio number (recto and verso indicated) in MSS *NPVX* or page number in the case of MS *K*.
Attribution – List of the manuscripts in which the poem is attributed to Richard de Semilli.
Music – List of the manuscripts that include notation of the melody.
Editions – List of all the editions of the text and the melody. Complete

references are found in the *Bibliography and List of Abbreviations*.

Structure – This section gives Mölk and Wolfzettel's number (MW) for the metrical structure of the piece and provides a detailed analysis of the metrical and musical structure. In the metrical structure, an apostrophe (') is used to indicate a feminine rhyme and capital letters indicate refrain lines. The musical structure is given in capital letters, and an apostrophe (') is used to indicate that the phrase is a repetition with some small variations of a previous phrase. If the poem served as a model for a counterfact, the Raynaud-Spanke number and the genre of the counterfact are given.

The Melodies

The melody of the song is then presented followed by notes on the variants.

The melodies are given in a simplified notation without stemmed notes or bar lines that would indicate relative duration. Notes in ligature are indicated by a slur, and plicas are indicated by a small note linked to the main note by a slur. Flat signs are given at the place where they appear in the base manuscript with a small arrow at the top of the staff showing where a new staff begins in the manuscript. Any discrepancies among the manuscripts in the use of the flat sign are discussed in the section *Music* in the notes.

Variants

The musical variants give all of the readings from other manuscripts in the group *KNPX*. Since MS *V* always has a different melody it has not been included in the variants. The position of the variant is indicated by the line number followed by a comma and the syllable number (2,3, for example, means second line, third syllable). Solfege syllables are used to give the tones, and a hyphen (–) shows notes in ligature, while a comma (,) indicates separate neumes. The notations *plica* and *no plica* indicate that one finds the same tone with or without a plica. If a variant reading would give a literal repetition of another melodic phrase, this is mentioned.

The Texts

The texts were prepared following the recommendations of Alfred Foulet and Mary Blakely Speer in their handbook, *On Editing Old French Texts*. Abbreviations have been expanded according to the scribe's normal usage, and the letters *i, j, u, v* have been resolved according to modern usage.

The lyrics have been typeset in such a way as to present, visually, certain structural aspects of the text. Lines are indented according to their length to show variations in the number of syllables, and refrains appear in italics. Square brackets indicate that the enclosed text does not appear in any manuscript; most often they indicate a refrain that is not repeated in its entirety after the first stanza, but on occasion they indicate an emendation of the text.

A second section of notes follows the text and gives the following information:

Rejected Readings – This section notes anything in the base manuscript that does not appear in the critical text. The notations "+1," "-1," and so on indicate the number of syllables by which a line is hyper- or hypometric.

Variants – The variants list readings in other manuscripts which differ from the base text. All textual and grammatical variants are included. In general, purely orthographic and dialectal variants are not noted, but a few interesting spelling variants have been included. Any abbreviations have been expanded according to the scribe's usual usage, and the letters *i, j, u, v* have been resolved according to modern usage. Hyper- and hypometric lines are indicated by plus and minus signs as in the *Rejected Readings*.

Notes – Comments on specific aspects of the text. They include glosses and interpretations of difficult lines and forms and remarks on such literary aspects of the text as image and theme.

Versification – Comments on the structure, formal genre, the rhymes, and the refrain.

Music – This section provides comments on various aspects of the music—structure and flow of the melodic line, tonal structure, differences among manuscripts in the use of the flat sign, and so forth. The idiosyncrasies of MS *V* are also noted.

The Lyrics and Music

1

L'autrier chevauchoie delez Paris

Bibliographies:	RS 1583, L 224–5, M 27
Refrains:	1 VB 537
	2 VB 620
	3 VB 1900
	4 VB 1282
	5 VB 462
Manuscripts:	*K* 170bis–170ter
	N 81r–81v
	P 185v–186r–186v
	V 45r–45v
	X 122r
Attribution:	*KN*
Music:	*KNPV*
Editions:	Steffens 354
	Aubry, *Arsenal* 59 (melody, 1 str.)
	Bartsch 242
	Gennrich, *Rhythmik* 36 (melody, 1 str.)
	Gennrich, *Rotrouenge* 35 (melody)
	La Borde II 214
	Monmerqué-Michel 32
	Rosenberg 249 (melody)
	Schläger xxi (melody, 1 str.)
	Spanke 431 (melody, 1/2 str.)
Structure:	MW 6,1, coblas singulars

Text:

a	a	a	a	a	a	a	a	v	R
10	10	10	10	10	10	10	10		

Music:

A	A'	A	A'	B	B'	B	B'	v	R
		v	R						

1	11b	11b	12b
2	8b	11b	4b
3	5b'	9b'	
4	5b	10b	5b
5	7b	7b	7b

1. L'au - trier che - vau - choi - e de - lez Pa - ris,

2. Trou - vai pas - to - re - le gar - dant ber - biz;

3. Des - cen - di a ter - re, lez li m'as - sis

4. Et ses a - mo - re - tes je li re - quis.

5. El me dist: "Biau si - re, par Saint De - nis,

6. J'aim plus biau de vous et mult melz a - pris.

7. Ja, tant con - me il soit ne sainz ne vis,

8. Au - tre n'a - me - rai, je le vos ple - vis,

9. Car il est et biax et cor - tois et se - nez.

10. *Dex,* je sui jo - nete et sa - dete et s'aim tez

11. *Qui* jones est et sa - des et sa - ges as - sez.

3,9 re-mi *P.* | 6,3–4 re, mi *P.* | 7,1–7 re, re, mi, fa, sol descending plica, mi-re *KNP* (–1). In all the manuscripts there is only a single neume for the word *conme,* which should count as two syllables. This phrase repeats phrase 5, which has enough syllables because *mi* and *re* are written as separate neumes. The phrase has been emended in accordance with line 5. | 8,3–4 re, mi *P.* 8,4 fa *N,* this reading gives a literal repetition of phrase 6. | 9,10 do-re *NP.* | 10,8 descending plica *N.* 10,9–10 do, re *P.* | 11,2 fa *N.* In all of the manuscripts the word *jones* has only one neume above it and is counted as one syllable rather than two. 11,7–8 do, re *NP,* literal repetition of phrase 9. 11,10 do-re *NP.*

1.   L'autrier chevauchoie delez Paris,
     Trouvai pastorele gardant berbiz;
     Descendi a terre, lez li m'assis
     Et ses amoretes je li requis.   4
     El me dist: "Biau sire, par Saint Denis,
     J'aim plus biau de vous et mult melz apris.
     Ja, tant conme il soit ne sainz ne vis,
     Autre n'amerai, je le vos plevis,   8
Car il est et biax et cortois et senez.
Dex, je sui jonete et sadete et s'aim tez
Qui jones est et sades et sages assez."

2.   Robin l'atendoit en un valet,   12
     Par ennui s'assist lez un buissonet,
     Q'il s'estoit levez trop matinet
     Pour coillir la rose et le musguet,
     S'ot ja a s'amie fet chapelet   16
     Et a soi un autre tout nouvelet.
     Et dist: "Je me muir, bele," en son sonet,
     "Se plus demorez un seul petitet,
        Jamés vif ne mi trouverez.   20
Tres douce damoisele, vous m'ocirrez
         Se vous voulez."

3.   Quant ele l'oï si desconforter,
     Tantost vint a li sanz demorer.   24
     Qui lors les veïst joie demener,
     Robin debruisier et Marot baler!
     Lez un buissonet s'alerent jöer,
     Ne sai q'il i firent, n'en qier parler,   28
     Mes n'i voudrent pas granment demorer,
     Ainz se releverent pour melz noter
        Ceste pastorele:
        Va li doriax li doriax lairele.   32

4.   Je m'arestai donc iluec endroit,
     Si vi la grant joie que cil fesoit
     Et le grant solaz que il demenoit
     Qui onques amors servies n'avoit,   36
     Et dis: "Je maudi amors orendroit,
     Qui tant m'ont tenu lonc tens a destroit;

Ge·s ai plus servies q'onme qui soit
N'onques n'en oi bien, si n'est ce pas droit;   40
   Pour ce les maudi.
Male honte ait il qui Amors parti
   Quant g'i ai failli!"

5.   De si loig conme li bergiers me vit,   44
    S'escria mult haut et si me dist:
    "Alez vostre voie, por Jhesu Crist,
    Ne nos tolez pas nostre deduit!
    J'ai mult plus de joie et de delit   48
    Que li rois de France n'en a, ce cuit;
    S'il a sa richece, je la li cuit
    Et j'ai m'amïete et jor et nuit,
       Ne ja ne departiron.   52
    Dancez, bele Marion!
    Ja n'aim je riens se vous non."

Rejected Readings
5. il *for* el ‖ 12. matendoit ‖ 23. el (–1) ‖ 44. con (–1)

Variants
1–28. *missing in* X ‖ 2. brebiz V. 3. delez (+1) V. 4. et et ses (+1) P. 5. ele
(+1) V. 6. biaus N; et et mult (+1) P. 7. com il (–1) V; ne mors ne vis V. 11.
qui joenne N, jennes V. ‖ 14. s'estoit] estoit N. 15. rose] rousee V. 16. ja
ja a s'amie (+1) N; fet un c. (+1) V. 17. unt N. 20. vis P; ne me NV; verrez
(–1) V. 21. Tres] he V; damoisele] besselete P; m'orcirrez N. ‖ 23. el N,
cele V. 24. lui P. 28. que il firent V; paller V. 29. granment] longuement
(+1) V. 32. lairele] la durele X. ‖ 33. et NPVX. 34. vit N. 35. granz N; qu'il
(–1) X. 36. servie V. 37. di PV. 38. m'ont tant P. 39. que honme (+1) V. 40.
ce n'est mie droiz V. 42. cil qui amours pert (–1) V. ‖ 44–54. *stanza omitted
in* PV. 44. con (–1) X. 48. mult *omitted* N (–1). 49. ce] se X; ce cuiit N. 50.
quit X.

Notes
1–28. MS X is missing a leaf (fol. 121) that undoubtedly included these
   stanzas. The leaf was replaced in the eighteenth century by a copy of the
   text of MS N.
10–11. The use of the nominative *tez* instead of the oblique *tel* seems to be
   an example of attraction caused by the subject relative pronoun *qui*
   (Moignet 90).

20. *mi*, me, Picard form (Moignet 38).
24. *li* (m.), him.
25. *Qui lors les veïst*, "You should have seen them!"
28. *Ne sai q'il i firent*, "I do not know what they did there."
32. Onomatopoetic refrain.
39. *ge·s*, contraction of *je les*.
42. *qui*, i.e., *cui*. "A curse on him whom Love has favored."
50. *cuit* PI 3 *quiter*, to give up, yield.

Versification
This pastourelle, consisting of five stanzas of eight decasyllabic lines, poses an interesting metrical problem. The normal division of a ten-syllable line in Old French lyric is 6 + 4 or 4 + 6. But many of the lines in this poem are of the *taratantara* type which divides the line into two five-syllable halves (5 + 5). This type of caesura occurs frequently in poetry of popular character but is very rare in the courtly *chanson* (Jeanroy, *Origines* 356; Dragonetti 495–99). However, some of the lines (7, 12, 14, 15, 24, 33, 45, 47, 48, 51) are one syllable short, having the division 5 + 4. According to Michel Burger, this variant of the ten-syllable line derives from the *arte mayor* and appears quite frequently in earliest pastourelles (see Burger 30–46, particularly 44–45 where he discusses this poem). Jeanroy, on the other hand, would prefer to regularize these lines (*Review* 443). Some lines can be regularized if a mute -e is not elided before a vowel (lines 15, 48, and 51, for example). But in other lines (12, 24, 45, and 47) there is no practical way of restoring the meter. Consequently, the text has not been emended.

It should be noted that all of the rhymes in the stanzas are masculine. The only feminine rhyme appears in the refrain of stanza 3.

The refrains of stanzas 1, 3, 4, and 5 appear only in this poem. The second refrain (VB 620) also occurs in two multiple-refrain love songs, RS 824 (str. 5) and RS 979 (str. 6).

Music
This song has a rather simple repetitive melody—AA'AA' BB'BB' vR—which reflects the metrical structure of decasyllabic lines in stanzas based on a single rhyme sound. The differences between A-A' and B-B' are very small, consisting of only a slight variation at the end of the phrase that makes it either open or closed. The manuscripts provide the music for the transitional line and refrain of only the first stanza, and these too show a similar repetitive structure: the two phrases of the refrain are open and closed versions of the transitional line (or C/C'C). The melodies of the refrains of stanzas 2–5 are not notated and are not found in any other sources.

The melody is interesting in that it shifts from one chain of thirds, *re-fa-la*, to another, *do-mi-sol*. The musical phrases A and A' begin with a variant of a recitation on *la* and have *re* and *la* as clear structural tones. In B and B' this chain is reduced to a third, *re-fa*, and the secondary chain, *do-mi-sol*, becomes more apparent, particularly in the second half of the line. These lines serve as a transition, in the first stanza at least, to the refrain and its introductory verse, where the chain *do-mi-sol* comes to dominate. The piece ends with *do* as the final tone.

Manuscript *V* has a completely different melody.

2

De chanter m'est pris corage

Bibliographies:	RS 22, L 224–2, M 1109
Manuscripts:	*K* 171
	N 81v-82r
	P 183v-184r
	V 45v-46r
	X 122r-122v
Attribution:	*KNX*
Music:	*KNPVX*
Editions:	Steffens 333
	Aubry, *Arsenal* 59 (melody, 1 str.)
	Aubry, *T et T* 102 (melody, 1 str.)
	Aubry, *T and T* 84 (melody, 1 str.)
	Cluzel 123
Structure:	MW 860,109, coblas doblas 1–2, coblas singulars 3–5

Text:

a′	b	a′	b	b	a′	a′	b
7	7	7	7	7	7	7	7

Music:

A	B	A	B	C	D	E	F

1. De chan - ter m'est pris co - ra - ge

2. Pour la tres be - le lö - er,

3. Ce que n'ai pas en u - sa - ge;

4. Mes a - mors me font chan - ter

5. Qui sou - vent me font tren - bler.

6. Li maus d'a - mors, c'est la ra - ge;

7. Bien sai, s'il ne m'a - so - a - ge,

8. Je ne puis lon - gues du - rer.

1,4 *omitted N.* 1,8 la *NX.* ❙ 2,3 no plica *X.* 2,5 fa *NPX,* this reading is an exact repetition of phrase 4. 2,6 *illegible N.* ❙ 3,1 la *X.* 3,8 la-ti *N;* no plica *X.* ❙ 4,3 descending plica *NP;* no plica *X.* 4,4 sol-fa-mi-re *X.* ❙ 6,4 no plica *X.* ❙ 7,4 do'-la *NPX.* All of the manuscripts (including *K*) have this version of the phrase in song 7 (RS 614) which shares the same melody. 7,5 la descending plica *P.* 7,6 sol *P;* no plica *X.* 7,7–8 fa-mi-re, do *NX.* ❙ 8,5 la-sol *NPX.*

1.   De chanter m'est pris corage
    Pour la tres bele löer,
    Ce que n'ai pas en usage;
    Mes amors me font chanter   4
    Qui souvent me font trenbler.
    Li maus d'amors, c'est la rage;
    Bien sai, s'il ne m'asoage,
    Je ne puis longues durer.   8

2.   Amors, je vous faz honmage,
    Car je me puis bien vanter
    Que je aim la plus tres sage
    Dont oïsse onques parler,   12
    Qui plus biau se set porter
    Sanz orgueil et sanz outrage,
    Ne ja pour son grant parage
    Ne voudra beuban mener.   16

3.   Je l'ai trop lonc tens amee,
    Onques ne li fis savoir;
    Ne voudroie que blasmee
    Fust de moi pour nul avoir,   20
    Car en son païs pour voir
    N'en a nule plus löee,
    Q'on dit q'il n'est ame nee
    Qui ses amors puisse avoir.   24

4.   G'en pert et solaz et joie
    Quant je n'i puis avenir,
    Qu'en me dit que melz porroie
    La roïne convertir;   28
    Si ne sai que devenir,
    Car siens sui ou que je soie,
    Ne ja, se s'amor n'est moie,
    Ne me puet joie venir.   32

5.   Chançon par amors trouvee,
    Salue moi la vaillant
    Et, se ton chant ne li gree,
    Di li qu'el le me remant;   36

Ja ne seras dite avant.
Mes soies de li amee,
Tu seras souvent chantee
De fin cuer baut et joiant.   40

Rejected Readings
40. bauz

Variants
3. n'a pas *N*. ‖ 11. car j'aim la tres plus sage (–1) *X*. 12. j'oïsse *N*, oïssiés *X*; paller *V*. 15. na ja por si grant outrage *N*. ‖ 17. tant lonc lonc tens (+1) *N*. 20. fu por moi *N*. 21. en sa rue *P*. 22. si loee *N*. 23. dist *V*. ‖ 25. L'en pert *PV*. 27. dist *V*. 30. car] que *V*. 31. ne ja *omitted V* (–2); l'amor *V*. ‖ 36. qu'ele me *NVX*. 38. soiez *P*, se es *V*. 40. baut] liez *P*; et baus et joiant (+1) *X*.

Notes
19–20. *que blasmee fust de moi*, "that she be blamed because of me."
34. *Salue moi*, dative of interest, "greet (her) for me."

Versification
This courtly *chanson* consists of five isometric stanzas of eight heptasyllabic lines. According to Dragonetti, this structure occurs frequently (387), and the combination of alternating rhymes followed by enclosing rhymes is the dominant type in courty lyric (441). MW list 128 pieces with this rhyme scheme of which nineteen have seven-syllable lines. Richard uses exactly the same structure in song 7 (RS 614).

Stanzas 1–2 of this poem present the only example of *coblas doblas* in the works of Richard.

Music
This melody has the typical structure of a courtly *chanson*, AB AB X. Unlike Richard's other melodies, it moves quite freely throughout the piece within the octave from *re* to *re'*. Phrase A begins with a recitation on *re'*, and like phrase D it develops the upper part of the range, while phrases C and F concentrate on the lower part. Phrases B and E make use of the whole range in a descending pattern which acts as a transition from the upper to the lower range. Richard used the same melody for song 7 (RS 614), another courtly love song which also shares the same rhyme scheme.

Manuscript *V* presents a distinct melody and has different melodies for songs 2 and 7 (RS 22 and 614).

3

Par amors ferai chançon

Bibliographies:	RS 1860, L 224–10, M 1237
Refrain:	VB 417, variable refrain
Manuscripts:	*K* 171–172
	N 82r-82v
	P 101r-101v-102r
	V 46r-46v
	X 122v-123r
Attribution:	*KNPX*
Music:	*KNPVX*
Editions:	Steffens 360
	Aubry, *Arsenal* 60 (melody, 1 str.)
	Noack 141
	Rosenberg 254 (melody)
Structure:	MW 890,3, coblas singulars

Text:	a	b	a	b	b	a	a	c′	A	C′
	7	7	7	7	7	7	7	8	7	8
Music:	A	B	A	C	D	E	F	G /	F	G

1. Par　a - mors　fe - rai　chan - çon

2. Pour　la　tres　be - le　lö - er;

3. Tout　me　sui　mis　a　ban - don

4. En　li　ser - vir　et　a - mer;

5. Mult　m'a　fet　maus　en - du - rer,

6. Si.n　a - tent　le　guer - re - don,

7. N'on - ques　n'en　oi　se　mal　non.

8. Hé　las,　si　l'ai　je　tant　a - me - e!

9. *Dame,　il　fust　mes　bien　se - son*

10. *Que　vostre　a - mor　me　fust　do - ne - e.*

The flat signs are given as they appear in MS *K*. A small arrow above the staff indicates the beginning of a new staff in the manuscript. See notes for a discussion of the flat signs in the other manuscripts. ❙ 1,4 do' *P; omitted X.* ❙ 5,3 ti-sol *NPX.* 5,4 la-ti *N.* ❙ 9,1 mi', fa' *K* (+1). 9,4 re' *X.*

1.   Par amors ferai chançon
        Pour la tres bele löer;
        Tout me sui mis a bandon
        En li servir et amer;
        Mult m'a fet maus endurer,   5
        Si·n atent le guerredon,
        N'onques n'en oi se mal non.
      Hé las, si l'ai je tant amee!
        Dame, il fust mes bien seson
     Que vostre amor me fust donee.   10

2.   Onques riens mes cuers n'ama
        Fors la bele pour qui chant,
        Ne jamés riens n'amera,
        Ce sai je bien autretant.
        Ma douce dame vaillant,   15
        Bien sai, quant il vos plera,
        En pou d'eure me sera
      Ma grant paine guerredonnee.
        Dame qui je aim pieç'a,
     Et quant m'iert vostre amor donee?   20

3.   Dame ou touz biens sont assis,
        Une riens dire vos vueil:
        Se vous estes de haut pris,
        Pour Dieu, gardez vous d'orgueil
        Et soiez de bel acueil   25
        Et aus granz et as petiz;
        Vos ne serez pas touz dis
      Ensi requise et demandee.
        Dame ou j'ai tout mon cuer mis,
     Et quant m'iert vostre amor donee?   30

4.   Se vous vivez longuement,
        Dame, il ert oncore un tens
        Ou viellece vous atent,
        Lors diroiz a toutes genz:
        "Lasse, je fui de mal sens,   35
        Que n'amai en mon jouvent,
        Ou requise iere souvent;
      Or sui de chascun refusee."

Dame que j'aim loiaument,
Et quant m'iert vostre amor donee?   40

5.   Chançon, va tost sanz delai
            A la tres bele au vis cler
            Et si li di de par moi
            Que je muir por bien amer,
            Car je ne puis plus durer   45
            A la dolor que je trai,
            Ne ja respas n'en arrai,
            Puis que ma mort tant li agree.
            Dame que j'aim de cuer vrai,
            Et quant m'iert vostre amor donee?   50

Variants

3. mis en abandon (+1) X. 6. si en atent (+1) P, j'en atent V. 9. bien mes seson N. ‖ 12. la la bele por qui je chant (+2) N. 13. n'amerai X. 14. sai je] sachiez V. 19–20. *omitted in* V. 19. qui] que NP; j'aim grant piecea X. 20. m'iert *omitted* P (–1). ‖ 25. soies PX. 26. au petiz N, a petis X. 28. et] ne V. 29. Dame il fust etc. V. 30. et quant etc. N. ‖ 32. uns tenz V. 35. mas sens N. 36. ma jouvent P. 37. iere] fui V. 39. Dame il fust etc. V. 40. et quant etc. N; doner X. ‖ 41. Chamçon N; va t'ent V, va t'en X. 42. cler vis V. 47. respas] respons N. 48. tant li gree (–1) V. 49. Dame etc. V; verai (+1) NX. 50. done N.

Notes

6. *si·n*, contraction of *si en*.
19. *qui*, i.e., *cui*, direct object.
26. *aus, as*, contraction of *a + les*.
31–38. The theme of this stanza, although it becomes well known later with the poetry of Ronsard ("Quand vous serez bien vieille"), is very rare in the poetry of this period. In fact, it is possible that this is the only example.

Versification

This love song has the structure of a courtly *chanson* to which a variable refrain has been added. The rhyme scheme, *abab baac'*, is of the type *cadena caudada* to which an extra rhyme has been added. This stanza derives from a courtly stanza of seven lines to which a rhyme *estramp* has been added (Dragonetti 436). This additional rhyme links the refrain to the stanza. MW list only three poems with this structure.

    This variable refrain is found only in this piece. The variations in the first line of the refrain are necessitated by the rhyme scheme, since the refrain repeats the rhyme and the number of syllables of the last two lines of the stanza. The meaning of the refrain remains the same in stanzas 2–5 in spite of the small variations in the first line. The change in the refrain between the first stanza and the others is more significant. In the first stanza, the poet declares that it is time that his lady give him her love. He believes he merits it by his service and his suffering. In the other stanzas, this declaration becomes a question that reveals his impatience (Johnson, *Refrain* 165–67). It is quite rare to have a significant change in the refrain at the beginning of a poem. Normally such changes occur in the final stanza.

Music

The manuscripts do not agree on which b's are to be flatted in the two melodic phrases of lines 7–10. All manuscripts indicate a flat (either before the note or at the beginning of the staff) for 10,7–8, but the flat appears only in *KNX* for the corresponding notes in line 8. MSS *KX* would seem to indicate a flat for 10,3, since the flat sign appears at the beginning of the staff in which the note appears, but none of the manuscripts show a flat before its counterpart in 8,3. The scribe of MS *X* places a flat sign at the beginning of every staff from 8,6 on. This would imply that 9,7 should be flatted as well. The other manuscripts do not indicate a flat at this point, and none of them show a flat before 7,7.

The structure of this melody, ABAC DEFG / FG, is more complex than those of the other songs, and it seems to be a variant of the common AB AB X structure. Phrase A of the *frons* introduces a melodic line which is repeated with a few changes in F. This phrase therefore links the three parts of the poem—*frons, cauda,* and refrain—and it also reinforces the rhyme scheme of the poem, since it appears consistently with the a- rhyme.

The melody has a wide range from *mi* to *sol'*. The opening phrase A, its variant F, and E explore the upper part of this range, while phrases B, C, and G concentrate on the lower part.

Manuscript *V* has a different melody.

4

Mult ai chanté, riens ne m'i puet valoir

Bibliographies:	RS 1820, L 224–8, M 1337
Refrains:	1 VB 1134
	2 VB 766
	3 VB 1852
	4 VB 582
	5 VB 505
Manuscripts:	*K* 172–173
	N 82v-83r
	P 98v-99r-99v
	V 46v-47r
	X 123r-123v-124r
Attribution:	*KNPX*
Music:	*KNPVX*
Editions:	Steffens 357
	Aubry, *Arsenal* 60 (melody, 1 str.)
	Cremonesi 219
	Toja 449
Structure:	MW 902,2, coblas singulars

	Text:	a	b	a	b	b	a	b	a	v	R
		10	10	10	10	10	10	10	10		
	Music:	A	B	A	B	C	D	E	F	v	R
				v		R					

1	8c	8c	8c
2	5c	7d'	5c
3	4c	5d	9c
4	8c'	6d	6c'
5	5c'	6c'	6c'

1. Mult ai chan - té riens ne m'i puet va - loir,

2. Car de mon chant a ma da - me n'en chaut;

3. Si ai plo - ré sou - vent par des - es - poir,

4. Mes ne chan - ter ne plo - rer ne m'i vaut.

5. Fox fu mes cuers quant il pen - sa si haut

6. Ou a - ve - nir ne puet pour nul a - voir,

7. La ou mer - ci crï - er riens ne li vaut,

8. Ne pri - e - re n'um - ble - ment sou - ploi - er;

9. Si puis vrai - e - ment chan - ter dont:

10. *Je sui li mains a - mez du mont*

11. *Et aim plus que tuit cil qui sont.*

2,3 do' descending plica *N.* 2,7 la-sol-fa *P.* ‖ 4,3 do' descending plica *N.* 4,4 la-sol *P.* 4,5 la *P.* 4,7 ti-la-sol *P.* ‖ 6,4 fa'-mi'-re' *P.* 6,6–7 no plica *X.* 6,8 descending plica *N.* ‖ 8,2 no plica *X.*

1. Mult ai chanté, riens ne m'i puet valoir,
    Car de mon chant a ma dame n'en chaut;
    Si ai ploré souvent par desespoir,
    Mes ne chanter ne plorer ne m'i vaut.   4
    Fox fu mes cuers quant il pensa si haut
    Ou avenir ne puet pour nul avoir,
    La ou merci crïer riens ne li vaut,
    Ne priere n'umblement souploier;   8
        Si puis vraiement chanter dont:
        Je sui li mains amez du mont
        Et aim plus que tuit cil qui sont.

2. Atornez sui, bien le voi, au languir,   12
    C'onques mes riens ne fu si entrepris,
    Car d'amer la ne me puis repentir
    Et si voi bien que avenir n'i puis;
    Pour ce chastoi cil qui n'ont pas apris   16
    Le grant ennui qui d'amors puet venir:
    Au conmencier se gardent bien touz dis,
    Car j'ai amors dont me couvient morir
            Tout sanz nul resort.   20
        Gardez bien voz amoretes,
        Les moies m'ont mort.

3. Ele me fet a duel ma vie user,
    Car je ne puis pour riens avoir s'amor;   24
    Ne me chausist ja de maus endurer
    Ne de paines plus q'un ribaut de for,
    Se cuidasse oncore au chief du tor
    En ma dame nule merci trouver.   28
    Biau sire Dex, verrai je ja le jor
    Que seul a seul li poïsse chanter
            Ceste chançon:
                Vous avez mon cuer   32
        Et j'ai vostre amor en ma prison.

4. Hors du païs m'en couvendra fouïr,
    Car je ne puis plus ces maus endurer
    Que ma dame m'i a fet tant sousfrir   36
    Et si ne puis en li merci trouver;

Si me vient melz ma vie ailleurs sauver
Que ci a duel et a torment morir;
Ne ça ne pens jamés jor retorner   40
Se ma dame ne venoit a plesir.
    Dex, qui set pour quoi el m'enchace?
     Di je donc, faz je donc
     Chose qu'autre ne face?   44

5.   Chançonete, tu me salueras
    La plus douce qui el mont n'a sa per,
    As ensaignes que a un soir tout bas
    Soe merci daigna a moi parler,   48
    Mes n'i osai pas granment demorer,
    Car je cuidai q'il ne li pleüst pas,
    Et si li di, pour Dieu ne li celer,
    Gart bien mon cuer qu'ele tient en ses las   52
     Et en sa baillie.
     Dex, de mon cuer n'ai mie,
     Ainz l'a ma douce amie.

Rejected Readings

5. mon cuer ‖ 8. nublement ‖ 10. le ‖ 12. a alanguir (+1) ‖ 52. gar

Variants

1. me puet *X*. 2. ne chaut *VX*, ne chant *N*. 4. ne plorer ne chanter *V*. 5. mon *P*; cuer *NP*; si si haut (+1) *N*. 8. nublement *NP*, humblement *V*. 9. veraiement (+1) *N*; chanter que *V*. 10. le *PX*; amé *P*. 11. j'aim *N*, si aing (+1) *V*; qui i sont (+1) *V*. ‖ 12. voi a languir *N*. 13. mes *omitted N* (–1); riens] nus *V*. 14. la] laz *V*. 16. ce *omitted N* (–1); cil] cel *V*. 18. si *P*, s'en *V*. 19. par Dieu amors *V*. 20. resort] deport *V*. 21. gardez vos bien d'amoretes *N*. ‖ 23. ma vie a duel user *N*. 25. ne ne me chausist (+1) *N*; des maus *NV*. 26. ne des paines *V*. 27. encor tout achever (–1) *V*. 29. je *omitted X* (–1). 30. chanter] conter *N*. 31. ceste chanter ceste chançon (+4) *P*. ‖ 36. me fet trop maux souffrir *V*. 38. aillors ma vie sauver *N*. 40. ça] ja *P*, sai *V*; jamés nul jor (+1) *X*. 42. e Diex (+1) *V*; ele (+1) *V*, il *X*; me chace *NV*. 44. que autre *P*. ‖ 45–55. *stanza omitted in V*. 49. osa *N*.

Notes

16. *cil*. All of the manuscripts have the nominative *cil* instead of the oblique *cels, ceus*. Lucien Foulet notes this usage and attributes it to the weakening of the case system (*Petite Syntaxe* 171). It is also possible that the nominative case is used because of the attraction of the subject relative pronoun *qui* (Moignet 90).

25–26. "I would not mind enduring torment and suffering any more than a scoundrel worries about the price (of things he steals), if I believed that in the end my lady would show me some mercy (*literally*, I would find any mercy in my lady)."

45. *Tu me salueras*, dative of interest, "You will greet for me, on my behalf."

47. *as*, contraction of *a* + *les*.

Versification

This multiple-refrain love song uses a typical courtly structure for its stanzas. The five *coblas singulars* are each followed by a transitional line of variable length that links the refrain to the stanza. The rhyme scheme *abab baba* is a variant of the eight-line stanza called *cobla encadenada*, with the rhymes appearing in reverse order in the *cauda* (Dragonetti 435). MW find forty-two pieces with this rhyme scheme.

The a-rhyme of the first stanza is noteworthy: *valoir, desespoir, avoir,* and *souploier*.

All of the refrains occur in other poems. The first (VB 1134) also appears in a single-refrain love song, RS 1387a; the second (VB 766) in a motet, M 82; the third (VB 1852) in a multiple-refrain pastourelle, RS 1372 (str. 5); the fourth (VB 582) in a multiple-refrain love song, RS 536 (str. 4); and the last (VB 505) in a single-refrain religious lyric, RS 902a.

Music

All of the manuscripts have a flat sign before 8,5, and the sign appears at the beginning of each staff after that to the end of the song.

The melody has the widest range of Richard's songs, extending from *re* to *fa'*. The structure is that of a courtly *chanson* (AB AB X) modified by the inclusion of a transitional line and refrains. The melody moves from the chain *fa-la-do'*, which dominates phrases A and B, to the tetrachord above which is explored in phrases C and D. After a rather dramatic build to *fa'* in D, phrase E returns to the lower part of the range, leading into the transition to the refrain. The two lines of the refrain are open and closed versions, with slight variations, of the same melodic line. The refrain returns and develops the lower end of the original chain, *fa-la*. The melodies of the refrains of stanzas 2–5 are not notated, and they are not found in any other source.

5

Chançon ferai plain d'ire et de pensee

Bibliographies:	RS 538, L 224–1, M 528
Refrain:	VB 605
Manuscripts:	*K* 174
	N 83r-83v
	P 97v-98r-98v
	V 47r
	X 124r-124v
Attribution:	*KNPX*
Music:	*KNPVX*
Editions:	Steffens 343
	Aubry, *Arsenal* 60 (melody, 1 str.)
	Cremonesi 217
	Gennrich, *Rotrouenge* 58 (melody)
	Noack 114
	Toja 446
Structure:	MW 449,1, coblas capcaudadas

Text: a′   a′   b   b   b   a′   C   C   C   A′
        10   10   6   6   7   6   6   6   7   6

Music: A   A   B   /   B

Model for RS 1182 (song to the Virgin)

1.   Chan - çon   fe - rai   plain   d'ire   et   de   pen - se - e

2.   Pour   ce - le   riens   el   mont   qui   plus   m'a - gre - e;

3.   Hé las!   on - ques   n'a - ma

4.   De   cuer   qui   li   blas - ma.

5.   Dex,   pour   quoi   es - con - dit   m'a?

6.   El   m'a   la   mort   do - ne - e.

7.   Dou - ce   da - me   de   pris

8.   Qui   je   lo   tant   et   pris,

9.   Si   m'a   vostre   a - mor   sor - pris,

10.   Plus   vous   aim   que   riens   ne - e.

1,4 *omitted X* (−1). 1,10 la, la-la-sol *X* (+1). 1,11 fa *NPX*, this reading gives an exact repetition of phrase 2. ❙ 4,1–5 mi, fa, sol, sol, fa-mi, fa-mi *X* (+1). ❙ 7,3 no flat indicated *P*. 7,6 descending plica *X*. ❙ 9,1–3 mi, fa, sol *X*. 9,3 fa, sol *N* (+1). ❙ 10,1–2 do, re *X*.

1.   Chançon ferai plain d'ire et de pensee
         Pour cele riens el mont qui plus m'agree;
             Hé las! onques n'ama
             De cuer qui li blasma.
              Dex, pour quoi escondit m'a?   5
             El m'a la mort donee.
             Douce dame de pris
             Qui je lo tant et pris,
        Si m'a vostre amor sorpris,
          Plus vous aim que riens nee.   10

2.   La fine amor qui m'est el cuer entree
         N'en puet partir, c'est dont chose passee.
             Bien voi, tuer me puis
             Ou noier en un puis,
              Car ja n'avrai joie puis   15
             Qu'a m'amor refusee.
             Douce [dame de pris,
             Qui je lo tant et pris,
         Si m'a vostre amor sorpris,
          Plus vous aim que riens nee].   20

3.   Ele est et bele et blonde et acesmee,
         Plus blanche assez que la flor en la pree;
             Ne sai de son ator
             N'en chastiau ne en tour
              Nule, s[i] en sui au tor   25
             De morir s'il li gree.
             Douce [dame de pris ˙
             Qui je lo tant et pris,
         Si m'a vostre amor sorpris,
          Plus vous aim que riens nee].   30

4.   Douce dame qui j'ai tant desirree,
         Ou j'ai tout mis cuer et cors et pensee,
             Jamés nul mal n'eüst
             Ne morir ne deüst
              Qui entre voz braz geüst   35
             Jusques a l'ajornee.
             Douce [dame de pris
             Qui je lo tant et pris,

Si m'a vostre amor sorpris,
Plus vous aim que riens nee]. 40

5.   Chançon que j'ai par fine amor trouvee,
Va devant l'uis, si seras citolee,
     Ou la tres bele maint
     Qui m'a fet ennui maint,
     Prie li qu[e] ele m'aint 45
     Ou ma joie est finee.
     [*Douce dame de pris*
     Qui je lo tant et pris,
Si m'a vostre amor sorpris,
Plus vous aim que riens nee]. 50

Rejected Readings

25. sen sui (–1) ‖ 36. jusques a lainz jornee ‖ 45. quele (–1)

Variants

1. plainz *V*; pesance *V*. 2. du mont *V*; que plus *P*. 4. mes cuers *PVX*; qui la
me blasma (+1) *N*. 6. el] et *V*. 8. que je *X*, qui ici lo (+1) *V*. ‖ 12. donc *N*;
chose prouvee *VX*. 15. car] et *V*; ja *omitted N* (–1). 16. qu'ele a (+1) *V*, que
m'amor *X*. 17. *refrain omitted in P*, D. dame *N*, D. d. de pris etc. *V*. ‖ 22.
f. que en la pree (+1) *V*. 24. en chasteau *N*. 25. s'en sui (–1) *NPVX*. 26. de
morir] d'amours *V*; agree (+1) *VX*. 27. D. dame de priz etc. *V*. ‖ 31. qui]
que *NP*. 32. j'ai] ja *N*; cuers *N*. 34. deüst] peüst *N*. 36. jusques a lainz jornee
NPX. 37. D. dame de priz *V*; *refrain omitted in P*. ‖ 41. que] qui *X*. 42.
devant li *V*; citolee] acolee *VX*. 45. priez *V*; qu'ele *NPVX*. 47. Douce *PX*,
Douce dame *NV*.

Notes

4. *qui*, "he who."
Refr. *qui*, i.e., *cui*, direct object.
16. *Qu'a m'amor refusee*, "since she has refused my love."
23–26. "I know of no lady of her character (nature) either in a castle or a
    tower, and so I am prepared to die (for her love), if she wishes."
25. This line is one syllable short in all of the manuscripts.
31. *qui*, i.e., *cui*, direct object.
42– 43. *l'huis* is the antecedent of the relative *ou*.
45. This line is a syllable short in all of the manuscripts.

Versification

This love song, completely courtly in its tone, shares its metrical structure
and music with the pastourelle that follows (song 6, RS 527). The refrain

repeats the metrical and musical structure of the last four lines of the stanza.

The rhymes of this poem present a unique *tour de force* in Richard's works. The poet, who normally prefers simple, sufficient rhymes, uses a variety of difficult rhymes here, especially in lines 3–5 of each stanza and in the refrain:

str. 1 leonine and paronymic rhymes: *ama, blasma, m'a*
str. 2 homonymic rhymes: *puis* (v.), *puis* (n.m.), *puis* (conj.)
str. 3 homonymic and paronymic rhymes: *ator, tour* (n.f.), *tor* (n.m.)
str. 4 leonine rhymes: *eüst, deüst, geüst*
str. 5 homonymic and equivocal rhymes: *maint* (v.), *maint* (adj.), *m'aint*
refr. homonymic and paronymic rhymes: *pris* (n.m.), *pris* (v.), *sorpris*.

In addition, the a-rhyme repeats the same rhyme sound in all of the stanzas, making the last rhyme of one stanza the first rhyme of the next, or *coblas capcaudadas*.

VB does not list any other examples of this refrain.

Music

Manuscripts *KNX* all have a b-flat sign after the clef in all staffs that contain a *b*. MS *P* also has b-flat signs in the initial staffs, but the sign is not found in the staff containing 7,3. Since this phrase repeats phrase 3 where all manuscripts indicate a b-flat, it would seem that the missing sign in *P* is a scribal error.

This song has the simple bipartite structure AA B/B. Gennrich designated it as a *rotrouenge* in which the second melodic phrase expands to four lines that are then repeated by the refrain. Phrase A is a recitation on *la* with a very limited range. The reading of MS *K* gives different notes for the final tones of lines 1 and 2, making them open and closed respectively. In MSS *NPX*, line 1 is a literal repetition of line 2, ending on *fa*. Lines 3–5 (and their repetition in 7–9) use a step-wise ascending-descending pattern to gradually descend and add the third member of the chain, *re*. Lines 6 and 10 have *re* and *fa* as structural tones and firmly establish the chain *re-fa-la*.

The same melody is used for song 6 (RS 527).

Manuscript *V* has a melody that shows none of the repetitions found in the other manuscripts, and it presents different melodies for songs 5 and 6 (RS 538 and 527).

6

Je chevauchai l'autrier la matinee

Bibliographies:	RS 527, L 224–4, M 536
Refrain:	VB 1299
Manuscripts:	*K* 174–175
	N 83v–84r
	P 97r–97v
	V 47r–47v
	X 124v–125r
Attribution:	*KNPX*
Music:	*KNPVX*
Editions:	Steffens 337
	Aubry, *Arsenal* 61 (melody, 1 str.)
	Bartsch 243
	Gennrich, *Rotrouenge* 54 (melody)
	Monmerqué-Michel 33
	Rosenberg 252 (melody)
	Schläger xxiii (melody, 1 str.)
Structure:	MW 480,1, coblas singulars

Text:

a′	a′	b	b	b	c′	D	D	D	C′
10	10	6	6	7	6	6	6	7	6

Music: A A B / B

1. Je che - vau - chai l'au - trier la ma - ti - ne - e;

2. De - lez un bois, as - sez pres de l'en - tre - e,

3. Gen - til pas - to - re truis.

4. Mes ne vi on - ques puis

5. (Ne) si plai - ne de de - duis

6. Ne qui si bien m'a - gre - e.

7. Ma tres dou - ce - te suer,

8. Vos a - vez tout mon cuer,

9. Ne vous le - roie a nul fuer;

10. M'a - mor vous ai do - ne - e.

5,1 mi *P.* 5,2–4 mi, fa-sol *KNPX* (–1). The phrase is one syllable short in all manuscripts. Phrase 9, which repeats this phrase, has the same pitches but with a different distribution that results in enough syllables—re, mi, fa, sol. The phrase has been emended in accordance with phrase 9.

1.   Je chevauchai l'autrier la matinee;
    Delez un bois, assez pres de l'entree,
        Gentil pastore truis.
        Mes ne vi onques puis
        [Ne] si plaine de deduis   5
        Ne qui si bien m'agree.
        Ma tres doucete suer,
        Vos avez tout mon cuer,
    Ne vous leroie a nul fuer;
        M'amor vous ai donee.   10

2.   Vers li me tres, si descendi a terre
    Pour li vöer et por s'amor requerre.
        Tout maintenant li dis:
        "Mon cuer ai en vos mis,
        Si m'a vostre amor sorpris,   15
        Plus vous aim que riens nee.
        Ma tres [doucete suer,
        Vos avez tout mon cuer,
    Ne vous leroie a nul fuer;
        M'amor vous ai donee]."   20

3.   Ele me dist: "Sire, alez vostre voie!
    Vez ci venir Robin qui j'atendoie,
        Qui est et bel et genz.
        S'il venoit, sanz contens
        N'en irïez pas, ce pens,   25
        Tost avrïez mellee."
        Ma tres [doucete suer,
        Vos avez tout mon cuer,
    Ne vous leroie a nul fuer;
        M'amor vous ai donee].   30

4.   "Il ne vendra, bele suer, oncor mie,
    Il est dela le bois ou il chevrie."
        Dejoste li m'assis,
        Mes braz au col li mis;
        Ele m'a geté un ris   35
        Et dit qu'ele ert tuee.
        Ma tres [doucete suer,
        Vos avez tout mon cuer,

Ne vous leroie a nul fuer;
    M'amor vous ai donee].   40

5.   Quant j'oi tout fet de li quanq'il m'agree,
          Je la besai, a Dieu l'ai conmandee.
              Puis dist, qu'en l'ot mult haut,
              Robin qui l'en assaut:
          "Dehez ait hui qui en chaut!   45
          Ç'a fet ta demoree."
          Ma tres doucete suer,
          [*Vos avez tout mon cuer,*
      Ne vous leroie a nul fuer;
          M'amor vous ai donee].   50

Rejected Readings
5. -1 (emendation Jeanroy)

Variants
1. chevauchoie *V*. 3. pastore i truis *N*. 4. mes] si *N*. 7. douce suer (–1) *V*; doucete suer vos suer (+2) *N*. 9. a nuel fuer *X*. 10. donne *N*. ‖ 13. veoir *VX*. 16. vous *omitted X* (–1). 17. ma t. douce seur etc. (–1) *V*. ‖ 21. m'a dit *V*. 22. R. que je ci atendoie (+2) *V*. 23. biaux *V*. 25. ne mariez pas (*m'av-riez?*) *V*. 26. avrïez la mellee (+1) *V*. 27. ma t. doucete *P*, ma t. douce seur etc. (–1) *V*. ‖ 35. el (–1) *N*; me geta *P*, me gete *VX*; un douz ris *V*. 36. dist *V*. 37. ma *NP*, ma t. douce suer etc. (–1) *V*. ‖ 41. j'oi de li fet tot *N*. 43. dit *NP*; p. d. qu'en l'en assaut *X*. 44. R. son ami en haut *X*. 45. hui *omitted NV* (–1). 47. *refrain omitted in P*; ma tres *NVX*.

Notes
5. This line is one syllable short in all of the manuscripts. Jeanroy suggested the emendation (*Review* 442).
12. *vöer*, i.e., *veoir*, voir. Jeanroy proposes this interpretation in his review of Steffens's edition (*Review* 442), and it is corroborated by the variant *veoir* in manuscripts *VX*.
22. *qui*, i.e., *cui*, direct object.
32. The verb *chevrier* has two meanings: to tend goats and to play the bagpipes (a musical instrument made of goatskin). Both meanings are possible here.
43–44. *Robin* is the indrect object of the verb *dist*.
45. *qui*, i.e., *cui*, indirect object.

Versification
This pastourelle uses one of the more complex forms of the *rotrouenge* as

defined by Gennrich. The second musical phrase (B) extends to the four lines at the end of the stanza which provide the metrical and musical structure of the refrain. This is the only piece listed by MW with this structure, but it closely resembles the preceding love song by Richard (song 5, RS 538) and an anonymous song to the Virgin (RS 1182). The *estramp* rhyme (*c'*) at the end of the stanza links the refrain to the stanza.

The refrain is found only in this poem. It is unusual for a pastourelle refrain in that it presents the thoughts of the knight and remains outside of the dialogue between the knight and the shepherdess in all of the stanzas, except perhaps stanza 2 (Johnson, *Refrain* 59–69).

Music
All of the manuscripts agree on the placement of the flat sign, and they also make line 2 a literal repetition of line 1 (in the preceding song MS *K* presents open and closed versions of this melodic line).

This song has the same melody as song 5 (RS 538); detailed notes accompany the preceding piece.

7

Quant la seson renouvele

Bibliographies:	RS 614, L 224–11, M 1111
Manuscripts:	*K* 175–176
	N 84r-84v
	P 96v-97r
	V 47v-48r
	X 125r-125v
Attribution:	*KNPX*
Music:	*KNPVX*
Editions:	Steffens 346
	Aubry, *Arsenal* 61 (melody, 1 str.)
Structure:	MW 860,111, coblas singulars

Text:	a′	b	a′	b	b	a′	a′	b
	7	7	7	7	7	7	7	7
Music:	A	B	A	B	C	D	E	F

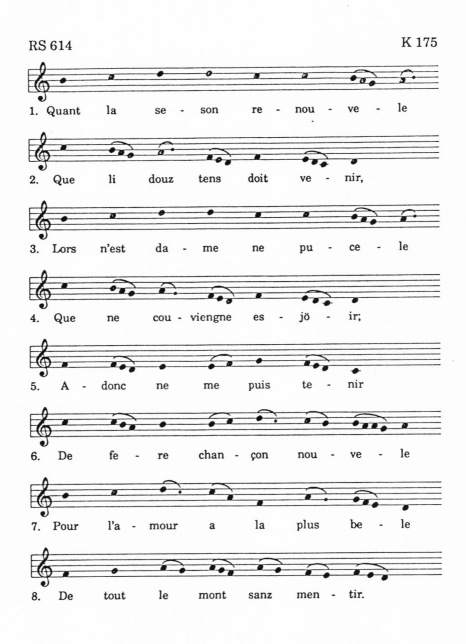

1. Quant   la   se - son   re - nou - ve - le

2. Que   li   douz   tens   doit   ve - nir,

3. Lors   n'est   da - me   ne   pu - ce - le

4. Que   ne   cou - viengne   es - jö - ir;

5. A - donc   ne   me   puis   te - nir

6. De   fe - re   chan - çon   nou - ve - le

7. Pour   l'a - mour   a   la   plus   be - le

8. De   tout   le   mont   sanz   men - tir.

1,8 la-ti *NX*. ‖ 2,3 descending plica *NPX*, exact repetition of phrase 4. ‖ 3,8 la-ti *NX*. ‖ 4,3 no plica *P*. 4,4 sol-fa-mi *P*. ‖ 6,4 ti ascending plica *NP*; ti *X*. ‖ 8,7 fa-mi-re, re *X* (+1).

1.   Quant la seson renouvele
    Que li douz tens doit venir,
    Lors n'est dame ne pucele
    Que ne couviengne esjoïr;   4
    Adonc ne me puis tenir
    De fere chançon nouvele
    Pour l'amour a la plus bele
    De tout le mont sanz mentir.   8

2.   Ne puis müer que ne die
    Les max qu'el me fet sentir,
    Qu'ele est de tel seignorie
    Que nus n'i puet avenir;   12
    Bien voi qu'il m'estuet morir
    Ne rien ne doing en ma vie,
    Car avenir n'i puis mie
    Ne mon cuer n'en puis partir.   16

3.   Oeil, se n'eüsse esperance
    De merci en li trouver,
    J·os feïsse sanz doutance
    Par droit anbesdeus crever,   20
    Qui me feïstes amer
    La plus tres bele de France.
    Certes ce fu grant enfance
    De si hautement penser.   24

4.   Ahi, cuer plain de sotie!
    Et conment t'i consentis?
    Certes ce fu grant folie,
    Ne te poïst venir pis;   28
    Car or pués tu mes touz dis
    Ensi mener dure vie,
    Ne ja n'en avras baillie,
    Car ele est de trop haut pris.   32

5.   Bien voi c'est perdue paine,
    Dolent sui quant me porpens;
    Melz porroit l'en toute Saigne
    Lancier en un pot dedenz   36
    Q'i avenisse a nul tens,
    Se pitié ne li amaine

     Et ce qu'ele est si tres plaine
     De cortoisie et de sens.   40

6.   Je dout mult qu'ele n'ait cure
     De ma chançon retenir,
     Mes qui touz les maus endure
     Se doit un pou enhardir;   44
     Coarz ne puet bien venir,
     Biaucop gist en aventure.
     Va dont, chançon, si li jure
     Qu'el me fet a duel morir.   48

Rejected Readings
19. je *for* j·os ‖ 38. pitiez

Variants
1. sesons *V*. 2. douz tens tens doit (+1) *N*. 4. que *omitted V*; resjoïr *V*. ‖ 9–
16. *stanza omitted in P*. 10. qu'el] que *N*. 12. puist *X*. 14. ne *omitted V* (–1);
riens *NVX*. ‖ 19. j ci os (+2) *N*, vous feïsse *V*; sanz] par *V*. 20. anbedeus
NVX. 23. esfance *P*. ‖ 25. Ashi *P*, Hai *V*. 26. et *omitted N*; t'i a consentis
N, comment le consentiz *V*. 29. or] ce *V*; touz] torz *N*. 30. mener ensi dure
vie *N*. 31. baillie] aïe *V*. ‖ 33–40. *stanza omitted in VX*. 34. sui quant sui
quant me porpens (+2) *N*. ‖ 41. Je] e *P*. 43. endure *omitted N* (–2). 44. en-
hardir] esbaudir *V*. 45. couart *V*. 47. chançon *omitted X* (–2).

Notes
19. *j·os*, contraction of *je vous*. This is a rare contraction that is found in
  texts of the north and west (Ménard § 48; Moignet 38–39).
35. *toute Saigne*, "the whole Seine." Jeanroy suggests this interpretation,
  which seems the best, in his list of typographical errors in Steffens's edition (*Review* 441 n. 4). Moignet notes that the definite article does not
  regularly accompany the forms of *tout* with toponyms (123).
39. *et ce qu'ele*, "and the fact that she."
43. *mes qui*, "but he who."

Versification
This love song is completely courtly in both tone and form. Stanzas of eight
heptasyllabic lines are encountered frequently in courtly lyric (Dragonetti
387), and the rhyme scheme, consisting of alternating rhymes followed by enclosing rhymes, is the preferred form of the trouvères (Dragonetti 441). MW
list 128 poems with this rhyme scheme of which nineteen have heptasyllabic
lines. Richard uses the exact same structure in song 2 (RS 22).

Music
This melody was also used for song 2 (RS 22). Detailed notes on the
melody accompany the earlier song.

8

L'autrier tout seus chevauchoie mon chemin

Bibliographies:	RS 1362, L 224–6, M 424
Refrain:	VB 437
Manuscripts:	*K* 176
	N 84v
	P 172r-172v
	V 48r
	X 125v
Attribution:	*KNX*
Music:	*KNPVX*
Editions:	Steffens 352
	Aubry, *Arsenal* 61 (melody, 1 str.)
	Bartsch 80
	Bec 17
	Cluzel 129
	Gennrich, *Grundriss* 54 (melody, 1 str.)
	Gennrich, *Rotrouenge* 56 (melody)
	Gennrich, *TTMM* 13 (melody)
	Gennrich, *TTMM trans.* 32 (melody)
	La Borde II 216
	Prunières I 71 (melody, 1 str.)
Structure:	MW 248, coblas singulars

Text:

a	a	a	b	C	B
11	11	11	6	11	6

Music: A A B / B

Model for RS 835 (song to the Virgin)

RS 1362

K 176

1. L'au - trier tout seus che - vau - choi - e mon che - min;

2. A l'ois - su - e de Pa - ris, par un ma - tin,

3. O - ï da - me bele et gente en un jar - din

4. Ces - te chan - çon no - ter:

5. Da - me qui a ´ mal ma - ri, s'el fet a - mi,

6. N'en fet pas a blas - mer.

1,1 sol *PX*. 1,2 la *P*. || 2,1 sol *P*. 2,2 sol *N*; la-ti *P*. || 3,8–11 sol, la, fa, sol *P*. || 4,1 re *P*. 4,4 la-fa *NPX*, exact repetition of phrase 6. || 6,2–3 re, mi *P*; mi-fa *NX*. The version of *NX* is an exact repetition of phrase 4.

1.   L'autrier tout seus chevauchoie mon chemin;
    A l'oissue de Paris, par un matin,
    Oï dame bele et gente en un jardin
        Ceste chançon noter:
    "Dame qui a mal mari, s'el fet ami,
      N'en fet pas a blasmer."   6

2.   Vers li me tres, si li dis: "Suer, dites moi
    Pour quoi parlez vous d'ami? Est ce desroi?"
    "Sire, je le vous dirai mult bien pourquoi,
        Ja ne·l vous qier celer:
    Dame [qui a mal mari, s'el fet ami,
      N'en fet pas a blasmer]."   12

3.   "A un vilain m'ont donee mi parent,
    Qui ne fet fors aüner or et argent,
    Et me fet d'ennui morir assez souvent,
        Q'il ne me let jöer.
    Dame [qui a mal mari, s'el fet ami,
      N'en fet pas a blasmer]."   18

4.   Je li dis: "Ma douce suer, se Dex me saut,
    Vez ci vostre douz ami qui ne vos faut;
    Venez vous en avec moi et ne vous chaut,
        Si le lessiez ester.
    Dame [qui a mal mari, s'el fet ami,
      N'en fet pas a blasmer]."   24

5.   "Sire, je n'iroie pas hors de Paris,
    J'avroie perdu heneur mes a touz dis,
    Mes ici l'acoupirai, se trouver puis
        Nus qui me vueille amer.
    Dame [qui a mal mari, s'el fet ami,
      N'en fet pas a blasmer]."   30

6.   Qant je vi qu'avecques moi ne vout venir,
    Je li fis le gieu d'amors au departir;
    Puis me pria et requist qu'au revenir
        Alasse a li parler.
    Dame qui a mal mari, [s'el fet ami,
      N'en fet pas a blasmer].   36

Rejected Readings
20. amis

Variants
1. touz *V*; seul *NP*; chemi *P*. 3. s'oï *P*. 4. iceste (+1) *V*; noter] chanter *N*. 6.
ne fet *N*. ‖ 7. Ver *N*. 8. pallez *V*. 9. je je vos *N*; dira *P*; *the stanza ends after*
mult bien *in V*. ‖ 16. mi *V*. 17. Dame qui a *N*, Dame etc. *PV*. ‖ 20. amis
PX. 21. avec mi *V*; et] si *N*. 22. le *omitted NV* (–1). 23. dame etc. *PV*. ‖ 25–
30. *stanza omitted in P*. 26. perdue *V*. 28. nus] nului (+1) *V*. 29–30. *refrain
omitted in V*. ‖ 31. vouloit (+1) *V*. 32. *the stanza ends after* le gieu *in X (a
leaf is missing)*. 33. mes puis me pria (+1) *V*; qu'a revenir *P*. 34. paller *V*. 35.
Dame *N*, Dame etc. *PV*.

Notes
This poem is interesting in that it completely fuses the themes of a
    pastourelle (or encounter song) and a *chanson de malmariée* (the song of
    an unhappily married woman). It has the typical opening of a pastou-
    relle, and the knight tries, as always, to seduce the woman he encoun-
    ters. But the "dame" here is an unhappily married woman who com-
    plains about her "vilain" husband (str. 3) and who is obviously quite
    ready to take a lover (str. 5). She sings a refrain that is typical of the
    chanson de malmariée, and in this situation it has the advantage of
    encouraging the knight in his pursuits.
10. *ne·l*, contraction of *ne le*.
22. *le*, i.e., the husband.
27. *l'*, i.e., the husband. "I will betray him."
28. *nus*, nominative case instead of oblique as a result of the attraction of
    the subject relative pronoun *qui*.

Versification
This piece has the typical form of a *rotrouenge* as defined by Gennrich. The
stanza, *aaab*, is followed by a two-line refrain that repeats the b-rhyme of
the stanza. The musical structure AA B/B is also that of a *rotrouenge*. MW
place the piece in structure 255 (11a 11a 11a 6b 7c 4c 6b), but the melodic
structure suggests the one given here, MW 248.
    Note that all of the rhymes are masculine.

Music
This melody has the AA B/B structure that Gennrich associates with the
rotrouenge. The first melodic phrase begins with a recitation on *do'* and is
clearly built on the chain *fa-la-do'*. The beginning of phrase B (lines 3 and
5) continues within this chain, starting at the top and slowly descending
to the lower part of the range. The second part of the phrase (lines 4 and
6) makes an excursion into the lower tetrachord, expanding the range of
the song to the octave from *do* to *do'*, and then returns to the base tone *fa*.

As always, MS *V* has a different melody. In fact, it presents two different melodies: the manuscript provides musical notation for the first three lines of the second stanza, and this melody does not correspond to the one given for the first stanza.

9

J'aim la plus sade riens qui soit de mere nee

Bibliographies:	RS 533, L 224–3, M 524
Refrain:	VB 1224
Manuscripts:	*P* 99v-100r
	K 177
Attribution:	*KP*
Music:	*KP*
Editions:	Steffens 340
	Aubry, *Arsenal* 62 (melody, 1 str.)
	Bec 122
	Cluzel 125
	Gennrich, *Rotrouenge* 51 (melody)
	Gérold I 132 (melody, 1 str.)
	Gérold II 279 (melody, 1 str.)
	La Borde II 213
	Paris, *Chansonniers* 734
Structure:	MW 438,1, coblas singulars

	a′	a′	B′	B′	B′
Text:	12	12	12	12	12
Music:	A	A /A′	A	A′	

The two manuscripts present different versions of this poem in that MS *P* includes two stanzas that are not found in MS *K*. Order of the stanzas:

K	1	2	3	4			7	8
P	1	2	3	4	5	6	7	8

MS *P* was chosen as the base for both philological and esthetic reasons. MS *P* has fewer erroneous readings than *K*. The stanzas that it adds develop the theme of the refrain and reveal more of the beloved's personality. They nicely complement and complete the physical description given in stanzas 1–4.

RS 533

K 177
(Text: P 99v)

4,1–6 sol, la, ti, la-sol, fa, mi *P*. Since this phrase should repeat phrase A it would seem that the scribe copied the first six neumes one tone lower. This variant led to the choice of MS *K* as the base for the music while the text is from *P*. || 5,7–8 sol, sol *P*. One might expect this phrase to repeat phrase 3, *fa-sol*. The two manuscripts do not agree and they both give a version of the phrase that differs from line 3.

1.   J'aim la plus sade riens qui soit de mere nee
     En qui j'ai trestot mis cuer et cors et pensee.
     Li douz Dex, que ferai de s'amor qui me tue?
     Dame qui veut amer doit estre simple en rue,
     En chambre o son ami soit renvoisie et drue!   5

2.   N'est rien qui ne l'amast, cortoise est a merveille,
     Plus est blanche que noif, conme rose vermeille.
     Li douz Dex, que feré de s'amor [qui me tue?
     Dame qui veut amer doit estre simple en rue,
     En chambre o son ami soit renvoisie et drue!]   10

3.   Ele a un chief blondet, euz verz, bouche sadete,
     Un cors por enbracier, une gorge blanchete.
     Li douz Dex, [que ferai de s'amor qui me tue?
     Dame qui veut amer doit estre simple en rue,
     En chambre o son ami soit renvoisie et drue!]   15

4.   Ele a un petit pié, si est si bien chaucie,
     Puis va si doucement desus cele chaucie.
     Li douz Dex, [que ferai de s'amor qui me tue?
     Dame qui veut amer doit estre simple en rue,
     En chambre o son ami soit renvoisie et drue!]   20

5.   Quant el vet au moustier, si simple est et si coie,
     Ja ne fera senblant de riens que ele voie.
     Li douz [Dex, que ferai de s'amor qui me tue?
     Dame qui veut amer doit estre simple en rue,
     En chambre o son ami soit renvoisie et drue!]   25

6.   Quant ele est e meson, tote seule sanz noise,
     Lors mande qui qu'el veut, si se gieue et envoise.
     Li douz Dex, [que ferai de s'amor qui me tue?
     Dame qui veut amer doit estre simple en rue,
     En chambre o son ami soit renvoisie et drue!]   30

7.   Q'iraie je disant? N'est nule qui la vaille!
     Se plaine est de pitié, il n'est riens qui i faille!
     Li douz Dex, que ferai de s'amor qui me tue?
     [Dame qui veut amer doit estre simple en rue,
     En chambre o son ami soit renvoisie et drue!]   35

8.   Chançon, va tost, si di la douce debounere
        Qu'el te chant sanz merci, el le saura bien fere!
        Li douz Dex, [que ferai de s'amor qui me tue?
        Dame qui veut amer doit estre simple en rue,
        En chambre o son ami soit renvoisie et drue!]   40

Rejected Readings
2. noif] flor ‖ 8. Sire Dex

Variants
1. neee K. ‖ 6. riens K. ‖ 16. pié petit K. 17. chauciee K. ‖ 21–30. *stanzas
5 and 6 omitted in K.* ‖ 32. n'est nule qui la vaille K.

Notes
16. *chaucie,* Picard form of the feminine past participle.

Versification
This love song, which has both courtly and popular elements, has a very
simple metrical structure, *a'a'B'B'B'*. MW list three other poems with this
structure. Dodecasyllabic lines are rare in courtly lyric but one finds them
as well in the "Tournoiement des dames" (song 11, RS 1044a) that was
probably also written by Richard.
    According to VB, this is the only example of this refrain.

Music
This melody is extremely simple and repetitive. Gennrich identified it as
a variant of the *rotrouenge,* although it must be noted that the second
melodic phrase (A') is first introduced in the refrain, not in the stanza. The
general, overall structure of the melody is similar to song 8 (RS 1362) in
that the first phrase works within a fifth while the end of the second jumps
down to the lower tetrachord, only to ascend again to the base tone.
    The first melodic phrase begins and ends on *la,* moving up and down
in single step intervals between *do'* and *fa.* The second phrase (A') begins
with an almost literal repetition of the first, but then ends by skipping
down to the *do* of the lower tetrachord, extending the range of the song to
an octave.

10

Nos veniom l'autrier de jöer

Bibliographies: RS 868, L 224-9, M 394
Refrain: VB 1192
Manuscripts: P 100r-100v
K 177-178
Attribution: *KP*
Music: *KP*
Editions: Steffens 349
Aubry, *Arsenal* 62 (melody, 1 str.)
Baumgartner 90
Cluzel 127
Gennrich, *ZfrP* 57,45 (melody, 1 str.)
La Borde II 217

Structure: MW 228,1, coblas singulars, coblas similaires 3 and 6 (*P*), 3 and 5 (*K*)

Text:	a	a	a	b'	B'	B'	(B'	B')
	9	4	8	6	6	6	(6	6)
Music:	A	B	C	D / D'	D	(D'	D)	

Model for RS 866 (religious lyric)

This poem, like the preceding one (RS 533), appears in only two manuscripts (*K* and *P*) which present rather different versions of the song. The two versions have five stanzas in common, but MS *P* includes an additional stanza after stanza 4 and has a refrain of four lines rather than two. The two manuscripts have totally different versions of the last stanza. Order of the stanzas:

K	1	2	3	4		6	8
P	1	2	3	4	5	6	7

In his edition, Steffens conflated the two versions. In general he followed the text of MS *K*—without the fifth stanza and with a two-line refrain—but for the last stanza he chose the text of MS *P*. This conflation is not completely satifactory since it does not respect the text of either manuscript. Since all other editions have reproduced Steffens's text (except Baumgartner, who uses the text of MS *K*), it seems worthwhile here to present the two texts as they exist in the manuscripts.

1. Nos   ve - ni - om   l'au - trier   de   jö - er

2. Et   de   res - ver,

3. Moi   et   mi   con - paig   et   mi   per,

4. Car   jo - lif   cuer   nos   mai - ne.

5. *L'a* - *mor*   *n'est*   *pas*   *vi* - *lai* - *ne*

6. *Qui*   *en* - *si*   *nos*   *de* - *mai* - *ne,*

7. *Ne*   *ja*   *por*   *nu* - *le*   *pai* - *ne*

8. *N'ert*   *qu'el*   *ne*   *soit*   *cer* - *tai* - *ne.*

3,4 re *K*. 3,5 fa descending plica *K*. ❙ 4,1 do *K*. 4,5 do *K*. ❙ 5,5 do *K*. ❙ 6,5 do *K*.
❙ 7,1 - 8,7 *omitted K*. MS *K* does not include the last two lines of the refrain in the text.

10a
Text of MS *P*

1.   Nos veniom l'autrier de jöer
          Et de resver,
      Moi et mi conpaig et mi per,
          Car jolif cuer nos maine.   4
          L'amor n'est pas vilaine
          Qui ensi nos demaine,
          Ne ja por nule paine
          N'ert qu'el ne soit certaine.   8

2.   De Paris encontrasmes, ce cuit,
          Le greigneur bruit
      Des dames qui vont en deduit
          Au pardon outre Saigne.   12
          L'amor [n'est pas vilaine
          Qui ensi nos demaine,
          Ne ja por nule paine
          N'ert qu'el ne soit certaine].   16

3.   La plus bele du mont i choisi,
          Dame a mari,
      Par pou que son non ne vos di,
          Toz jorz m'a mis en paine.   20
          L'amor [n'est pas vilaine
          Qui ensi nos demaine,
          Ne ja por nule paine
          N'ert qu'el ne soit certaine].   24

4.   Ele ot euz verz, un chief si blondet,
          Vis vermeillet,
      Douce bouche, douz mentonet,
          Une doucete alaine.   28
          L'amor [n'est pas vilaine
          Qui ensi nos demaine,
          Ne ja por nule paine
          N'ert qu'el ne soit certaine].   32

5.   Ele ot biaus braz, un cors si tres gent,
          Baz chaucement;

        Et puis va si doucetement
        Conme une magdalaine.   36
        L'amor [n'est pas vilaine
        Qui ensi nos demaine,
        Ne ja por nule paine
        N'ert qu'el ne soit certaine].   40

6.   Tuit li deduit du mont sont en li,
        Onc ce ne vi,
        Car ele chante sanz merci
        Cler conme une seraine.   44
        L'amor [n'est pas vilaine
        Qui ensi nos demaine,
        Ne ja por nule paine
        N'ert qu'el ne soit certaine].   48

7.   Plus a solaz en ses biens nonmer
        Et regreter
        Q'autre besier . . .
        Cent foiz en la semaine.   52
        L'amor [n'est pas vilaine
        Qui ensi nos demaine,
        Ne ja por nule paine
        N'ert qu'el ne soit certaine].   56

Notes

10. *le greigneur bruit,* "the most illustrious, distinguished."
12. *Saigne,* the Seine.
18. *dame a mari,* "a married woman."
51. The end of the line is missing. Jeanroy suggests the phrase "ou acoler" to complete it (*Review* 443).

10b
Text of MS *K*

1. Nous venions l'autrier de jöer
    Et de resver,
    Moi et mi conpaing et mi per,
    Car jolif cuer nos maine.
    L'amour n'est pas vilaine
    Qui ensi nos demaine.   6

2. De Paris encontrasmes, ce cuit,
    Le greigneur bruit
    Des dames qui vont en deduit
    Au pardon outre Sainne.
    L'amor [n'est pas vilaine
    Qui ensi nos demaine].   12

3. La plus bele du mont i choisi,
    Dame a mari,
    Par pou que son nom ne vous di,
    Touz jorz me met en paine.
    L'amor [n'est pas vilaine
    Qui ensi nos demaine].   18

4. Ele ot euz verz, un chief si blondet,
    Vis vermeillet,
    Douche bouche, douz mentonet,
    Une doucete alaine.
    L'amor [n'est pas vilaine
    Qui ensi nos demaine].   24

5. Tuit li deduit du mont sont en li,
    Onc ce ne vi,
    Car ele chante sanz merci
    Cler conme une seraine.
    L'amor [n'est pas vilaine
    Qui ensi nos demaine].   30

6. Je ne chant pas pour ce qu'ele m'aint
    Ne ne bé point,
    Car plus vaillant trouveroit maint,

Plus est blanche que laine.
L'amor [n'est pas vilaine
Qui ensi nos demaine].   36

Notes
33. "For she would find more than one more worthy (than I)." This
    assumes that the lady is the subject of the phrase but the syntax is not
    clear.

Versification
This piece is popular in its structure, having monorhymed stanzas followed by a refrain. In fact the metrical structure is analogous to that of the
rotrouenges by Richard, but the musical structure does not fit the definition
given by Gennrich.

The final line of the stanza, with its unique rhyme *estramp* (*b'*), links the
refrain to the stanza by its rhyme and number of syllables. This is the only
example of this refrain noted by VB.

Music
The stanza proper of this song (lines 1–4) provides the only example of a
through-composed melody in the works of Richard. This structure
(unusual for Richard but not uncommon in the troubadour and trouvère
repertoire as a whole) is in keeping with the varying line lengths of the
text—9a 4a 8a 6b'. While the melody and meter of the first three lines
show great variety, they are united by a shared rhyme sound. The fourth
line introduces a musical phrase that is repeated with slight variations in
the refrain, and it is at this point that we find the repetitions so typical of
Richard's songs. The refrain alternates a literal repetition of musical phrase
D with an open version of that same phrase.

The first two musical phrases have *la* and *do'* as their structural tones.
Phrase C acts as a transition, making regular use of the *la* of the first two
phrases but also descending to include the lower elements of the chain, *fa*
and *re*. Phrases D and D' explore the lower end of the range: *re* and *fa* are
the main structural tones but *la* (although it appears only once in each of
these lines) also has a prominent place since it is always followed by a skip
down to *re*.

11

Le Tournoiement des dames

Bibliographies:	RS 1044a, L 224–7, M 17
Refrain:	VB 518, variable internal refrain
Manuscript:	X 127r (no attribution, music for only the last hemistich)
Edition:	Jeanroy, *Notes* 237
Structure:	MW 4,2, coblas singulars, epic caesura

Text:

a	a	a	a	A	a
12	12	12	12	12	12

Most of the melody and the first stanza of this piece have disappeared with a leaf that is now missing. Only the notation for the last hemistich remains: *sol, la, sol, la-sol, sol-fa, sol, sol.*

1.   . . . .
     . . . .
     . . . .
     . . . .
     . . . .
     . . . . qui ne soit bien armee.   6

2.   L'une est la chastelaine devers Mon[t] le Heri,
     Et l'autre est Jaqueline, qu'en claime de Vitri.
     Grant paor ai des dames, greigneur que je ne di,
     Qu'il ne sont pas aprises de soufrir tant d'ennui.
     Dex, gardés moi mes dames, mesire Saint Merri!
     Qu'il ne sont pas aprises de soufrir tant d'ennui!   12

3.   Joustes ont fiancies et grant tornoiement,
           Ne pes ne püent faire ne ami ne parent;
           Mes itant ont les dames establi sagement
           Qu'il n'i avra ja lance ou il ait ferrement.
           Dex, gardés moi mes dames, messire Saint Climent!
           Si ont il toutes armes, quant qu'il a dame apent.   18

4.   Venons a la mellee, qu'irïons nos faisant?
           Sist soi la chastelaine sus un cheval ferrant,
           De trestoutes les autres senble la plus vaillant;
           N'a de l'autre partie qui paor n'en ait grant.
           Dex, gardés moi mes dames, mesire Saint Amant!
           Si ne doutent il lance ou il n'a fer devant.   24

5.   [J]aqueline ert armee sus un morelet bas;
           El se fiert en la preisse assés plus que le pas,
           Et fiert la sarazine con s'el ne l'amast pas;
           S'el ne seüst tant d'armes, cheoite fust sans gas.
           Dex, gardés moi ma dame, sire Saint Nicholas!
           Ele est mout bien armee, si a bon talevas.   30

6.   Atant es un message poignant de par le roi,
           Qui leur comande a toutes qu'il laissent leur desroi.
           Ma dame la roïne a tout ce pris sur soi,
           N'i a puis si hardi[e] qui die ce ne quoi.
           Dex, gardés moi mes dames, mesire Saint Eloi!
           Et si doutent il lances desferrees mout [poi].   36

Rejected Readings
25. Laqueline ‖ 36. pou *for* poi

Notes
This poem belongs to a rare genre that has been called the "Tournoiement des dames". There are only three lyric examples of the genre in Old French: Richard's poem, one by Huon d'Oisi, and an anonymous piece published by Holger Petersen Dyggve (*Personnages* 145–92). There is also a narrative poem of 1794 lines composed by Pierre Gencien.

    These pieces narrate a joust or melee in which all of the combatants are ladies. Jeanroy relates this genre to enumerative lyrics of the Middle Ages (*Notes* 232), and both Jeanroy and Petersen Dyggve note that there is a clear satirical intent in the poem by Huon d'Oisi and the anonymous piece. If satire is a characteristic of this genre (but we do not have enough examples to know this with any certainty), Richard's poem does not show this trait. The poet merely expresses a somewhat exaggerated fear for the safety of these beautiful warriors (exaggerated because they are fighting with blunted lances) and asks a variety of saints to protect them. The arrival of the king's messenger brings a peaceful and friendly end to the battle.

Holger Petersen Dyggve tried to identify the historical personnages in this poem. The two rival camps are led by Jacqueline de Vitry (Vitry, Seine-et-Marne, or perhaps Vitry-sur-Seine, Seine) and the Chatelaine de Montlhéry (Seine-et-Oise). According to Petersen Dyggve, the king who sends a messenger to end the fight must be Philippe-Auguste, and consequently *ma dame la roïne* who is mentioned in line 33 must be one of his wives (*Personnages* 145).

1–6. The first stanza, except for the last hemistich, has disappeared with a missing leaf (fol. 126).
9. *grant paor ai des dames*, "I am greatly afraid for the ladies."
10. et passim *il = elles*. This dialectal form of the feminine personal pronoun is found frequently in the north and west (Moignet 38). Jeanroy systematically replaced it with *els* (*Notes* 237).
Refr. *gardés moi*, "protect (them) for me," dative of interest.
12. It would seem that the scribe mistakenly repeated line 10.
13. *fiancies*, Picard form of the feminine past participle.
22. "There is no one on the other side who is not greatly afraid."
31. "Now, here comes a messenger from the king, galloping on his horse."

Versification
The use of twelve-syllable lines and epic caesura indicate the earliness of the piece. Dodecasyllabic lines, which are rare in lyric poetry, are also used in song 9 (RS 533). MW list nineteen poems with this rhyme scheme, but this is the only one with twelve-syllable lines.

This variable internal refrain is found only in this poem. Richard obviously chose his saints as needed to fit the rhyme scheme.

Index of Proper Names

Glossary

The glossary is selective in that words that have continued into Modern French, unchanged in meaning or form, have generally been omitted. Verbal forms are entered under their infinitives, which are given in parentheses if the infinitive itself does not appear in the texts. Conjugated forms that may not be readily recognized are listed separately with a cross-reference to the infinitive. The verb entries contain a complete listing of all the forms that occur. The persons of the verb are indicated by the numbers 1 to 6. Declinable words are entered under the accusative singular form if more than one form is used, otherwise they are listed under the form that occurs in the text. The references give the number of the poem in this edition followed by the line number.

Abbreviations

adj.	– adjective	nom.	– nominative
adv.	– adverb	obl.	– oblique
conj.	– conjunction	pers.	– personal
contr.	– contraction	pl.	– plural
dem.	– demonstrative	poss.	– possessive
dimin.	– diminutive	prep.	– preposition
f.	– feminine	pron.	– pronoun
impers.	– impersonal	refl.	– reflexive
indef.	– indefinite	refr	– refrain
infin.	– infinitive	rel.	– relative
interrog.	– interrogative	sg.	– singular
m.	– masculine	subst.	– substantivized
n.	– noun	v.	– verb
C	– conditional	PI	– present indicative
F	– future	PP	– past participle
I	– imperative	Pret	– preterit
II	– imperfect indicative	PrP	– present participle
IS	– imperfect subjunctive	PS	– present subjunctive

a *prep.* with, 3:46; in, 4:39, 7:48; for, 1:16-17; of, 7:7

acesmee *adj. f.* elegant, 5:21

(acoupir) *v.* to be unfaithful to one's husband / wife; *F 1* **acoupirai,** 8:27

acueil *n.m.* **de bel acueil** gracious, cordial, 3:25

adonc *adv.* now, 7:5

(agreer) *v.* to please; *PI 3* **agree,** 3:48, 5:2, 6:6, 6:41

ahi *exclamation* alas, 7:25

aim *PI 1* amer

aint *PS 3* amer

ainz *adv.* instead, 1:30

ainz *conj.* but, 4:55

ajornee *n.f.* dawn, 5:36

alaine *n.f.* breath, 10a:28, 10b:22

(aler) *v.* to go; *PI 3* **va,** 9:17, 10a:35, **vet,** 9:21; *PI 6* **vont,** 10a:11, 10b:9; *Pret 6* **alerent,** 1:27; *IS 1* **alasse,** 8:34; *C 1* **iraie,** 9:31, **iroie,** 8:25; *C 4* **irïons,** 11:19; *C 5* **irïez,** 6:25; *I 2* **va,** 5:42, 7:47, 9:36; *I 5* **alez,** 1:46, 6:21

ama *Pret 3* amer

amai *Pret 1* amer

amaine *PI 3* amener

amast *IS 3* amer

amee *PP f.* amer

(amener) *v.* to persuade; to lead, guide; *PI 3* **amaine,** 7:38

amer *v.* to love, 3:4, 4:14, 7:21, *etc.;* to like, 11:27; *PI 1* **aim,** 2:11, 6:16 *etc.;* *Pret 1* **amai,** 3:36; *Pret 3* **ama,** 3:11, 5:3; *F 1* **amerai,** 1:8; *F 3* **amera,** 3:13; *PS 3* **aint,** 5:45, 10b:31; *IS 3* **amast,** 9:6, 11:27; *PP* **amez,** 4:10, **amee,** 2:17, 3:8

amïete *n.f. dimin.* sweetheart, 1:51

amoretes *n.f. dimin.* love, 1:4, 4:21

anbesdeus *adj. pl.* both, 7:20

(apendre) *v.* to be appropriate, suitable; *PI 3* **apent,** 11:18

apris, aprises *adj.* well educated, well brought up, 1:6; trained, 11:12

(aprendre) *v.* to learn; *PP* **apris,** 4:16

(arester) *v. refl.* to stop; *Pret 1* **arestai,** 1:33

arrai *F 1* avoir

asoage *PI 3* assoagier

(assaillir) *v.* to assault, attack; *PI 3* **assaut,** 6:44

assaut *PI 3* assaillir

assés *see* assez

(asseoir) *v. refl.* to sit; *Pret 1* **m'assis,** 1:3, 6:33; *Pret 3* **s'assist,** 1:13

assez, assés *adv.* rather, 6:2, 8:15; much, 5:22; very, 11:26

assis *adj.* well placed, 3:21

(assoagier) *v.* to relieve, soothe; *PI 3* **asoage,** 2:7

atant *adv.* then, at that moment, 11:31

(atendre) *v.* to wait for; *PI 1* **atent,** 3:6; *II 1* **atendoie,** 6:22; *II 3* **atendoit,** 1:12

ator *n.m.* character, nature, 5:23

(atorner) *v.* to be in a state; *PP* **atornez,** 4:12

aüner *v.* to hoard, amass, accumulate, 8:14

autre *n. m. or f.* another, 1:8, 4:44, 10a:51

autretant *adv.* as well, 3:14

autrier *adv.* the other day, recently, 1:1, 6:1, 8:1, 10a:1, 10b:1

avant *adv.* in the future, 2:37

avenir *v.* to reach; to obtain, 2:26, 4:6, 4:15, 7:12, 7:15; *IS 1* **avenisse** 7:37

aventure *n.f.* chance, luck, 7:46

avoir *n.m.* fortune; **pour nul avoir** for any fortune, at any price, 2:20, 4:6

(avoir) *v.* to have; *PI 1* **ai,** 2:17, *etc.;* *PI 3* **a,** 2:22, *etc.;* *PI 5* **avez,** 4:32, 6:refr; *PI 6* **ont,** 8:13, 11:13, 11:15, *etc.;* *II 3* **avoit,** 1:36; *Pret 1* **oi,** 1:40, 3:7, 6:41; *Pret 3* **ot,** 1:16, 10a:25, 10b:19; *F 1* **avrai,** 5:15, **arrai** 3:47; *F 2* **avras,** 7:31; *F 3* **avra,** 11:16; *PS 3* **ait,** 1:42, 7:41, 11:16; *IS 1* **eüsse,**

7:17; *IS 3* **eüst**, 5:33; *C 1* **avroie**,
8:26; *C 5* **avriez**, 6:26

baillie *n.f.* possession, power, 4:53,
7:31

baler *v.* to dance, 1:26

bandon *n.m.* **a bandon** entirely,
without restraint, 3:3

bas *adj.* calm, not high-spirited,
11:25; **tout bas** in a low, hushed
voice, 4:47

baut *adj.* joyous, gay; ardent, 2:40

baz *adj.* low-cut, 10a:34

(**beer**) *v.* to strive for; to dream of; *PI
1* **bé**, 10b:32

berbiz *n.m.* sheep, 1:2

bergiers *n.m.* shepherd, 1:44

besier *v.* to kiss, 10a:51; *Pret 1* **besai**,
6:42

beuban *n.m.* arrogance, haughtiness,
2:16

biau, biaus, biax *adj. m.* handsome,
beautiful, 1:5, 1:6, 1:9, 10a:33

biau *adv.* graciously, 2:13

biaucop *n.m.* much, a lot, 7:46

bien *adv.* truly, 2:10

bien *n.m.* good (thing), 1:40

biens *n.m. pl.* good qualities, 3:21,
10a:49

blanchete *adj. f. dimin.* white, 9:12

blasmer *v.* to blame, accuse, 8:refr;
Pret 3 **blasma**, 5:4; *PP f.* **blasmee**,
2:19

blondet *adj. m. dimin.* blond, 9:11,
10a:25, 10b:19

braz *n.m. pl.* arms, 5:35, 6:34, 10a:33

buissonet *n.m. dimin.* bush, 1:13, 1:27

ça *adv.* here, 4:40

c' *conj.* since, 4:13

ce *dem. pron. neuter* this, 1:49, 3:14,
6:25, *etc.;* **pour ce** for this reason,
because of this, 1:41, 4:16; **ce ne
quoi** anything at all, 11:34; **ce que**
the fact that, 7:39; **pour ce que** so
that, in order that, 10b:31

cele *dem. adj. f.* that, 5:2, 9:17

celer *v.* to hide, conceal, 4:51, 8:10

certes *adv.* certainly, 7:27

ceste *dem. adj. f.* this, 1:31, 4:31, 8:4

(**chaloir**) *v. impers.* to concern, matter, 4:2, 4:25, 6:45; to worry, 8:21;
PI 3 **chaut**, 4:2, 6:45, 8:21; *IS 3*
chausist, 4:25

chançonete *n.f. dimin.* song, 4:45

chant *n.m.* melody, 2:35; song, 4:2

chanter *v.* to sing, 2:1, 4:9; *PI 1*
chant, 3:12, 10b:31; *PI 3* **chante**,
10a:43; *PS 3* **chant**, 9:37; *PP*
chanté, 4:1, **chantee**, 2:39

chapelet *n.m.* garland of flowers,
1:16

chascun *indef. pron.* everyone, 3:38

chastelaine *n.f.* chatelaine, lady of a
manor, 11:7

chastiau *n.m.* castle, 5:24

(**chastoier**) *v.* to rebuke, admonish;
PI 1 **chastoi**, 4:16

chaucement *n.m.* shoe, slipper, 10a:34

chaucie *n.f.* street, road, 9:17

chaucie *PP f. Picard* **chaucier**, to be
well outfitted with shoes, 9:16

chausist *IS 3* **chaloir**

chaut *PI 3* **chaloir**

(**cheoir**) *v.* to fall; *PP f.* **cheoite**, 11:28

(**chevauchier**) *v.* to ride (on a horse);
II 1 **chevauchoie**, 1:1, 8:1; *Pret 1*
chevauchai, 6:1

(**chevrier**) *v.* to tend goats; to play
the bagpipes; *PI 3* **chevrie**, 6:32

chief *n.m.* head, 9:11, 10a:25, 10b:19;
au chief du tor in the end, 4:27

(**choisir**) *v.* to catch sight of; *Pret 1*
choisi, 10a:17, 10b:13

chose *n.f.* matter, 5:12

ci *adv.* here, 4:39; **vez ci** here is, 6:22,
8:20

cil *dem. pron. m. nom. sg. and pl.* this
one, he, 1:34; those, 4:11, 4:16

(**citoler**) *v.* to play on a citole (a
stringed instrument resembling
perhaps a guitar); *PP f.* **citolee**, 5:42

(**clamer**) *v.* to call, name; *PI 3* **claime**,
11:8

cler *adj.* bright, clear, 3:42

cler *adv.* clearly, 10a:44

coarz *n.m. nom.* coward, 7:45

coie *adj. f.* calm, quiet, 9:21

coillir *v.* to gather, 1:15

(comander) *v.* to command, order, 11:32; **a Dieu conmander** to commend to God, say good-bye, 6:42; *PI 3* **comande,** 11:32; *PP f.* **conmandee,** 6:42

con *adv.* as, 11:27

conme *adv.* like, as, 9:7, 10a:36; **tant conme** as long as, 1:7

conmencier *subst. infin.* beginning, 4:18

conpaing, conpaig *n.m. nom.* companion, comrade, 10a:3, 10b:3

(consentir) *v.* to consent to, agree to; to approve; *Pret 2* **consentis,** 7:26

contens *n.m.* dispute, quarrel; fight, 6:24

convertir *v.* to persuade, convince, 2:28

corage *n.m.* desire, wish, 2:1

cors *n.m.* body, 9:12, 10a:33; body, life, 5:32, 9:2

cortois, cortoise *adj.* courtly, courteous, refined, 1:9, 9:6

cortoisie *n.f.* courtly refinement, noble behavior, 7:40

(couvenir) *v. impers.* to be necessary, must, 4:19, 4:34; to be proper, right, 7:4; *PI 3* **couvient,** 4:19; *F 3* **couvendra,** 4:34; *PS 3* **couviengne,** 7:4

cuer, cuers *n.m.* heart, 2:40, 6:refr; 9:2, *etc.*; **de cuer, de cuer vrai** sincerely, 3:49, 5:4

(cuidier) *v.* to think, believe; *PI 1* **cuit,** 1:49, 10a:9, 10b:7; *Pret 1* **cuidai,** 4:50; *IS 1* **cuidasse,** 4:27

cuit *PI 1* cuidier, 1:49, 10a:9, 10b:7

cuit *PI 1* quiter, 1:50

cure *n.f.* **avoir cure** to wish, desire, 7:41

de *prep.* with, 6:41, 9:refr; because of, on account of, 2:20; *introducing a*

comparison than, 1:6

debounere *n.f.* woman of noble birth, 9:36

debruisier *v.* to bend, sway (while dancing), 1:26

dedenz *prep.* into, 7:36

deduit, deduis *n.m.* pleasure, delight, 1:47, 6:5, 10a:41, 10b:25; **aller en deduit** to enjoy oneself, 10a:11, 10b:9

dehez *n.m.* **dehez ait** a curse upon, 6:45

dejoste *prep.* next to, 6:33

dela *prep.* beyond, 6:32

delez *prep.* near, 1:1, 6:2

delit *n.m.* delight, pleasure, 1:48

demener *v.* to govern, control, lead, 10:refr; to display (emotions), 1:25, 1:35; *PI 3* **demaine,** 10:refr; *II 3* **demenoit,** 1:35

demoree *n.f.* delay, 6:46

demorer *v.* to delay, tarry, 1:19, 1:24; to stay, remain, 1:29, 4:49; *PI 5* **demorez,** 1:19

departir *subst. infin.* departure, 8:32

(departir) *v.* to part, separate; *F 4* **departiron,** 1:52

(descendre) *v.* to dismount; *Pret 1* **descendi,** 1:3, 6:11

desconforter *v.* to lose heart, to be discouraged, 1:23

desferrees *adj. f. PP* **desferrer** from which the metal point has been removed, 11:36

desroi *n.m.* foolish talk, 8:8; foolishness; wrongdoing, misconduct, 11:32

destroit *n.m.* distress, torment, 1:38

desus *prep.* on, 9:17

deüst *IS 3* devoir

devant *adv.* at the tip, 11:24

devers *prep.* from, 11:7

(devoir) *v.* to have to; *IS 3* **deüst,** 5:34

dire *v.* to say, to tell, 3:22; *PI 1* **di,** 10a:19, 10b:15, 11:9; *PI 3* **dit,** 2:23,

2:27, 6:36; *Pret 1* **dis**, 1:37, 6:13, 8:7, 8:19; *Pret 3* **dist**, 1:5, 1:18, 1:45, 6:21, 6:43; *F 1* **dirai**, 8:9; *F 5* **diroiz**, 3:34; *PS 1* **die**, 7:9; *PS 3* **die**, 11:34; *I 2* **di**, 2:36, 3:43, 4:51, 9:36; *I 5* **dites**, 8:7; *PrP* **disant**, 9:31; *PP f.* **dite** 2:37

dis *n.m. pl.* days; **touz dis** always, 3:27, 4:18; **mes (a) touz dis** for ever more, 7:29, 8:26

doing *PI 1* **doner**

dolent *adj.* sad, sorrowful, wretched, 7:34

dolor *n.f.* pain, grief, 3:46

donc *adv.* then, 1:33

(doner) *v.* **ne doner de** to care little about, attach little importance to; *PI 1* **doing** 7:14

dont *conj.* therefore, 4:9, 5:12, 7:47

doucete *adj. f. dimin.* sweet, 10a:28, 10b:22; dear, 6:refr

doucetement *adv.* softly, 10a:35

doutance *n.f.* doubt, hesitation, 7:19

(douter) *v.* to doubt, 7:41; to fear, 11:36; *PI 1* **dout**, 7:41; *PI 6* **doutent**, 11:36

douz, douce, douche *adj.* mild, 7:2; sweet, 10a:27, 10b:21; dear, 8:19, 9:refr, 9:36, *etc.*

droit *n.m.* **par droit** rightfully, 7:20

drue *adj. f.* amorous, loving; lively, vivacious, 9:refr

duel *n.m.* grief, sorrow, 4:23, 4:39, 7:48

durer *v.* to last; to continue to exist, 2:8, 3:45

e *prep.* in, 9:26

el *pers. pron. f.* she

el *contr.* **en + le** in the, 4:46, 5:2, 5:11

en *pron.* one, people, 2:27, 6:43, 7:35, 11:8

enbracier *v.* to embrace, 9:12

(enchacier) *v.* to chase away, drive away; *PI 3* **enchace**, 4:42

(encontrer) *v.* to come upon, meet; *Pret 4* **encontrasmes**, 10a:9, 10b:7

endroit *adv.* **iluec endroit** at that spot, 1:33

endurer *v.* to endure, suffer, bear, 3:5, 4:25; *PI 3* **endure**, 7:43

enfance *n.f.* childishness, foolishness, 7:23

ennui *n.m.* pain, torment, 4:17, 5:44, 11:10; boredom, 1:13, 8:15

ensaignes *n.f.* **as ensaignes que** the proof being that, 4:47

ensi *adv.* thus, 3:28, 7:30, 10:refr

entrepris *adj.* in a bad, sorry state, 4:13

(envoisier) *v.* to enjoy oneself; *PI 3* **envoise**, 9:27

ert *II 3* **estre**, 11:25; *F 3* **estre**, 3:32, 6:36

es here comes, 11:31

(escondire) *v.* to reject, refuse; *PP* **escondit**, 5:5

esjoïr *v.* to delight, gladden, 7:4

(establir) *v.* to decide; *PP* **establi**, 11:15

ester *v.* **laissier ester** to let be, let alone, 8:22

estes *PI 5* **estre**

(estovoir) *v. impers.* must; *PI 3* **estuet**, 7:13

estre *v.* to be, 9:refr; *PI 1* **sui**, 2:30, 5:25, 7:34, *etc.*; *PI 3* **est**, 2:1, 2:31, 6:23, *etc.*; *PI 5* **estes**, 3:23; *PI 6* **sont**, 10a:41, 10b:25, 11:10, 11:12, *etc.*; *II 1* **iere**, 3:37; *II 3* **ert**, 11:25, **estoit**, 1:14; *Pret 1* **fui**, 3:35; *Pret 3* **fu**, 4:5, 7:23; *F 2* **seras**, 2:37, 5:42; *F 3* **ert**, 3:32, 6:36; **iert**, 3:refr, **sera**, 3:17; *F 5* **serez**, 3:27; *PS 1* **soie**, 2:30; *PS 3* **soit**, 1:7, 9:1, 11:6; *IS 3* **fust**, 2:20, 3:9, 3:10, 11:28; *I 2* **soies**, 2:38; *I 5* **soiez**, 3:25

estuet *PI 3* **estovoir**

eure *n.f.* time, 3:17

eüsse *IS 1* **avoir**

eüst *IS 3* **avoir**

euz *n.m. pl.* oil eyes, 9:11, 10a:25, 10b:19

face *PS 3* **faire**

(faillir) *v.* to fail, 1:43, 8:20; to be lacking, 9:32; *PI 3* faut, 8:20; *PS 3* faille, 9:32; *PP* failli, 1:43

faire, fere *v.* to do, to make, 9:37, 11:14; to write, compose, 5:1, 7:6; faire a + *infin.* to deserve to be, 8:refr; *PI 1* faz, 2:9, 4:43; *PI 3* fet, 4:23, 7:10, 7:48, 8:14, 8:refr; *PI 6* font, 2:4; *II 3* fesoit, 1:34; *Pret 1* fis, 2:18, 8:32; *Pret 5* feïstes, 7:21; *Pret 6* firent, 1:28; *F 1* ferai, 3:1, 5:1, 9:refr; feré, 9:8; *PS 3* face, 4:44; *IS 1* feïsse, 7:19; *PrP* faisant, 11:19; *PP* fet, 1:16, 3:5, 4:36, 5:44, 6:41, 6:46

faut *PI 3* faillir

faz *PI 1* faire

feïsse *IS 1* faire

feïstes *Pret 5* faire

fer *n.m.* metal tip, point of a lance, 11:24

ferai *F 1* faire

fere *see* faire

feré *F 1* faire

(ferir) *v.* to strike, 11:27; *refl.* to charge, 11:26; *PI 3* fiert, 11:26, 11:27

ferrant *adj.* iron-gray, 11:20

ferrement *n.m.* iron tip, point, 11:16

fesoit *II 3* faire

fet *PI 3* faire; *PP* faire

(fiancier) *v.* to agree to by oath; *PP f. Picard* fiancies, 11:13

fiert *PI 3* ferir

fin, fine *adj.* loyal, 2:40; perfect, true, 5:11

(finer) *v.* to end; *PP f.* finee, 5:46

flor *n.f.* flower, 5:22

foiz *n.f. pl.* times, 10a:52

for *see* fuer

fors *prep.* except, 3:12, 8:14

fouïr *v.* to flee, 4:34

fox *adj. m. nom.* crazy, insane, 4:5

fu *Pret 3* estre

fuer, for *n.m.* price, 4:26; a nul fuer at any price, on no account, 6:refr

fui *Pret 1* estre

fust *IS 3* estre

(garder) *v.* to watch, tend, 1:2; to attend to, take care of, 4:21, 4:52, 11:refr; *v. refl.* to be careful, 4:18; to beware of; to guard oneself against, 3:24; *PS 3* gart, 4:52; *PS 6* gardent, 4:18; *I 5* gardés, 11:refr, gardez, 4:21, 3:24; *PrP* gardant, 1:2

gas *n.m.* sans gas no kidding, without a doubt, 11:28

gent, gente, genz *adj.* handsome, beautiful; pleasing, nice, 6:23, 8:3, 10a:33

gentil *adj.* pretty, 6:3

genz *n.f.* people, 3:34

(gesir) *v.* to lie, 5:35; gesir en to depend on, be subject to, 7:46; *PI 3* gist, 7:46; *IS 3* geüst, 5:35

(geter) *v.* geter un ris to laugh; *PP* geté, 6:35

geüst *IS 3* gesir

gieu *n.m.* game; faire le gieu d'a-mors to make love, 8:32

gieue *PI 3* jöer

gist *PI 3* gesir

granment *adv.* for a long time, 1:29, 4:49

(greer) *v.* to please; *PI 3* gree, 2:35, 5:26

guerredon *n.m.* reward, 3:6

(guerredoner) *v.* to reward, recom-pense; *PP f.* guerredonnee, 3:18

hardie *adj. f.* bold, 11:34

haut *adv.* in a loud voice, out loud, 1:45, 6:43

hautement *adv.* in a high place, i.e., a woman of such high rank, posi-tion, 7:24

heneur *n.f.* honor, 8:26

honmage *n.m.* homage, 2:9

honte *n.f.* shame, dishonor, 1:42

hui *adv.* today, 6:45

iere *II 1* estre

iert *F 3* estre

il *pers. pron. f. pl. dialectal form* they

(f.), 11:10, 11:12, *etc.*
iluec *adv.* **iluec endroit** at that spot, 1:33
iraie *C 1* **aler**
ire *n.f.* sadness, sorrow, grief, 5:1
iroie *C 1* **aler**
itant *adv.* then, 11:15
ja *adv.* already, 1:16; **ne ... ja** never, 2:15, 2:31, 5:15
jamés *adv.* never, 1:20, 3:13, 4:40, 5:33
jöer *v.* to enjoy oneself, have fun, 1:27, 8:16, 10a:1, 10b:1; *PI 3* **gieue**, 9:27
joiant *adj.* joyful, 2:40
jolif *adj. m.* joyous, gay; tender, loving, 10a:4, 10b:4
jones *adj. m. nom.* young, 1:11
jonete *adj. f. dimin.* young, 1:10
jor, jorz *n.m.* day; **jamés jor** never, 4:40
joustes *n.f. pl.* single combat, joust, 11:13
jouvent *n.m.* youth, 3:36
(laier) *v.* to leave, 6:refr; to let allow, 8:16; *PI 3* **let**, 8:16; *C 1* **leroie**, 6:refr
(laissier) *v.* to leave off, stop, 11:32; **laissier ester** to let be, let alone, 8:22; *PS 6* **laissent**, 11:32; *I 5* **lessiez**, 8:22
lancier *v.* to throw, 7:36
languir *subst. infin.* languidness, languor, 4:12
las *n.m. pl.* snare, trap, 4:52
lasse *interjection* alas, 3:35
leroie *C 1* **laier**
lessiez *I 5* **laissier**
let *PI 3* **laier**
(lever) *v. refl.* to get up; *PP m.* **levez**, 1:14
lez *prep.* next to, near, 1:3, 1:13
löer *v.* to praise, 2:2, 3:2; *PI 1* **lo**, 5:refr; *adj. PP f.* **löee**, 2:22
loiaument *adv.* faithfully, sincerely, 3:39
loig *adv.* **de si·loig conme** as soon

as, 1:44
lonc *adj.* **lonc tens** for a long time, 1:38, 2:17
longuement *adv.* for a long time, 3:31
longues *adv.* for a long time, 2:8
lors *adv.* then, at that time, 1:25, 3:34, 7:3
magdalaine *n.f.* repentant sinner (from Mary Magdalaine), 10a:36
(maindre) *v.* to live, dwell; *PI 3* **maint**, 5:43
maine *PI 3* **mener**
mains *adv.* least, 4:10
maint *adj.* many, 5:44; *indef. pron.* many, more than one, 10b:33
maint *PI 3* **maindre**
maintenant *adv.* **tout maintenant** immediately, 6:13
mal *adj.* bad, nasty, wicked; unpleasant, 8:refr
mal, maus, max *n.m.* sorrow, pain, 2:6, 3:7, 4:35, 5:33, 7:10
(mander) *v.* to summon; *PI 3* **mande**, 9:27
matinet *adv.* **trop matinet** very early in the morning, 1:14
(maudire) *v.* to curse; *PI 1* **maudi**, 1:37
mellee *n.f.* scuffle, fight, 6:26, 11:19
melz *adv.* better, 1:6; more easily, 2:27, 7:35; **venir melz** to be better, preferable, 4:38
mener *v.* to lead, 7:30, 10a:4, 10b:4; to show, display (emotions), 2:16; *PI 3* **maine**, 10a:4, 10b:4
mentonet *n.m. dimin.* chin, 10a:27, 10b:21
merci *n.f.* mercy, pity, 4:28, 4:37, 7:18; **soe merci** *title* her Grace, 4:48
merveille *n.f.* **a merveille** wondrously, 9:6
mes *adv.* now, 3:9; **mes (a) touz dis** for ever more, 7:29, 8:26
mes *conj.* but, 2:38, 4:4

mesire, messire *title* my lord, 11:refr
meson *n.f.* house, 9:26
message *n.m.* messenger, 11:31
mi *poss. adj. pl. nom.* my, 8:13, 10a:3, 10b:3
mi *pers. pron. obl. Picard* me, 1:20
mie *n.f.* **ne ... mie** not at all, 6:31, 7:15; nothing at all, 4:54
moie, moies *poss. pron. f. sg. and pl.* mine, 2:31, 4:22
mont *n.m.* world, 4:10, 5:2, 7:8, 10a: 17, 10b:13, 10b:25
morelet *n.m. dimin.* morel black horse (of Moorish origin), 11:25
morir *v.* to die, 4:19, 5:34, 7:13, 7:48, 8:15; to kill, 4:22; *PI 1* **muir**, 1:18, 3:44; *PP* **mort**, 4:22
mort *n.f.* death, 3:48, 5:6
mort *PP* **morir**
moustier *n.m.* church, 9:21
mout *see* **mult**
müer *v.* to restrain oneself, to stop oneself, 7:9
muir *PI 1* **morir**
mult, mout *adv.* very, 6:43, 8:9, 11:30, 11:36; much, 1:6, 1:48; a lot, a great deal, 3:5, 4:1, 7:41
musguet *n.m.* lily of the valley, 1:15
ne *conj.* nor, 5:34, 7:16, 10b:32; and, 1:40, 3:7, 3:47, 4:40, 7:14; **ne ... ne** neither ... nor, 4:8, 5:24, 6:5–6, 7:3, 11:14
noier *v. refl.* to drown, 5:14
noif *n.f.* snow, 9:7
noise *n.f.* noise, commotion, 9:26
nonmer *v.* to enumerate, list, 10a:49
nos *pers. pron. nom.* we, 10a:1, 11:19; *obl.* us, 1:47, 10:refr
noter *v.* to sing; to play, 1:30, 8:4
nouvelet *adj. m. dimin.* new, 1:17
nul, nule, nus *adj.* any, 2:20, 4:6, 4:20, 5:33, 6:refr; some, 4:28; **a nul tens** ever, 7:37
nul, nule, nus *indef. pron.* no one, 2:22, 5:25, 7:12, 9:31; anyone, some-one, 8:28

o *prep.* with, 9:refr
(ocire) *v.* to kill; *F 5* **ocirrez**, 1:21
oi *Pret 1* **avoir**
(oïr) *v.* to hear; *PI 3* **ot**, 6:43; *Pret 1* **oï**, 8:3; *Pret 3* **oï**, 1:23; *IS 1* **oïsse**, 2:12
oissue *n.f.* gate, entry; edge, out-skirts, 8:2
onc *adv.* **onc ... ne** never, 10a:42, 10b:26
oncor, oncore *adv.* yet, 3:32; still, 4:27; again, 6:31
onme *n.m.* man, 1:39
onques *adv.* never, 5:3, *etc.*; ever, 2:12; **onques mes** never, 4:13
or *adv.* now, 3:38, 7:29
or *n.m.* gold, 8:14
orendroit *adv.* now, from now on, 1:37
ot *PI 3* **oïr**, 6:43
ot *Pret 3* **avoir**, 1:16, 10a:25, 10b:19
ou *rel. pron.* in whom, 3:21, 5:32
outrage *n.m.* presumption, 2:14
outre *prep.* beyond, on the other side of, 10a:12, 10b:10
paine, paines *n.f.* sorrow, sadness, 3:18, 4:26, 10a:20, 10b:16; effort, 7:33
païs *n.m.* country, land, 2:21, 4:34
paor *n.f.* fear, 11:9
par *prep.* **de par** on behalf of, 3:43, 11:31; **par pou que** almost, nearly, 10a:19, 10b:15
parage *n.m.* nobility, rank, 2:15
pardon *n.m.* religious festival at which indulgences were granted, 10a:12, 10b:10
partie *n.f.* opposing side, 11:22
partir *v.* to leave, 5:12; to part, 7:16; to favor, 1:42; *Pret 3* **parti**, 1:42
pas *n.m.* **plus que le pas** quickly, rapidly, 11:26
(passer) *v.* to decide, settle; *PP f.* **passee**, 5:12
pastore *n.f.* shepherdess, 6:3
pastorele *n.f.* shepherdess, 1:2; a pastourelle (a type of song), 1:31

pensee *n.f.* thought, 5:32, 9:2; worry, care, 5:1

(penser) *v.* to think; *PI 1* **pens**, 4:40, 6:25

per *adj. et n.* equal, peer, 4:46

per *n.m.* companion, 10a:3, 10b:3

(perdre) *v.* to lose; *PI 1* **pert**, 2:25

pes *n.f.* peace, 11:14

petitet *n.m.* moment, 1:19

pié *n.m.* foot, 9:16

pieç'a *adv.* for a long time, 3:19

pis *n.m.* anything worse, 7:28

plain, plaine *adj.* full (**de**, of), 5:1, 6:5, 7:25, 7:39, 9:32

(plaire) *v.* to please; *F 3* **plera**, 3:16; *IS 3* **pleüst**, 4:50

plera *F 3* **plaire**

plesir *n.m.* **venir a plesir** to please, 4:41

pleüst *IS 3* **plaire**

(plevir) *v.* to pledge, promise; *PI 1* **plevis**, 1:8

plorer *v.* to weep; to bemoan one's fate, 4:4; *PP* **ploré**, 4:3

plus *adv.* **plus que le pas** quickly, rapidly, 11:26

poi *see* **pou**

(poindre) *v.* to gallop; *PrP* **poignant**, 11:31

poïsse *IS 1* **pooir**

poïst *IS 3* **pooir**

(pooir) *v.* to be able, can; *PI 1* **puis**, 4:9, 7:15, *etc.*; *PI 2* **pués**, 7:29; *PI 3* **puet**, 2:32, 4:6, 5:12, 7:12; *PI 6* **püent**, 11:14; *PS 3* **puisse**, 2:24; *IS 1* **poïsse**, 4:30; *IS 3* **poïst**, 7:28; *C 1* **porroie**, 2:27; *C 3* **porroit**, 7:35

por *see* **pour**

(porpenser) *v. refl.* to reflect on, think about; *PI 1* **porpens**, 7:34

porroie *C 1* **pooir**

porroit *C 3* **pooir**

porter *v. refl.* to behave, 2:13

pou, poi *n.m.* little, 3:17, 7:44, 11:36; **par pou que** almost, 10a:19, 10b:15

pour *prep.* in spite of, 2:15; because

of, 3:44; in the name of, 1:46, 3:24, 4:51; **pour voir** in truth, 2:21; **pour ce** for this reason, because of this, 1:41, 4:16; **pour ce que** so that, in order that, 10b:31

pree *n.f.* field, 5:22

preisse *n.f.* throng, fray, 11:26

(prendre) *v.* (*with dat.*) to come, to occur to someone, 2:1; **prendre sur soi** to take, assume responsibility for, 11:33; *PP* **pris**, 2:1, 11:33

pris *n.m.* worth, merit, 3:23, 5:refr, 7:32

pris *PI 1* **prisier**

pris *PP* **prendre**

(prisier) *v.* to estime, value; to praise; *PI 1* **pris**, 5:refr

püent *PI 6* **pooir**

pucele *n.f.* girl, maiden, 7:3

pués *PI 2* **pooir**

puet *PI 3* **pooir**

puis *n.m.* well, 5:14

puis *adv.* since then, after that, 6:4, 11:34; then, 8:33; **puis que** since, 5:15–16

puis *PI 1* **pooir**

qant *see* **quant**

qier *PI 1* **querre**

quanque *pron.* all that, 6:41

quant *conj. and interrog.* when, 2:26, 6:41, 7:1, *etc.*; **quant que** all that, 11:18

que *conj.* because, 8:16, 11:10, 11:12; for, 3:36, 7:11; since, 1:14; so that, in such a way that, 6:43, 7:2

que *rel. pron.* when, 4:30; *indef. rel. pron.* what, 1:28

(querre) *v.* to wish, desire; *PI 1* **qier**, 1:28, 8:10

qui *indef. pron.* he / she who, 5:4, 6:6, 7:43; if anyone, 1:25

qui *rel. pron. obl., i.e.,* **cui** whom, 1:42, 3:19, 5:refr, 5:31, 6:22, 6:44

(quiter) *v.* to give up, yield; let someone have something; *PI 1* **cuit**, 1:50

quoi *indef. pron.* **ce ne quoi** anything at all, 11:34

rage *n.f.* madness, insanity, 2:6

regreter *v.* to tell, 10a:50

(remander) *v.* to send back; *PS 3* **remant**, 2:36

(renouveler) *v.* to change; *PI 3* **renouvele**, 7:1

renvoisie *adj. f.* charming, alluring, 9:refr

requerre *v.* to request, ask for, 6:12; *Pret 1* **requis**, 1:4; *Pret 3* **requist**, 8:33; *PP f.* **requise**, 3:28

resort *n.m.* help, 4:20

respas *n.m.* cure, 3:47

resver *v.* to roam, wander about for pleasure, 10a:2, 10b:2

retorner *v.* to return, 4:40

revenir *subst. infin.* return, 8:33

ribaut *n.m.* rogue, scoundrel, 4:26

richece *n.f.* wealth, 1:50

rien, riens *n.f.* creature, person, 9:1; anyone, 1:54, 9:6; thing, 3:22; **ne ... riens** nothing, 4:1, 9:32; anything, 7:14; **riens nee** anything, anyone that exists, 5:refr, 6:16

ris *n.m.* **geter un ris** to laugh, 6:35

sade, sades *adj.* charming, pleasing, 1:11, 9:1; *dimin. f.* **sadete**, 1:10, 9:11

sai *PI 1* **savoir**

sainz *adj. m. nom.* healthy, sound, 1:7

sanz *prep.* without, 2:14, 6:24, 9:37, *etc.*

(sauver) *v.* **se Dex me saut** I assure you; *PS 3* **saut**, 8:19

savoir *v.* to know, 2:18; *PI 1* **sai**, 2:7, 5:23, *etc.*; *PI 3* **set**, 2:13, 4:42; *F 3* **saura**, 9:37; *IS 3* **seüst**, 11:28

se *adv.* so, 9:32

se, s' *conj.* if, 2:7, 2:31, 2:35, 5:26, 6:24, 7:17, 8:refr, 11:28

seignorie *n.f.* noblilty, rank, 7:11

senblant *n.m.* **ne faire senblant de rien** to feign ignorance or indifference, 9:22

(senbler) *v.* to seem; *PI 3* **senble**, 11:21

senez *adj. m. nom.* sensible, prudent, 1:9

sens *n.m.* good sense, intelligence, wisdom, 7:40; **estre de mal sens** foolish, unreasonable, 3:35

(seoir) *v. refl.* to be seated; *Pret 3* **sist**, 11:20

seraine *n.f.* siren, 10a:44; 10b:28

seson *n.f.* season, 7:1; time, 3:9

set *PI 3* **savoir**

seul, seus *adj.* alone, 8:1; **seul a seul** in private, 4:30

seüst *IS 3* **savoir**

si *adv.* so, thus, 2:29, 6:11, 9:16, *etc.*; so, 5:refr, 6:5–6, 9:16–17, *etc.*

si *conj.* so, therefore, consequently, 5:25, 9:36, *etc.*; yet, nevertheless, 11:36

siens *poss. pron. m. nom.* hers, 2:30

simple *adj.* mild, gentle; modest, unassuming, 9:refr, 9:21

sist *Pret 3* **seoir**

soe *poss. adj. f. sg.* **soe merci** *title* her Grace, 4:48

soi *pers. pron., tonic* himself, 1:17; herself, 11:33

soie *PS 1* **estre**

soies *I 2* **estre**

soiez *I 5* **estre**

solaz *n.m.* joy, pleasure; solace, 1:35, 2:25, 10a:49

sonet *n.m.* song, 1:18

(sorprendre) *v.* to charm, captivate; *PP* **sorpris**, 5:refr, 6:15

sotie *n.f.* foolishness, folly, 7:25

soufrir, sousfrir *v.* to suffer, bear, endure, 4:36, 11:10, 11:12

souploier *v.* to beseech, implore, beg, 4:8

suer *n.f. nom.* sister, *term of address* my dear, darling, 6:refr, 8:7

sui *PI 1* **estre**

sus *prep.* on, 11:20, 11:25

talevas *n.m.* shield, 11:30

tant *adv.* so much, 3:48; so long, 4:36;

tant conme so long as, 1:7

tantost *adv.* immediately, 1:24

tel *adj.* such great, 7:11

tenir *v. refl.* to restrain oneself, to stop oneself, 7:5

tens *n.m.* a while, time, 3:32; weather, 7:2; lonc tens for a long time, 1:38, 2:17; a nul tens ever, 7:37

tez *pron. m.* such a one, 1:10

(tolir) *v.* to take away; *I 5* tolez, 1:47

tor *n.m.* estre au tor de to be in a state, frame of mind, 5:25; au chief du tor in the end, 4:27

torment *n.m.* torment, pain, 4:39

tornoiement *n.m.* tournament, 11:13

tost *adv.* quickly, 3:41, 9:36; soon, 6:26

tour *n.f.* tower, 5:24

tout, touz, tuit, toute, toutes *adj.* all, 6:refr, 7:8, 10a:41, *etc.*; the whole, entire, 7:35; touz dis always, 3:27, 4:18; mez (a) touz dis for ever more, 7:29, 8:26; touz jorz always, 10a:20, 10b:16

tout *adv.* all, 1:17, 8:1; entirely, completely, 3:3, 4:20; tout maintenant immediately, 6:13

tout, *etc. pron.* all, everything, 5:32, 11:32

(traire) *v.* to suffer, bear, 3:46; *refl.* to go, move towards, 6:11, 8:7; *PI 1* trai, 3:46; *Pret 1* tres, 6:11, 8:7

trenbler *v.* to tremble, 2:5

tres *Pret 1* traire

tres *adv. intensifier, e.g.,* la plus tres bele, the most beautiful, 2:11, 7:22

trestot, trestoutes *pron.* all, 9:2, 11:21

trop *adv.* very, 1:14, 2:17

trouver *v.* to find, 1:2, 1:20, 6:3, 10b:33; to compose, 2:33, 5:41; *PI 1* truis, 6:3; *Pret 1* trouvai, 1:2; *F 5* trouverez, 1:20; *C 3* trouveroit, 10b:33; *PP f.* trouvee, 2:33, 5:41

truis *PI 1* trouver

tuit *see* tout

uis *n.m.* door, gate, 5:42

umblement *adv.* humbly, 4:8

usage *n.m.* habit, custom, 2:3

user *v.* user sa vie to spend one's life painfully, 4:23

vaillant *adj.* brave, 11:21; of great worth, merit, 2:34, 3:15; worthy, 10b:33

vaille *PS 3* valoir

valet *n.m.* dale, small valley, 1:12

valoir *v.* to be of equal merit, worth, 9:31; to be of use, 4:1, 4:4, 4:7; *PI 3* vaut, 4:4, 4:7; *PS 3* vaille, 9:31

veïst *IS 3* veoir

vendra *F 3* venir

venir *v.* to come, 2:32, 6:22, *etc.*; to come back, return, 10a:1, 10b:1; *v. refl.* to come, 8:21; *v. impers.* to happen, 7:28; bien venir to succeed, 7:45; venir a plesir to please, 4:41; venir melz to be better, preferable, 4:38; *PI 3* vient, 4:38; *II 3* venoit, 4:41, 6:24; *II 4* veniom, 10a:1; venions, 10b:1; *Pret 3* vint, 1:24; *F 3* vendra, 6:31; *I 4* venons, 11:19; *I 5* venez, 8:21

(veoir), vöer *v.* to see, 6:12; *PI 1* voi, 4:12, 4:15, 5:13, 7:13, 7:33; *Pret 1* vi, 1:34, 6:4, 8:31, 10a:42, 10b:26; *Pret 3* vit, 1:44; *F 1* verrai, 4:29; *PS 3* voie, 9:22; *IS 3* veïst, 1:25

vermeillet *adj. dimin.* rosy, 10a:26, 10b:20

verz *adj. m.* green, 9:11, 10a:25, 10b:19

vet *PI 3* aler

vez; vez ci here is, 6:22, 8:20

vi *Pret 1* veoir

viellece *n.f.* old age, 3:33

vif, vis *adj.* alive, 1:7, 1:20

vilain *n.m.* a man of lowly birth, 8:13

vilaine *adj. f.* lowly, base, 10:refr

vis *adj. see* vif, 1:7

vis *n.m.* face, 3:42, 10a:26, 10b:20

vit *Pret 3* veoir

vöer *see* veoir

voi *PI 1* veoir

voie *n.f.* way, 1:46, 6:21

voir *adj.* **pour voir** in truth, 2:21

vos *pers. pron. nom. and obl.* you, 1:8, 6:refr, 6:14, 8:20, *etc.*

vostre *poss. adj. sg.* your, 5:refr, 6:15, 8:20, *etc.*

(vouloir) *v.* to want, wish, desire; *PI 1* **vueil**, 3:22; *PI 3* **veut**, 9:refr; *PI 5* **voulez**, 1:22; *Pret 3* **vout**, 8:31;

Pret 6 **voudrent**, 1:29; *F 3* **voudra**, 2:16; *C 1* **voudroie**, 2:19; *PS 3* **vueille**, 8:28

voudrent *Pret 6* **vouloir**

voudroie *C 1* **vouloir**

vout *Pret 3* **vouloir**

voz *poss. adj. pl.* your, 4:21, 5:35

vraiement *adv.* truly, 4:9

vueil *PI 1* **vouloir**

vueille *PS 3* **vouloir**

The Lyrics of Richard de Semilli is a critical edition of the complete poetic works of the late twelfth-century trouvère, Richard de Semilli, presented here for the first time with their accompanying melodies in a modernized version of the medieval notation. Though he is best known for his *pastourelles* Richard's corpus also includes courtly love songs, love songs in the non-courtly or *popularisant* register, a *Tournoiement de Dames* (one of the rare examples of this genre), and an interesting piece that fuses the themes of the *pastourelle* with the *chanson de malmariée*. This thematic diversity is matched by a variety of metrical and musical structures.

Johnson's Introduction discusses Richard's life and works, the manuscript tradition, the language of the texts, and the metrical and musical structure of the songs. The volume also includes complete critical apparatus— standard reference numbers, previous editions, rejected readings, variants, and notes—for both the texts and their melodies, and a bibliography and glossary, making it a comprehensive yet focused study of this innovative poet and of the medieval lyric as a complete art-form.

Susan M. Johnson is Assistant Professor of French at Memphis State University. Her other publications include "The Role of the Refrain in the Pastourelles *à refrain*," in *Literary and Historical Perspectives of the Middle Ages: Proceedings of the 1981 SEMA Meeting* (1982), and "Christian Allusion and Divine Justice in *Yonec*" (forthcoming).

mRts

medieval & Renaissance texts & studies
is the publishing program of the
Center for Medieval and Early Renaissance Studies
at the State University of New York at Binghamton.

mRts emphasizes books that are needed —
texts, translations, and major research tools.

mRts aims to publish the highest quality scholarship
in attractive and durable format at modest cost.

Jim Pearson has been a successful leader in both the world of business and the world of ministry. His heart's desire is to see Christians excel in the marketplace while achieving spiritual excellence. This book will help you navigate safely through the minefields he has identified.

Steve Alford
Men's Basketball Coach, University of Iowa

Jim Pearson is truly a rare commodity! As he writes, he speaks with authority from years of experience in both ministry and the business world. In Minefields in the Marketplace, *he speaks straight from the heart and, at times, straight from the gut. His book is a winner!*

R. Kirk Nowery, President
INJOY Stewardship Services
Author, *The Giving Christian* and
The Stewardship of Life

As a former businessman, Jim Pearson knows firsthand the minefields in the marketplace. This book will give you practical ways to avoid them and also insights for maintaining spiritual sharpness. Jim challenges you to live the type of life God expects.

Paul A. Steiner, Retired Chairman and
President,
Brotherhood Mutual Insurance Company

This book scared me! My desire to honor my God, my wife, and my children seems to be directly related to one word—choice…. Wow!! Jim challenges Christian businessmen to finish the race faithfully, staying focused on the prize.

Tommy Mitchell, Founder & Executive Director
Race to Win Ministries

There is a real world out there with real minefields. Jim Pearson gives real insight as to how to avoid them. His personal experience in the business world and the church world uniquely qualify him to speak to both.

Dan Southerland, Founder
Church Transitions
Author, *Transitioning, Leading Your Church through Change*

In an "anything goes" culture with its theme song, "If it feels good, do it," Pastor Jim Pearson warns that the slippery slope of moral compromise is ever before those who are in the marketplace. Pastor Jim draws upon his own experience and the truth of God's Word to help professionals identify and avoid the spiritual minefields waiting for the uninitiated and the unaware. An excellent read for those of us in the marketplace who are committed to set a standard of ethical, moral, and spiritual excellence.

Daryle Doden, President
Ambassador Steel Corporation

Jim Pearson masterfully challenges our awareness of godliness and integrity in our personal and professional journeys. His encouragement guides us down the path of abundant living and genuine success.

Randy Dunton, Men's Basketball Coach
Liberty University

Discussing Jim Pearson's book in a group or pondering his insights in quiet moments before the Lord may save your Christian walk, witness, and family. Minefields *is a refreshing approach to the issues that can derail our lives in a pressure-packed world. I was challenged and convicted, but also encouraged and given hope.*

Dr. William J. Hamel, President
Evangelical Free Church of America

Jim Pearson speaks with experience and insight. A proven leader in the business world and a proven leader in the church world, he passes on to us proven principles for effective living in the marketplace.

Rick Hawks, Senior Pastor
The Chapel, Fort Wayne, Indiana

Jim Pearson is one of those guys who has been there and done that. His stories are interesting and the lessons penetrating. And you will also enjoy a few good laughs as he walks you through the minefields we all encounter. His insights are fresh and his storytelling engaging.

Bill Hull
Author, *Choose the Life; Jesus Christ, Disciplemaker; The Disciple-Making Pastor; The Disciple-Making Church*

From the first chapter, Minefields *will grab your mind and heart with 'I've been there' narratives that illustrate just how easily we can slide toward unthinkable compromises to our most cherished values.* Minefields *is great reading that exposes insidious workplace threats to our character and offers biblically grounded, actionable answers. This book should be on every Christian manager's must-read list.*

Mark G. Holbrook, President
Evangelical Christian Credit Union
Chairman of the Board, Christian Management
Association

MINEFIELDS IN THE MARKETPLACE

Ethical Issues Christians Face
in the World of Business

By

James M. Pearson

with
Kelly Hahn

BMH Books
Winona Lake, Indiana
www.bmhbooks.com

Minefields in the Marketplace
Ethical Issues Christians Face in the World of Business

Copyright ©2005 by James M. Pearson

ISBN 10: 0-88469-302-3
ISBN 13: 978-0-88469-302-4
Printed in the United States of America

Published by BMH Books
BMH Books, P.O. Box 544, Winona Lake, IN 46590 USA
www.bmhbooks.com

In order to keep the identities of some individuals confidential, the names of people and companies have been changed.

Dedication

To my world-class family:
Linda, you have been my beloved wife and
friend for more than thirty years; I truly
marvel at your energy, creativity, and
unfailing support. Drew and Kyle, a father
could not have two better sons. Thanks for so
many proud moments. May God richly bless
you as you continue to live for Him!

Acknowledgments

I want to acknowledge so many individuals who made this book possible. "Thank You . . ."

Linda Pearson for encouraging me to write.

Kelly Hahn for your expertise and partnership in this project.

Terri Tracy for all your work on the manuscript.

Cheryl Dillman for your assistance in finalizing the manuscript.

The pastoral staff of Brookside Church for putting up with me.

The Brookside congregation for the privilege of serving you these past eight years.

Dave Boyer for your expert advice to a first-time author.

Dave and Marilyn Knuth, we are friends forever.

And last, my mom and late father, you raised me well. You loved me every day.

Contents

Foreword

Prisons have fostered far more art, wonderful literature, and mystical spiritual insight than any Arts Council, English Department, or church. Adversity gives birth to genius.

Every day millions of men and women fling themselves into the crucible of the place the Apostle John called "The World," and if they are faithful disciples, they will be tested.

Many call "The World" the Marketplace. It is a difficult place to be if you are committed to truth. Yet, the people we are called to reach, to love, to influence, to touch with the Gospel also call the marketplace home.

And most don't get up on Sunday morning and think, "I wonder how I can make that church on Fifth and Elm successful." They are not interested in church and why should they be? There is no indication or command in Scripture that they should be in church.

The Scripture does, however, command the church to go to the world, and that is different from just living in it. One could even think of the world as a harvest field.

Christians are to be workers in the field, not just residents. The church is the church only when it exists for others. Therefore, the church is at its best when the doors are locked, the lights are out, and the parking lot is empty. That is the test—what are we like 98 percent of the time when we are not "in churches"?

That is what *Minefields in the Marketplace* is about. What kind of people are we when it really counts? Anyone can hold it together for a couple of hours surrounded by stained glass and religious-sounding people. But what if telling the truth will cause you to lose the sale, your commission, and probably the promotion?

You might reason, "No one really cares or will know about it anyway;" or "Hey, God loves me, He will forgive me and ten percent of my commission will go to the church."

It sounds very convincing, doesn't it? "After all, two more people can go on the mission trip to Uganda if I lie." But, have you ever thought about the long-term effect of honesty, of the dynamic of God's blessing—or lack of it—based on your conduct?

iv

Have you considered the wound to your soul, the inner knowledge that you haven't really experienced the fruit of what God can do with a person of integrity? Have you thought about what those close to you at work think about God because of you?

How we live and talk with our colleagues either opens doors or closes them for the Gospel.

If you haven't thought about it, Jim Pearson has. Jim is one of those guys who has been there and done that. His stories are interesting and the lessons penetrating. And you will also enjoy a few good laughs as he walks you through the minefields that we all encounter. His insights are fresh and his storytelling engaging.

Jim is the kind of guy you would like to spend time with over a cup of coffee. In fact, Jim is a good model for all those who want to influence others with their character.

The most difficult problem for the church is not how to organize an outreach program; it is how to get its people to do outreach. Its companion problem is to convince them that reaching others is not primarily about having a gospel tract in your wallet. It is about one's character and conduct, and what effect you are having on those you see every day.

Just as a prison can bring out the very best in a person, a disciple in the marketplace can mean a more glorious ministry than can be had in any church, monastery, or crusade.

Bill Hull
Writer and Teacher
Author: *Choose the Life; Jesus Christ, Disciplemaker;*
The Disciple-Making Pastor; The Disciple-Making Church

Introduction:
The Danger of Minefields

My father served in the British army for seven years. From 1938-1945, he faithfully fought for the Allied cause in World War II. Seven years is a substantial segment of anyone's life, yet my father rarely spoke about that period of time. Like most young boys, I occasionally watched war movies. Afterward, I would often attempt to get my father to open up and share with me some of his wartime experiences. Usually, he would say very little. However, every now and then he would allow me a brief glimpse into what his military experience was like.

On a few occasions, my dad spoke about his experiences with minefields. One of his responsibilities was working with a team to discover where the minefields were located, and then remove them so that his squadron could safely advance. It was, needless to say, an extremely hazardous assignment. On one occasion, one of my dad's colleagues stepped on a mine while the team was gingerly attempting to clear a path. The man froze with terror. Somehow, my father and the rest of the team were able to keep the mine from exploding. It was an experience one never forgets.

Minefields are dangerous! Every step is potentially your last. Every soldier seeks to avoid the mines and somehow cross the field safely. There is no margin for error, no room for carelessness. It takes both vigilance and a certain amount of luck.

This book is about minefields. But not the kind my father encountered in World War II. The minefields discussed in these chapters are those that Christians in the business world encounter on a regular basis. The marketplace is filled with minefields. For the most part, they are not ones that threaten your physical safety. Most do not threaten to end your career, though some certainly could. The minefields discussed in this book are those that threaten your spiritual well-being. They also threaten your family relationships and your testimony for Jesus Christ.

To be sure, these minefields are not peculiar to the world of business. However, in my eight years in the corporate world, and in my subsequent counseling ministry with businessmen and businesswomen, I have seen the same minefields victimize Christians again and again. As a businessman, I saw them wreak havoc in the lives of my Christian colleagues. And in my ministry, I have watched them bring destruction to the lives of members of my congregations. Over the last sixteen years, I have counseled many Christians who stepped on a landmine while pursuing careers in the marketplace. All too often, a lack of attention to their walk with Christ led to spiritual disaster.

Whether you are a college student contemplating a business career, a salesman just getting started, or a CEO of a *Fortune 500* company, this book is written for you. Though written from a man's perspective, it will challenge and be of value to women as well. Biblical principles are biblical principles.

It is my prayer that this book will challenge businessmen and businesswomen to maintain an authentic walk with Christ. You *can* stay close to the Savior while climbing the corporate ladder. God has called us to a high standard. Let's watch out for the minefields.

Jim Pearson
Fort Wayne, Indiana
August, 2005

Chapter 1

A Parable

Grant tapped his pen irritably as he reread Question 7a. for the tenth time. His pen cast a long shadow down the right side of his cluttered desk as the sun dipped lower across the San Francisco skyline. The question itself seemed to symbolize everything that was wrong with the company. If he were to make vice-president according to his projected timeline, these kinds of questions soon would no longer annoy him.

"**What is your personal mission statement?**" the question stared up at him again.

What's the point? Grant argued within himself. *What does my personal mission have to do with developing ad campaigns? If I can put a deal together that earns the company a cool million, will anybody care about my personal pursuits? I don't think so.*

Still, the question had lines underneath it—two thick parallel lines, to be exact—and they demanded a response. It was Medley's idea to do these Personal Inventory Assessments as a way of team-building and promoting personal growth. The PIAs would help their division grow holistically, Medley had said—body, soul, relationships, bottom line. At the time of the announcement, Grant had thought it all seemed like a colossal waste of time. But Medley was the boss, and there was no point in protesting. Medley had asked for them to be completed by the next quarterly off-site—a good two months to spend a generous amount of introspective time on it. But Grant had blown it off, and now the deadline was tomorrow. Hence, he was sitting in his office at 6:30 p.m., stewing over two thick parallel lines that demanded a response.

What made the situation worse was the other set of papers flanking the PIA. They were slightly creased and their yellowish tint suggested they were a few years old. They were seven years old, in fact, and they were the first Personal Inventory Assessment he had ever filled out—the day he was hired. "We ask every new hire to complete one," his previous boss, Hal Cleverly, had told him. "That way we can pull them out in a few years and see if you're still on track with your life goals." Back then, it had sounded like a great idea to Grant Roth—new employee and world-beater. He had had no idea how much those few hours would come back to haunt him later.

Grant hadn't spent much time looking through his previous assessment. Viscerally, he knew he didn't want to see how much he had changed in seven years. He had thumbed through portions of it; mostly the analytical stuff like his Taylor-Johnson Temperament Analysis and the Leadership Development Assessment. But other than that, he really just wanted to avoid the whole thing.

Shifting in his chair, Grant blinked at the clock: 6:45. This was becoming ridiculous. If he didn't start scribbling something, he'd be chained to his office all night. *Maybe I'll just copy*, Grant thought. *How in-depth is anyone going to look at this anyway? After all, if my current mission statement matches the one from seven years ago, maybe I'll have to participate less.* Satisfied with this shortcut possibility, Grant adjusted his previous PIA so it sat to the left of the fresh one and opened both to question 7a.

The type font was different, but the lines hadn't changed. The two thick parallel lines had been filled in on the first assessment. On his first day of work seven years earlier, Grant Roth had written as his personal mission statement:

My personal mission is to be a devoted father and husband, to honor God in my work through productivity and integrity, and to leave a legacy built on ethics and character.

Lord, it was worse than he thought! It sounded as if Mr. Rogers had ghostwritten it for him. He couldn't take *that* into tomorrow's off-site; practically everyone would know he faked it. If only he had written something bland like, *My mission is to serve my company and exercise my talents to their full capacity.* Then, he could have worked with it. But

4

not this—this was the work of an alter ego he thought he'd killed, or at least exiled.

Grant read it again and winced. It was like looking at old pictures of himself with fishbowl haircuts and parachute pants. *That's not me,* he would think, and he thought it now. Yet apparently this *had* been his personal mission at one time. Grant looked at the first part of the statement: "*...to be a devoted father and husband.*" A picture of his family sat on his credenza next to the quartz timepiece that now read 6:50. It was a juxtaposition that he hated and struggled with daily: his family and the clock. They sat side-by-side on his desk, but battled constantly in his heart and home. The picture was taken shortly after Christmas, when he had taken a rare three-day weekend. The photo of the four of them was good. Tension and strain were pleasantly absent. As a savvy advertising executive, Grant had mastered the art of disguising his true emotions.

Leann, his wife of seven years, was sitting on the left. William, three years old, stood between her and Grant. Grant Jr., eighteen months, rested on Leann's lap. Aside from his hectic work in advertising, they filled the rest of his life. The quartz timepiece, he told people, had been a gift from his late father. It wasn't true. He had bought it at Wal-Mart.

When he thought about how his family life might look from an outsider's perspective, he saw a comfortable family living a comfortable life. But Grant knew better, of course. It wasn't that Grant didn't want to be a good husband and dad. It was just that being good at either required so much *time*—time to talk about Leann's day; time to listen to William's stories about tiny soldiers who lived and fought in their backyard; time to help with the baby; time to pray with Leann and model prayer as the family leader. Unfortunately, time was a commodity in which he was thoroughly bankrupt.

His 401k was growing by leaps and bounds, but he had no time to give anyone—not even to himself. Catching the morning train to work required him to rise at 5:30 and leave the house by 6:15. And while business was paying off in terms of promotions, larger accounts, and bonuses, it was costing him everywhere else. Most days he wouldn't get home until 7:30. And when he arrived, Leann usually had all the warmth of his leftover supper. On particularly bad days at the office, Grant would actually sleep in his office chair rather than go home for another round of verbal beatings.

William seemed mostly to ignore Grant. When he came home, William would often be parked in front of the TV, pacifier in his mouth, oblivious to anything going on around him—even when occasional shouting matches erupted in the kitchen. Grant Jr. was usually asleep by the time he got home. Grant could go days without ever seeing his son awake. When the weekends came, Grant Jr. would play with a wary eye on his dad, not entirely sure who he was.

Obviously, Grant could no longer put the same words he had written about his family seven years ago onto the new PIA. Everybody on his work team knew he put in nearly 65 hours a week. Saying his personal mission was to be a devoted father and husband would raise eyebrows for sure, if not provoke outright laughter. So he couldn't do it. But there was another reason that was even more personal and hidden: Grant couldn't say he was committed to being a devoted husband while he was simultaneously considering an affair with Natalie in the production department.

Grant knew there is a certain truth to the idea that sometimes the people you work with become more of a family than your actual family. It's not that you like these people more; it's just that you're around them and adapt to their rhythms over time. For Grant, the few hours he spent awake at home felt more like living with in-laws.

And over time, his path had crossed with Natalie's often enough to create an attraction. As Leann went through pregnancy, delivery, and life with Grant Jr., she became less and less interested in showing affection to Grant. For a while, Grant convinced himself that the harmless flirting with Natalie was a reasonable way to make up for the lack of love at home. But now home was becoming an increasingly uncomfortable place to be. And Natalie was stopping by the office more, seeing if his schedule was clear for coffee, smiling in his direction …

In his heart, he didn't want to do it. But in some ways he felt almost *compelled* to do it. All his aspirations for business success had been realized and yet that success was ruining every other aspect of his life. He felt his compromised dreams owed him *something*, even if just one night.

Grant switched his mind from Natalie back to the PIA: "…*honor God in my work through productivity and integrity…*" He shrugged slightly. He was productive—no one could argue that. Arguing for his integrity would be less convincing, however. At one time his mission really was to conduct business with the character of Jesus Christ. The thought seemed somewhat laughable now, but even as he stared at the parallel lines, he felt a sudden surge of energy—like a flicker of something that had once engulfed him but had since disappeared.

When he and Leann were newly married and he had just begun his climb up the corporate ladder, Grant had been part of a small group of businessmen who met every couple of weeks for an extended time of lunch and fellowship. They would eat, pray, and work through a book of the Bible or another book designed to help them grow as Christian businessmen. Most of the sessions centered on honesty, integrity, values, and respect. "How would Jesus organize His day, relate to co-workers, pitch a strategy, or approach a failure?" the leader would ask. "How can you live for Christ in the business world?"

Grant had rarely missed a luncheon. Sometimes he had even led the session. At work, he had tried to approach his tasks and relationships as Jesus would. But about two years into his tenure, that all changed.

One week, he and the resident company "wonder boy," Tom, flew to Tampa to meet with executives of an arena football league. Tom was a hard-nosed, opinionated company rogue who ran roughshod over people and controlled situations. He reminded Grant of a young Robert DeNiro. Tom was widely disliked, but no one could deny that he was a charmer when making presentations and overseeing negotiations. He had talent, and that talent made lots of money for the company.

In Tampa, the negotiations went better than expected. Grant let the more experienced Tom handle the flow of conversation and by the end of the day, the executives agreed to a contract they would sign the following day. Grant and Tom were soaring. Tom suggested they celebrate over dinner. That's where the problems began.

Dinner wasn't a steak and potato deal at Outback Steakhouse. Tom instead picked a ritzy bistro called Sal's. Entrees *began* at $39.99. Tom ordered expensive champagne. Then, he ordered surf and turf at the market price, $79.95. Grant picked the $39.99 menu item. Tom called him a sissy and suggested that after dinner they hit the strip bars. Grant protested, but tipsy from the champagne, and slightly frightened of Tom, he agreed to go.

In the end, Tom racked up $400 on the company card at the restaurant and another $500 at the strip club. Apparently, this wasn't new for him. What was new for him was that the next morning, both he and Grant overslept and the executives of the arena football league nixed the deal. To this point, the company had allowed Tom certain liberties as long as he brought home the deals. This time, he didn't bring home the deal. In fact, this was the third time it had happened in recent months.

His boss had been suspicious for some time about Tom's expense accounts. As long as the lucrative contracts were coming in, he was willing to look the other way. But now, the "wonder boy" wasn't getting it done. This time, Tom was grilled about his expense account. The boss even pulled some old reports out of a file and began to ask pointed questions. Tom admitted to turning in phony receipts. The company had him dead to rights. Not only had he manufactured false receipts to account for the exorbitant expenses, he had also used false receipts to line his pockets with a little extra cash. Tom was fired on the spot.

Though Grant was not squeaky clean in the whole matter, he came out faring pretty well. He ended up taking over most of Tom's accounts. And along with those accounts, he took some of Tom's ability to compromise. His ethics deteriorated, and so did his participation in the businessmen's luncheons. Friends called to ask whether anything was wrong. Nothing was wrong, he had said. He was just busy. He was still living for Christ, but was just busier. And then, as if lying to the group was the last straw, he stopped going to the group—and to church—altogether.

So, no, "honoring God in my work through productivity and integrity" could not go on this PIA. Neither could "leaving a legacy of ethics and character." He wasn't sure what kind of legacy he was going to leave behind, but it surely wasn't the one he had envisioned seven years earlier.

Grant shook his head and closed the older PIA. He had no personal mission. He was trying to make money and do just enough so he wasn't buried by excessive guilt. All his altruistic aspirations had been washed away in a tidal wave of contracts, fights with Leann, disconnection with William, guilt over his lies, thoughts about Natalie, and a growing emptiness within.

I really wanted to be someone with a mission to do things that showed I love God and others, he muttered to himself. Surprisingly, his voice cracked just a little when he said "God." Puzzled by the unfamiliar crack in his composure, he steeled himself and picked up the old Personal Inventory Assessment. Slowly and deliberately, he crumpled it into a ball. When he could crumple it no further, he tossed it absent-mindedly across the room.

But this is business, he thought to himself. *And business is a whole other kind of life. It's one thing to believe in God, go to church, love my family, and tell the truth when I'm on my own time. But the business world doesn't allow me to be soft. The only way to make it in the business world is to live a fragmented life. I think God will understand. After all, He made me to love business and be good at it. I didn't ask for Leann to shut me out, and I didn't ask for Natalie to come on to me. I am trying to do the best I can, but I won't throw my career away. I've come too far. I've worked too hard. God can forgive the occasional lie. My mission is to be the best businessman I can be, and I will not let anyone interfere with that.*

The sun disappeared behind a row of high-rises. Grant decided not to go home that night.

Think It Can't Happen to You?

How does someone like Grant end up beginning his business career wanting to serve Christ in the marketplace and yet end up hardened, estranged from his family, unethical and flirting with adultery? His story is like that of many Christian businessmen who failed to make it safely through the six minefields we will explore in the following chapters. Think it can't happen to you? Think again. Remember these words in the Bible:

> *O God, you are my God; earnestly I seek you; my soul thirsts for you; my flesh faints for you, as in a dry and weary land where there is no water* (Psalm 63:1, ESV).

> *I love you, O LORD, my strength. The LORD is my rock, my fortress and my deliverer; my God is my rock, in whom I take refuge* (Psalm 18:1-2).

Those words were written by the same man of whom it is also written: "One evening David got up from his bed and walked around on the roof of the palace. From the roof he saw a woman bathing. The woman was very beautiful, and David sent someone to find out about her. The man said, 'Isn't this Bathsheba, the daughter of Eliam and the wife of Uriah the Hittite?' Then David sent messengers to get her. She came to him, and he slept with her" (2 Samuel 11:2-4a).

Even David, who loved God and was credited by God as being a man after His own heart, was caught in a destructive minefield. If it can happen to him, it certainly can happen to you. Spend some time praying before you read these chapters. Ask God to open your heart and reveal where you're entering into a minefield, trapped with mines all around you. Then yield yourself to what He tells you. My prayer is that you will be a businessperson who lives for Christ as a whole person—all facets of your life working together to serve God and glorify Him. May we, through the process of refining by the Spirit, be the kind of people who exemplify David's words in Psalm 15:

> LORD, who may dwell in your sanctuary?
>   Who may live on your holy hill?
> He whose walk is blameless
>   and who does what is righteous,
> who speaks the truth from his heart
>   and has no slander on his tongue,
> who does his neighbor no wrong
>   and casts no slur on his fellowman,
> who despises a vile man
>   but honors those who fear the LORD,
> who keeps his oath
>   even when it hurts,
> who lends money without usury
>   and does not accept a bribe against the innocent.
> He who does these things
>   will never be shaken.

Chapter 2

The Minefield of Ethical Compromise

Once you lose your integrity, the rest comes easy.
– J. R. Ewing, Dallas

A good name is more desirable than great riches;
to be esteemed is better than silver or gold.
– Proverbs 22:1

"Don't Tell Him the Truth!"

My secretary stood up as I entered the office. She quickly moved in my direction. I had been in the building for only a few moments, but something about the atmosphere told my subconscious there was a problem. A big problem. I greeted her with a hearty smile and a resounding, "Good Morning!" as a hopeful way to stave off any lurking bad news. But as she curtly motioned toward my office, I knew my premonition was true. As I took off my coat and removed items from my briefcase, I prepared myself for whatever was going to come.

"Jerry from RW Johnson called at seven. Our truck never arrived this morning. All production is held up without the shipment. Jim, he is *furious*! You better find out what's going on."

Her words were like a punch in the gut. RW Johnson was one of my oldest and most productive accounts. But I knew that delayed or missed shipments could quickly turn loyal customers into former customers. Trying not to panic, I dialed Jerry's number. Jerry was as tough as the scrap iron we sold him, but surely he'd look into the facts before jumping to conclusions—or jumping accounts. It was a hopeful thought, but I braced myself for an earful either way.

"Hi, Jerry? This is Jim Pearson."

"*Where is your truck?*" he screamed into the phone. "I have men waiting for your shipment so they can get to work. This is costing me all kinds of wages and down time! If I can't rely on you and your company, *I'll find somebody else to be my supplier!*"

I quickly apologized and promised I would call him back as soon as I could discover why the shipment hadn't arrived. *A flat? Construction? Mechanical problem? Surely there has to be a reasonable explanation for this*, I thought. I immediately called the shipping department to get answers.

"We blew it, Jim," the dispatcher groaned. "The truck is being loaded right now. It won't get there for several hours."

I slumped in my chair and felt the stress coursing through my body. It really was the worst-case scenario. There was no mechanical problem, no snaky set of construction detours, no torrential downpours forcing the driver to pull over. There was nothing to tell Jerry but the...

"Look, Jim, make up a lie," the dispatcher pleaded. "Tell him the truck broke down. Tell him it had a flat. Tell him the driver got sick and had to pull into a rest area. Whatever you do, *don't tell him the truth!* If he knows we just plain forgot, they'll ditch us for sure."

After hanging up the phone, I stared out the window for a few moments to gather my thoughts. *What do I tell him?* The internal debate began. It would have been easy to make up a story. After all, trucks do break down and tires do go flat. Jerry would still be angry, but at least we wouldn't look incompetent. At the end of the day, he'd still have his shipment and we'd still have our client. Why make an ugly situation even worse by supplying a reason for RW Johnson to fire us? Sure, it wasn't the truth, *but sometimes isn't it better to hide the truth in order to avoid an unnecessary catastrophe?* The dispatcher's plea echoed: *Whatever you do, don't tell him the truth!*

12

My secretary popped her head in the door. "What are you going to do?" she asked. I knew there really was only one thing to do. I would have to call Jerry and tell him what really happened. Oh, the internal debate had surfaced a number of reasons for not telling the truth. But all along I knew what I would ultimately end up doing. Deep in my heart, I knew lying was not an option.

Knowing this didn't make calling Jerry any easier. With trembling fingers, I placed the call. Before he could say anything (or scream anything), I gave the truth in a straightforward measure: "Jerry, I'm sorry, we blew it. The truck hasn't even left yet." Then I braced for a new education in the world of modern expletives.

Oddly, It didn't come.

"Pearson," he said, almost as if he had to consciously remember who I was, "You're the least of my worries. I just found out my overhead crane will be down for most of the day. By the time we're ready to run, your truck will be here. But make sure this doesn't happen again, and send over two additional truckloads right away."

It was one of those moments when you leap from your chair, pump your fist in the air, and shout, "Yes!"

Of course, the result could have been much different. Had the crane not broken down, Jerry might have turned his frustration on me. My company could have lost its position as RW Johnson's primary supplier. My own means for making a living may have been jeopardized.

If I had lied my way out of the situation, it is unlikely Jerry would have ever found out. Most likely, our relationship would have continued. It would have been business as usual. I might have felt guilty about it for awhile, but I also would have reminded myself that it was the best decision for that circumstance.

But no matter how I might have dressed up my deception, it is an unmistakable fact that I would have willingly stepped directly onto the minefield of ethical compromise.

What Would You Do?

So what would you do if you had been sitting at my desk? It's your hand dialing Jerry's number. You have a boss who depends on your account. You have a wife and kids at home who depend on your income. You have an angry plant superintendent who considers honest mistakes unacceptable. You have to make the call and tell Jerry something. Force yourself to answer with brutal honesty: *What would you say?*

Every day, in corporations across the globe, people make private and public decisions to compromise ethical standards. Parts are approved for shipment, even though inspectors know they don't meet the customer's specifications. Bribes are offered in order to get a "last peek" at what is supposed to be a secret bid. Invoices are falsified to boost profit margins. If you're in the marketplace, you know—directly or indirectly—how it's done.

"Business is business," some say. "Hey, you can't compete if you always play the game in an honest manner." The more they say it, the better it sounds. To them, it becomes a maxim or a proverb objectively portraying how the world of business *really* works. They echo the thoughts of H. L. Mencken when he mused, "It is hard to believe that a man is telling the truth when you know that you would lie if you were in his place."[1]

And it would be a mistake to think that all ethical compromises are made strictly to profit the company. Far more often, breaches of integrity occur for personal convenience. Employees may refuse to bend their ethical standards at the request of middle management, but when it comes to padding their expense accounts to create an extra hundred dollars a month, they say, "Why not? Everybody else is doing it. And besides, I deserve it."

Let me be very direct. Ethical compromise is a sin. Lying, cheating and stealing may be commonplace in the corporate world; however, the Christian in the marketplace is not supposed to operate at that level. We are called to a higher standard. The Apostle Paul wrote, "Do not conform...to the pattern of this world, but be transformed by the renewing of your mind" (Romans 12:2a). If he were writing this book, he would say, "I don't care how other people are doing it. I don't care how your co-workers are profiting from dishonesty. *You don't conform to that standard.* You live by a higher standard. Renew your mind and get God's take on ethical compromise. Don't settle for what the *world* is doing."

In 2 Corinthians 10:5, Paul says, "We demolish arguments and every pretension that sets itself up against the knowledge of God, and *we take captive every thought* to make it obedient to Christ" (emphasis added). Every thought. Living in reverent submission to Christ means subjecting all our thoughts to His standard of truth. That means even our inner ethical debates must be laid in front of the Lord Jesus Christ and pass His

test. So let's do that. Let's take some of the most common ar
favor of ethical compromise and see if they are obedient to Ch

"I'm Not Paid Enough, So Taking a Little Extra Makes Up for Their Stinginess."

I have never enjoyed feeling unappreciated. I imagine you don't enjoy it either. There is a measure of personal pain that hits every one of us who commits time and energy to an eight, nine, or ten hour work day, only to leave feeling as if no one cares and no one notices. One of the chief ways we feel appreciated is by how we're compensated. That doesn't always mean money; it often also means receiving praise, special opportunities, meaningful work, and celebration. But in many corporate climates, the primary compensation is financial. When we feel unappreciated by our bosses and the monetary compensation is lacking, the temptation to cheat the company arises. By padding your expenses a little each month, or by taking other shortcuts, you can live at the level of compensation you "deserve."

2 Kings 5 tells the story of a servant named Gehazi, who may remind you of yourself. He was an assistant to the great prophet Elisha, and he witnessed many incredible acts in Elisha's ministry—including a resurrection (2 Kings 4:8-35). Gehazi played an important administrative role for Elisha, often delivering messages and taking care of details.

But Gehazi wasn't perfect and he was by no means immune to temptation. In 2 Kings 5, Elisha heals a man named Naaman of leprosy. Naaman is overjoyed and in his gratitude, he offers a gift to Elisha. Elisha refuses Naaman's gift. Why? Naaman's words in 2 Kings 5:18 give a hint: "When my master enters the temple of Rimmon to bow down and he is leaning on my arm and I bow there also—when I bow down in the temple of Rimmon, may the LORD forgive your servant for this."

Naaman acknowledged God—even to the point of desiring forgiveness from Him—but he also worshiped a god named Rimmon. The LORD was great in Naaman's eyes, but Rimmon was pretty good, too, and because the king liked Rimmon, that's where Naaman's job security was. This blending of religions is called syncretism, and it would ultimately be Israel's undoing as the rest of 2 Kings unfolds.

So what would have happened if Elisha had accepted Naaman's gift? It's possible that people would have seen it as an acceptance of syncretism. Instead of being a nation uncompromisingly devoted to one God—the LORD—now it would be okay to accept gifts and create networks with nations who worship Rimmon. Doing such a thing would break the standards set forth by God in Exodus 20:3—the first commandment: "You shall have no other gods before me." God does not share power interdependently with a board of other gods. He is God alone and expects to be worshiped as God alone. For Elisha to accept the gift from Naaman would be to bend that standard. Elisha stood firm, and he needed to since Naaman, an army commander, was not used to taking "no" for an answer: "And even though Naaman urged him, he refused" (2 Kings 5:16b).

Gehazi, on the other hand, saw Elisha's refusal differently: "After Naaman had traveled some distance, Gehazi, the servant of Elisha the man of God, said to himself, 'My master was too easy on Naaman, this Aramean, by not accepting from him what he brought. As surely as the LORD lives, I will run after him and get something from him" (2 Kings 5:19-20).

Gehazi either did not see, or was not interested in, rejecting any form of syncretism. He saw only a missed opportunity to make a little extra income. After all, Naaman was a pagan foreigner! Naaman was an army commander, so he had wealth at his disposal. What good could come from letting Naaman walk away healed by God and not having financially helped the servants of God? Why should Gehazi and Elisha have to eat gourd stew and depend on handouts (4:38-44) while this commander lived in luxury? And there was a famine in the land! (4:38). The more he thought to himself (isn't it great the way the Bible reveals the characters' thoughts—and ours?) the more he determined Elisha was wrong.

Gehazi sets out after Naaman, and Naaman—who had wanted to give Elisha a gift—gives Gehazi two talents (a generous gift). Gehazi returns home, feeling justified in his actions. After putting the talents away in the house, Gehazi is confronted by Elisha:

"'Where have you been, Gehazi?' Elisha asked.

"'Your servant didn't go anywhere,' Gehazi answered" (2 Kings 5:25).

Apparently, Gehazi was not 100 percent convinced that Elisha had erred in not taking Naaman's gift. Instead of coming clean, Gehazi lied to Elisha's face! Think about that! If your company's CEO were to discover falsified expense reports and confront you with it, how confidently could you defend your case that you cheated the company because you're underappreciated and not paid enough? How defendable are those inner convictions when they're face to face with someone who may not hold the same point of view?

Elisha had given Gehazi a chance to come clean and he blew it. Elisha reveals that he knew what Gehazi had done. As punishment, Gehazi is afflicted with leprosy that didn't just affect him, but his future descendants as well.

If you were to ask Gehazi, "Why did you do it? Why did you take the gift even though you had to have known somewhere in your heart and mind that Elisha had refused it for a reason?" I think Gehazi would respond, "I felt justified. Being a prophet's assistant is a hard life. I was tired of getting second-best. I was angered that we were in the midst of a famine and Elisha refused a gift that could have relieved our hunger. I wasn't getting what I felt I deserved, and so I took something to make me feel better about my job and my life."

I think Gehazi's story is included in the Bible to warn us about the justifications we create and defend within ourselves. God does not promise us an easy life. He promises us that a life lived in Him will not be lived in vain. But along the way there are pitfalls and pity parties, dungeons, and doldrums. The answer doesn't lie in grasping what's not rightfully yours; the answer is in refocusing your hope on God.

Don't make enough money? Who does? Dependence upon God makes us rich in His grace. It's not a bad thing to depend on God for our provision. Since all things come from God, we depend on Him whether we're in plenty or in need. If your compensation is below the industry norm, take the road of integrity and speak to your supervisor. If a better agreement can't be worked out, pray for direction. If God is leading you to stay where you are, pray for a greater sense of contentment with what you earn. If God is leading you to pursue other opportunities, do it with integrity. Continue producing good work while you look. But whatever you do, don't justify taking from the company by saying you're underpaid and underappreciated. It's an argument that only you will believe.

Ethics Are Relative: "It All Comes Down to What I Can Live With."

I stand with our third President Thomas Jefferson's belief, "I have never believed there was one code of morality for a public and another for a private man."[2]

Are ethics relative? Do I have a self-created ethical code based on my conscience that may be different from yours? If I refuse to view adult movies while on a business trip away from home because of my ethical standards, yet find no harm in withholding some of my income from the IRS, is that okay? If I base my ethical decisions on what I can personally live with, does that make me immune to possible consequences?

"Personal" ethics don't really exist, as John Maxwell points out in his book, *There's No Such Thing As "Business" Ethics*: "People try to use one set of ethics for their professional life, another for their spiritual life, and still another at home with their family. That gets them into trouble. Ethics is ethics. If you desire to be ethical, you live it by one standard across the board."[3] And if you are a believer in Jesus Christ, your ethics have been chosen for you.

In their book *Execution: The Discipline of Getting Things Done*, Honeywell Industries CEO Larry Bossidy and organizational consultant Ram Charan write, "Whatever leadership ethics you may preach, people will watch what you do. If you're cutting corners, the best will lose faith in you. The worst will follow in your footsteps. The rest will do what they must to survive in a muddy ethical environment."[4]

Think about that word-picture for a moment. A "muddy ethical environment" sounds like a place where the most popular ethics are the ones that don't interfere with the bottom line. Is that what you want for yourself? Is that the kind of legacy you want to leave? Is that the kind of career you can proudly present to God one day?

It's a bad deal any way you look at it. Don't try to justify decisions you know to be unethical simply because your conscience won't give you an ulcer. Don't contribute to a muddy ethical environment. You might read Maxwell's book for a deeper look at the Golden Rule, or you might simply apply loving others as you love yourself to your decisions. My recommendation for resisting ethical compromise is this: Whenever you are about to make a decision that "wiggles"—a decision that isn't cut and dried, black or white; one that has potential to hurt someone—ask yourself this question: "Is this going to honor God? Does it honor God when I promise a customer a Wednesday shipment when I know full well that getting it there by Saturday is a long shot? Is my description of this product accurate in a way that God is honored by my truth-telling?" Treating others as you would want to be treated is important, but ultimately we live our lives for an audience of One. It's His judgment about our ethical decisions that matters.

"I'm Not Really Hurting Anybody If No One Knows but Me."

This argument is similar to the one above in that conscience is once again the game breaker. What is really being said is that if I am breaching a rule of ethics, and yet only I know and I can live with it, no harm, no foul. This is a private lie that we come to believe because we think that if no one else knows about it, no one else is available to question or critique the decision.

My friend, don't step into this minefield by assuring yourself you are the only one who knows. Unless you are God (and you're not), you cannot be absolutely sure your unethical deed is known to you alone. The more you worry about who might find out, the more you'll realize the deed was never worth it in the first place.

When I was a "rookie" in the scrap iron and steel business, I made a colossal purchasing mistake. I bought 100 tons of material that was worth $50 a ton less than what I paid for it. Any way you slice it, I made a $5,000 mistake. When a copy of the purchase contract crossed the desk of the company president, he called me immediately.

"Why did you pay so much for that order?" He demanded. "Only an idiot would pay more for a product than what it is worth!" By "idiot," he was referring to me.

In the moment of panic, I was tempted to tell a whopper. I could have told him the price on the contract was incorrect, and I would immediately make a correction. The chances that a busy company president would follow up on the contract correction were slim to none, and only I would ever have known about the defensive fib. It was tempting! But I knew it would have been a lie, even if no one ever found out. John Wayne could have been talking about my situation when he said, "There's right and there's wrong. You get to do one or the other. You do the one, and you're living. You do the other, and you may be walking around, but you're as dead as a beaver hat."[5]

I told the truth. "I'm sorry. In the heat of the moment, I made a mistake. I read the wrong price on my price list and paid too much. I'll try not to do it again."

He obviously wasn't pleased, but you know what? He'd probably forgotten about my blunder by the time the weekend rolled around. But if I had breached my integrity, the consequences would have stayed around much longer.

19

No Such Thing as "a Simple Plan"

A few years ago, an excellent exposition on the consequences of ethical compromise came out in the movie *A Simple Plan*, starring Bill Paxton and Billy Bob Thornton. Paxton played a small-town laborer named Hank Mitchell while Thornton played his feeble brother, Jacob. The two of them, along with a third man, Lou, stumble upon a crashed plane with a dead pilot and four million dollars in cash aboard. The ethical tug-of-war begins. Jacob and Lou want to keep the money. Hank hedges. It would be wrong, but his wife is pregnant and they're always living paycheck to paycheck. They could bury it and divvy it up later. No one would know but them. Armed with that comfort and the rationalization that it was probably drug money anyway, Hank agrees to take the cash.

But that decision sets off a chain of events that plunges Hank into a continuous barrage of ethical choices, each one with greater risks and greater consequences. Suddenly, Hank is participating in cover-ups and lies that never would have been options before. Soon, they are struggling to cover-up their cover-ups, and the money is becoming more and more of a curse they cannot escape. The movie is tragic, yet human in its treatment of its characters. It challenges the viewer to ask himself or herself, "If you found four million dollars and were certain no one would know about it but you, would you take it?" Early in the film, the answer might be easily reached in favor of taking it. But as the story unfolds, the lesson is clear that with such a decision, you must take whatever consequences arise.

There is a biblical parallel to the movie *A Simple Plan*. It's found in Acts 5 and it involves a husband and wife named Ananias and Sapphira. They, too, thought they had a simple plan about which no one would ever know.

"Now a man named Ananias, together with his wife Sapphira, also sold a piece of property. With his wife's full knowledge he kept back part of the money for himself, but brought the rest and put it at the apostles' feet" (Acts 5:1-2).

To fully understand the significance of Ananias' action, we must make a brief trip back to Acts 4:32-35. The church is growing—not just in number—but in servanthood and generosity. Verse 32 says, "All the believers were one in heart and mind. No one claimed that any of his possessions was his own, but they shared everything they had." People with plenty were sharing with people in need, so that no one in the community of the church would be classified "rich" or "poor." Rather, there would be *no* rich or poor. Verses 34-35 of chapter 4 give more detail: "There were no needy persons among them. For from time to time those who owned lands or houses sold them, brought the money from the sales and put it at the apostles' feet, and it was distributed to anyone as he had need."

The grace of Jesus Christ was showing up in the way people handled their possessions. The community of the church was characterized by its giving and sharing. What a wonderful community to be a part of!

We can assume that Ananias enjoyed being a part of the community, and that he wanted to be seen as spiritual and committed to giving and sharing as others were. So he, like many others, sold a piece of property. He didn't have to give all the proceeds to the church; he didn't have to give *any* of the proceeds to the church. But he must have liked the way the church appreciated the giving spirit of those who were expressing generosity. Suddenly, a plan appeared in Ananias' mind. He could keep part of the property proceeds for himself and still appear to be a generous giver in the eyes of the church. He gets to keep some of the money and still look good. *It's a simple plan and nobody will know it but Sapphira and me!*

But simple plans usually result in monumental failures. As Ananias lays the proceeds at Peter's feet, Peter confronts Ananias about his dishonesty. Presumably God, who sees the inner workings of every human heart, gave Peter the knowledge of Ananias' deed. You probably know the rest of the story. Peter rebukes Ananias and he falls dead on the spot. Later, his unsuspecting wife, Sapphira, tells Peter the same lie. She, too, falls over dead. The real stinger lies in the content of Peter's rebuke: "Didn't [the land] belong to you before it was sold? And after it was sold, wasn't the money at your disposal? What made you think of doing such a thing? You have not lied to men but to God" (Acts 5:4). What seemed like a small breach to Ananias was not a small breach to God. The text implies that had Ananias been up front in his intentions, Peter would have gladly accepted whatever portion Ananias had honestly given. There was no pressure on Ananias; just the responsibility to tell the truth.

It was a scheme to keep back a little money while still giving Ananias and Sapphira the opportunity to appear a little more godly. God wasn't supposed to know. Peter wasn't supposed to know. It certainly wasn't supposed to get them killed! But it did. Such is often the fate of craftily laid plans that hinge on ethical compromises.

So what is my point?

My point is that ethical compromise is not justified by circumstances, it is not justified by conscience, and it is never justified because you *think* you're the only one who knows. A former colleague once told me something I have never forgotten. In the midst of a discussion on the prevalence of padding expense accounts, he looked at me and said, "Jim, everyone has a little bit of larceny in their blood." He was right. Without knowing it, he was delving into some basic theology. No matter how mature in our faith we may become, we will always be subject to temptation. It is a part of our human condition. It's lurking under the surface and will rear its ugly head when you least expect it. How you deal with those situations will depend on whether or not you adhere to God's standard of ethics.

Jesus said, "I am the light of the world. If you follow me you won't be stumbling through the darkness" (John 8:12, NLT). Jesus never sought to do anything that wouldn't in some way honor His heavenly Father. Jesus knew all about temptation. The devil planted specific landmines for Jesus to detonate. But Jesus also knows all about victory. If you begin to base your ethical decisions on whether or not your move will honor God, your Lord and Savior, Jesus Christ will be a fail-safe guide through the minefield of ethical compromise.

Notes

[1] John M. Shanahan, *The Most Brilliant Thoughts Of All Time (in Two Lines or Less)* (New York: Collins, 1999), p. 79.

[2] Robert G. Torricelli, *Quotations For Public Speakers: A Historical, Literary, and Political Anthology* (New Brunswick, NJ: Rutgers University Press, 2000), p. 31.

[3] John C. Maxwell, *There's No Such Thing As "Business" Ethics: There's Only One Rule For Making Decisions* (New York: Warner Business Books, 2003), p. xi.

[4] Larry Bossidy & Ram Charan, *Execution: The Discipline of Getting Things Done* (New York: Crown Business, 2002), p. 81.

[5] Jessica Allen, *Quotable Men of the Twentieth Century* (New York: William Morrow and Company Inc., 1999), p. 87.

Chapter 3

The Minefield of Materialism

I think greed is healthy. You can be greedy
and still feel good about yourself.[1]
– Ivan Boesky

Do not store up for yourselves treasures on earth, where moth and
rust destroy, and where thieves break in and steal. But store up for
yourselves treasures in heaven, where moth and rust do not destroy,
and where thieves do not break in and steal.
– Matthew 6:19-20

Henry Blackaby said, "You can't be a pastor for long before you have someone in your office weeping over the lost years spent seeking the things of this world instead of seeking first the kingdom."[2] I can attest that Blackaby's words are true. And believe it or not, I almost became one of those victims.

Living the High Life

Like many young couples, my wife, Linda, and I survived on a very modest income during the early years of our marriage. Living paycheck to paycheck was an unavoidable way of life. The first two years were especially difficult. I remember regularly walking to the same pay phone to make calls because we didn't have the deposit needed for telephone installation. A big night out consisted of a trip to the local diner for the Wednesday night $1.49 spaghetti special. What a relief it was to keep the macaroni on the shelf and splurge on undercooked pasta and burnt garlic toast!

We were poor but happy. We were actively involved in our local church, we kept a clean apartment and—most importantly—we had each other. Occasionally, I would feel a twinge of envy when another young couple in our Sunday School class bought their first home, or perhaps a new car. But for the most part, we were content.

But in June of 1978, our financial woes came to an abrupt end. I said good-bye to teaching and began a career in business. Suddenly, I went from $8,000 a year to $12,000—with a company car! At the same time, my wife graduated and began full-time employment of her own. In a matter of a few weeks, the Pearson family income increased by 150%. And, as often happens with individuals and families that fall into the materialistic trap, along with that extra income came the inner sense of urgency to begin spending it.

My first indulgence was a brand new Pontiac Grand Prix. Purchasing it created powerful feelings of upward mobility and worth. I washed it every day and waxed it once a week. When I drove it, I felt the "scraping by" life we had known disappearing in my rearview mirror.

That fall we purchased our first home. It was a 1,400 square foot ranch with three bedrooms and an attached garage. The purchase price was $35,000. It was no mansion, but it was all ours—in our minds, anyway. When you're inebriated with spending, you tend to forget that the bank really owns the house; you simply own the keys.

In the evenings, we would take walks through the neighborhood. Surveying the lovely homes around us, with their putting green lawns and detailed landscaping, creating feelings of pride and achievement. We had finally arrived. We had taken our place in Middle America. We were grabbing our share of the American Dream. No more getting excited about crummy, undercooked $1.49 spaghetti dinners. Payphones and bus rides were fading distant memories. No more thinking, "Someday, this will all change." That "someday" had arrived. Life was good. And wasn't this the way things were supposed to be?

Then one evening, I saw new homes under construction in an upscale neighborhood across the highway. Our home was nice, but these homes were luxurious. And without realizing it, a strange thing happened: I started looking at our cozy ranch a little differently. Instead of enjoying our house's amenities—which were a far cry from our austere, phoneless apartment—I began mentally to critique its shortcomings. I began to compare it to the houses springing up across the highway. *Look at those houses! Sprawling lawns! Eye-catching views! Probably hardwood floors!* Yes, life was good, but I began to think the living might be better in a nicer and newer house.

Judgment Day came over lunch when a banker friend informed me interest rates were about to go through the roof. "If you want to buy a new home," he intoned, "buy it now."

We did.

By 1980, we were in yuppie heaven. Life was now *really* good—a steady stream of college football weekends, great vacations, fine dining, and the assurance of financial security. Yet, something else had taken place. Something beneath the surface. An inner, driving force that was gaining control of me, though I tried everything to ignore it.

Ka-Boom!

Without realizing it, my spiritual life had taken on water. My commitment to Christ—my burning zeal for being His faithful disciple, had cooled. College football weekends were a blast, but I sometimes couldn't find the necessary energy the next day to attend church. I still believed the same doctrines, but my day-to-day living reflected a different doctrine—a doctrine of prosperity, entitlement and materialism. The things of this world were more important to me than the things of God. The contentment we had known in the early years had been replaced by a perpetual desire for more and better. It hadn't happened overnight—it seldom does for anyone; nonetheless, I was living a weak Christian life and digging myself deeper into the ditches of wants, things and stuff.

In 1982, I was transferred to my company's home office in Fort Wayne, Indiana. It was a great opportunity; one more step up on the corporate ladder. But while it could have entrenched me further in a materialistic mindset, it turned out to be the beginning of getting my life back in perspective. By God's grace, we found a wonderful church in our new city. Each Sunday we not only heard great expository preaching, but also participated in a Sunday school class with about twenty other couples near our age. Successful in similar industries, we often chatted about our cars, our investments, housing additions—typical yuppie things. However, several guys in the class also exhibited a great deal of spiritual depth. Though they were enjoying the fruits of their careers, they left no doubt that their walk with Christ was indispensable to them. I'd like to say the Holy Spirit tapped lightly on my shoulder, but He didn't; it was more like a two-by-four across the nose. Week after week, I was humbled and deeply challenged.

After several of these Sundays, I left on one of my usual business trips. As the day's agenda came to a close, I made a departure from my normal routine. Instead of entertaining customers, I begged off and returned to my room. I stared out the window at the city lights, brake lights, and streetlights below. I spent a great deal of time reflecting on the drift that had taken place in my life. Only a few years before, I had felt I'd arrived. But now I was remorseful over where I had ended up.

Before retiring for the night, I knelt next to my bed and asked God to forgive me for putting the things of this world ahead of Him. I promised I would never let anything come between me and my relationship with Him again. That was more than twenty years ago and I can say with all integrity that I believe I have kept my promise. Don't get me wrong; I'm not saying materialism is no longer a threat. As much as I'd love to say every ounce of materialistic temptation has been forever banished from my being, I know that's not true. I still love shiny new cars. But I also know that between Linda and the Holy Spirit, I have the necessary accountability to keep me from driving one home.

Your Money or Your Life

One of the frequently voiced misconceptions about money and possessions is that they are evil and to be renounced and despised. You've just read my story. Was my Pontiac Grand Prix a bastion of evil? Was our purchase of a nice home a grotesque sin in God's eyes? Is a gaudy bank account symbolic of a depraved soul? The answer is clearly no. If God has blessed you with a large amount of this world's goods, that in itself does not mean you've become a victim of materialism. Where the line is crossed is when the wealth and possessions you have become more important to you than the things of God.

John Piper writes, "The issue is not how much a person makes. Big industry and big salaries are a fact of our times, and they are not necessarily evil. The evil is in being deceived into thinking a $100,000 salary must be accompanied by a $100,000 lifestyle."[3] It's when prolonging and expanding the affluent *lifestyle* becomes more important than living the *life* God created you for, that you've sold out to materialism.

Jesus summed it up perfectly (as He always did) when He spoke about materialism: "No one can serve two masters. Either he will hate the one and love the other, or he will be devoted to the one and despise the other. You cannot serve both God and Money" (Matthew 6:24). According to Jesus, it is impossible to serve two masters with your one life. Someone will get cheated. Either you will cheat your devotion to God by giving your desire for nice things preeminence in your life, or you will cheat your commitment to materialism by wholeheartedly following God—which often involves sacrifice, giving, simplicity, and servanthood. Someone is going to be cheated and every decision will tear you apart if you're trying to serve two masters. Jesus said it cannot be done. Trying to prove Jesus wrong is an exercise in folly and frustration.

You may be saying, "Wait a minute, Jim. I'm not making that much money. The economy has been so soft lately; I can't afford anything anyway." Or, you might be saying, "I'm not trying to become the next Donald Trump; I'm just trying to feed my family." But consider this: You may have a career in business well into your sixties or even your seventies. Economic downturns? They eventually come to an end. Promotions come when you least expect them. You might be struggling now, but if you work hard and increase your skills, more than likely success will come your way. When it does, the temptation of materialism will come with it like a tick on a dog.

One of my favorite movies is the 1980's hit *Wall Street*. Charlie Sheen plays Bud Fox, a young stock broker with a burning desire to become a major player in the world of finance. When he connects with Wall Street tycoon Gordon Gekko (played by Michael Douglas), he finally gets his chance. The movie chronicles his ascent from the trading floor to the corporate suites. Though his father warns him about the dangerous path he's on, Bud is hooked on the good life. The deeper the infection, the more expensive the suits. Bud continues to ascend the Wall Street hierarchy—getting his own corner office and an upscale high-rise condo. But the revenues of hard work aren't enough to take Bud where he wants to go, and his lust for more leads him to participate in insider trading.

Ultimately, he is arrested and scandalized. In the movie's final scene, he is heading to court. He knows he's facing jail time. All the fine things in his life will be taken away. To use our working metaphor, he is a casualty of the minefield of materialism.

I don't think I'm exaggerating when I say there's a little bit of Bud Fox in all of us. How many of us have lain awake at night, scheming to get that set of new golf clubs, that Lexus, or that key to the executive washroom? How many of us have told ourselves, "Life would be perfect, if I had…" How many of us have found ourselves precariously balancing on ethical lines, reaching for something that will stay out of our grasp unless we step over those lines? Chuck Colson writes, "Practicing the religion of consumerism is like drinking salt water; the more you drink, the thirstier you get. There is never enough wealth and power to satisfy, never enough material possessions to blot out guilt."[4]

For the Christian in the market place, materialism is a subtle danger. It's not as obvious as stealing or sleeping around, but it's no less lethal to your emotional, relational, and spiritual lives.

Of course, I'm not dooming every resident of the upper crust to a life of greed and groaning. I believe anyone can make it safely across the terrain. Whether you do or not will depend on three critical attitudes: an attitude of stewardship, an attitude of contentment, and an attitude of availability.

Stewardship vs. Ownership

One of the best ways to avoid the mine field of materialism is to embrace a very basic biblical principle. The earlier in life you adopt it, the better. The principle is this: *No matter how little or how much you possess, God owns it all.* Consider the following passages:

> *The earth is the LORD's, and everything in it,*
> *the world, and all who live in it* (Psalm 24:1).

> *To the LORD your God belong the heavens, even the highest*
> *heavens, the earth and everything in it* (Deuteronomy 10:14).

If you're trying to evaluate your life based on what you own, you've already set yourself up for failure, because the concept of ownership is built on a foundation of sand. You don't really "own" anything. When you came into the world, you had nothing—not even a garment to cover your nakedness. But as you've accumulated various assets in life, the world has assured you they are yours. But everything you have in your possession—your car, your house, your stock portfolio, your family, even your life—belongs to God. Genesis 1:1 says "In the beginning God created the heavens and the earth." If He created the heavens and the earth, then everything in heaven and on earth belongs to Him from the smallest pillbug to the continent of North America to the air you breathe. The Latin term for God's method of creation is "ex nihilo" or "from nothing." From nothing, God made everything. Had He not created in this way, you would not have anything that you do.

Often, God needs to remind us that He is the source of everything. In Joshua 24:12b-13, God speaks through Joshua with these words: "It was not your swords or bows that brought you victory. I gave you land you had not worked for, and I gave you cities you did not build—the cities in which you are now living. I gave you vineyards and olive groves for food, though you did not plant them" (NLT).

How many of us need to be reminded on a regular basis that we are working with hands we did not create, capitalizing on favorable market conditions we did not create, or living in a free nation we did not create? How easily do we forget that everything comes from the gracious hand of God? Having an attitude of stewardship doesn't mean thinking of God as a divine Rent-a-Center; it means receiving His gifts in appreciation of the loving parent He is.

Does this disappoint you? Does stewardship mean you can't enjoy what you have? Does ownership equal enjoyment while stewardship equals diminished value? Quite the contrary! Rick Warren gives a great illustration that shows enjoyment has nothing to do with ownership:

> *Years ago, a couple let my wife and me use their beautiful, beach-front home in Hawaii for a vacation. It was an experience we never could have afforded, and we enjoyed it immensely. We were told, "Use it just like it's yours," so we did! We swam in the pool, ate the food in the refrigerator, used the bath towels and dishes, and even jumped on the beds in fun! But we knew all along that it wasn't really ours, so we took special care of everything. We enjoyed the benefits of using the home without owning it.[5]*

When we cling to attitudes of ownership and thus entitlement, our flawed perspective stretches to how we view giving back to God. Sometimes Christians think that because God owns the first 10% (a tithe), then the other 90% must belong to them. Don't misunderstand me, tithing is a good thing—an act of gratitude and faith. However, the purpose of the tithe is not to create a profit-sharing plan with God. God is interested in how you manage *all* He's given you. I like to put it this way: I literally possess much, but I own nothing. In *The Screwtape Letters*, C. S. Lewis' fictional demon Screwtape muses on this subject of ownership: "The sense of ownership in general is always to be encouraged. The humans are always putting up claims to ownership which sound equally funny in Heaven and in Hell, and we must keep them doing so."[6]

Wise men have seen our culture's addiction to ownership and have warned us not to follow. Richard Foster wrote, "Most of us could get rid of half our possessions without any serious sacrifice.... Learn to enjoy things without owning them. Owning things is an obsession in our culture. If we own it, we feel we can control it; and if we can control it, we feel it will give us more pleasure. The idea is an illusion."[7] A. W. Tozer also surmised, "There can be no doubt that this possessive clinging to things is one of the most harmful habits in life. Because it is natural, it is rarely recognized for the evil that it is. But its outworkings are tragic."[8]

What are they saying? They are merely expounding on the banking advice of Jesus in Matthew 6:19-21: "Do not store up for yourselves treasures on earth, where moth and rust destroy, and where thieves break in and steal. But store up for yourselves treasures in heaven, where moth and rust do not destroy, and where thieves do not break in and steal. For where your treasure is, there your heart will be also." Gravitation toward ownership creates a treason of the heart, while stewardship keeps the heart in its proper allegiance.

In order to please God with our finances, we must bring God into our financial decisions. We must challenge ourselves with questions we may be used to ignoring. "Is this a wise investment?" "If I buy this house, or new car, will I be forced to cut back on my giving to the Lord?" "Do I have more faith in my financial investments than I do in God's providing for me?" When we embrace the principle that God owns it all, every major spending decision becomes a spiritual decision. We begin to approach financial decisions by saying, "Lord, is this a good way for me to spend your money?"

We can avoid stepping on the landmine of materialism if we see ourselves as stewards of all we have rather than owners.

Contentment vs. Credit

I almost titled this chapter, "The Joneses Are Miserable, Too!" So many of us have developed a not-so-subtle addiction to outdoing our neighbors when it comes to materialistic acquisitions. Recognizing this tendency, some credit card companies have even devised commercials that play off and encourage this urge. But this is nothing new. As far back as the book of Genesis, Abel had something that Cain wanted and Cain killed him over it (God's favor—the story is told in Genesis 4). And who can dispute the truth of Ecclesiastes 4:4, written in approximately 935 B.C.: "...most people are motivated to success by the envy of their neighbors" (NLT). If you have four oxen, I want to have five. If you have three servants, I want to have four. Has anything really changed?

This, among other destructive behaviors that lead to out-of-control spending, has created a society that lives and feasts on credit. Credit card applications flood our mailboxes. Low introductory rates and the wide availability of retailers that accept credit cards have made spending cash almost obsolete. It's also made the idea of spending only what you actually have, antiquated. Having the option of owning (really? owning?) something now, yet paying for it later has sucked many of us into the consumer debt trap.

And I'm not going to soften the punch: *God discourages debt.*

Notice I didn't say "God prohibits debt." He doesn't. However, the discouragements against accumulating debt for the future to live comfortably now are clear. Consider the following verses:

> *The rich rule over the poor,*
> *and the borrower is servant to the lender* (Proverbs 22:7).

> *Let no debt remain outstanding* (Romans 13:8).

Easy credit has led to financial and spiritual disaster through the minefield of materialism. And I can guarantee that a high percentage of people who read these words are squirming uncomfortably right now. Carrying a credit card balance has just become a way of life for us as

Americans. But God's wisdom and direction always trumps cultural norms. An $8,000 balance might not seem like much to you, but God sees the invisible hooks that tether your heart and soul to your lender. He sees that rather than living in peace and contentment with what He's given you, you can buy a dose of happiness with money you don't have. Debt creates a spiritual cancer that seeks immediate gratification whatever the consequences.

In a *Money* magazine article on spending sprees, the magazine cited the story of Chad Pitt, a 25-year-old Orlando DJ. Pitt loves to hit the malls and purchase expensive clothes and accessories. But night DJ's don't make an overwhelming amount of money, so he puts a majority of his spending on his credit cards. The result? He's currently in debt to the tune of over $100,000. *Money* adds, "On days he can't make it to the mall, he finds himself feeling 'bittersweet,' thinking not about his considerable debts but about the deals he may be missing."[9]

The antidote to this destructive reliance on credit cards is twofold: The first is to embrace an attitude of stewardship as mentioned in the section above. If you remind yourself that you are a steward of God's gifts, you won't be driven to consumer debt by pursuing ownership of things. The second attitude to embrace is called contentment.

How you approach contentment reveals the content of your hope. If your hope is primarily located in this world, you will never be satisfied with what you have. If your hope is in Jesus Christ and living in His mansion for eternity (John 14:2-3), you will be more likely to be satisfied with what you have. You intuitively understand and embrace the words of Leonard Sweet: "There is no cause-and-effect relationship between well-off and well-being."[10]

Aware of the human impulse to measure success by acquisition and wealth, Paul advised Timothy:

> ...*godliness with contentment is great gain. For we brought nothing into the world, and we can take nothing out of it. But if we have food and clothing, we will be content with that. People who want to get rich fall into temptation and a trap and into many foolish and harmful desires that plunge men into ruin and destruction. For the love of money is a root of all kinds of evil. Some people, eager for money, have wandered from the faith and pierced themselves with many griefs* (1 Timothy 6:6-10).

32

Notice how a spirit of contentment flows from an attitude of stewardship! *"For we brought nothing into the world, and we can take nothing out of it."* Paul had seen the tragic consequences of individuals putting all their energy into accumulating wealth in this world. In fact, one of the reasons he wrote this letter to Timothy was because of false teachers poisoning the community of God in Ephesus through erroneous and harmful teaching (1 Timothy 1:3-7). Their motive? "These people always cause trouble. Their minds are corrupt, and they don't tell the truth. *To them religion is just a way to get rich*" (6:5, NLT, emphasis added). They did not live with a spirit of contentment, and their greed compromised the very content of their teaching. They shamed the Christian church because of their lust for gain.

Living with contentment focuses on a different hope. As John Piper said, "…God is most glorified in us when we are most satisfied in him."[11] We display our spiritual bearings when we embody contentment. And, perhaps most importantly, it enables us to embrace a third crucial attitude.

Availability vs. Unavailability

When you live as a steward of God's gifts and allow that attitude to breed contentment, you make yourself available for God to use you. Quite simply, people who are overextended financially, vocationally, and recreationally do not make themselves available to serve God. They're too focused on climbing the next rung on the corporate ladder, planning the next vacation, or purchasing their next big toy. Carve out time to minister to others in a small group? "I'm just too busy right now." Isn't that usually an indictment of our priorities rather than the shortness of time? And aren't those priorities often based on commitments to ownership, affluence, and upward mobility?

You may be saying, "But Jim, I go to church. I even serve as a greeter or an usher sometimes." That's good and certainly important. But how would you rate your *availability* to God? Is your life free of materialistic clutter so that when God taps your shoulder, you are not bound to credit card debt, unbearable workloads, and a house filled with "stuff" that needs care, maintenance, and regular use? If God ordered you to minister among the poor in India, could you cut your strings without significant difficulty? You see, the more we become committed to playing the world's game of ownership and acquisition, the less we have open hearts that shout to God, "Here am I. Send me" (Isaiah 6:8).

As you consider what I've written so far about stewardship, contentment, and availability vs. ownership, credit, and unavailability, how you do understand Jesus' words in Luke 14:16-24?

> *Jesus replied: "A certain man was preparing a great banquet and invited many guests. At the time of the banquet he sent his servant to tell those who had been invited, 'Come, for everything is now ready.' But they all alike began to make excuses. The first said, 'I have just bought a field, and I must go and see it. Please excuse me.' Another said, 'I have just bought five yoke of oxen, and I'm on my way to try them out. Please excuse me.' Still another said, 'I just got married, so I can't come.' The servant came back and reported this to his master. Then the owner of the house became angry and ordered his servant, 'Go out quickly into the streets and alleys of the town and bring in the poor, the crippled, the blind and the lame.' 'Sir,' the servant said, 'what you ordered has been done, but there is still room.' Then the master told his servant, 'Go out to the roads and country lanes and make them come in, so that my house will be full. I tell you, not one of those men who were invited will get a taste of my banquet.'"*

In the parable, the invited guests were more interested in other pursuits than they were in attending the great banquet. By their commitments to their own agendas, they made themselves unavailable for the party. Contrast this unavailability with God's challenge in 2 Chronicles 16:9: "For the eyes of the LORD range throughout the earth to strengthen those *whose hearts are fully committed to him*" (emphasis added). God sees availability and commitment in terms of the heart. If our hearts are consumed with keeping up with the Joneses or building a bigger bank account, God will consider us unavailable for His use and His strengthening.

If you're going to get through the minefield of materialism, your end goal must be availability to the God of the universe. If you're available, you will prefer being content with what you have rather than indebting yourself to credit card companies or banks in the pursuit of "more." And contentment is only possible when you remember that God, in His grace, gives you much in this life and He expects you to take care of it without getting attached to it. In the words of Joe Stowell, "The real point of materialism is not how much we have, but what has us."[12]

What, or Who, has you makes all the difference in safely crossing the minefield of materialism.

Notes:

[1] This statement was made by Boesky in 1986 while giving a Commencement address at the University of California School of Business.

[2] Henry and Tom Blackaby, *The Man God Uses* (Nashville: Broadman & Holman, 1999), p. 133.

[3] John Piper, *Desiring God: Meditations of a Christian Hedonist* (Sisters, OR: Multnomah, 1986), pp. 172-173.

[4] Charles Colson and Nancy Pearcey, *How Now Shall We Live?* (Wheaton: Tyndale House, 1999), p. 224.

[5] Rick Warren, *The Purpose Driven Life: What On Earth Am I Here For?* (Grand Rapids: Zondervan, 2002), p. 45.

[6] C. S. Lewis, *The Screwtape Letters* (New York: Simon and Schuster, 1961), p. 80.

[7] Richard Foster, *Celebration of Discipline: The Path to Spiritual Growth* (San Francisco: HarperSanFrancisco, 1978), pp. 92-93.

[8] A. W. Tozer, *The Pursuit of God: The Human Thirst for the Divine* (Camp Hill, PA: Christian Publications, 1982), p. 28.

[9] David Futrelle, "Do You Shop Too Much?" *Money*, November, 2003, pp. 141-146.

[10] Leonard Sweet, *SoulSalsa: Seventeen Surprising Steps to Godly Living in the 21st Century* (Grand Rapids: Zondervan, 2000), p. 57.

[11] John Piper, *Desiring God*, p. 50.

[12] Joseph M. Stowell, *Shepherding the Church Into the 21st Century: Effective Spiritual Leadership in a Changing Culture* (Wheaton: Victor Books, 1994), p. 241.

Chapter 4

The Minefield of Power

The lust for power is not rooted in strength, but in weakness.[1]
– Erich Fromm

*Now Moses was a very humble man, more humble than
anyone else on the face of the earth.*
– Numbers 12:3

Pete the Powerful

In my time in the marketplace, I had several bosses. Most were benevolent, encouraging, and supportive. However, one boss I had was very much the opposite. He was demeaning, spiteful, and callous. I will always remember him as a boss who failed to navigate safely through the minefield of power. I watched him become a casualty time after time after time.

The memories I have of this man are quite painful. These are not memories that have been packaged in the healing balm of time and wisdom. The images and sounds are as fresh and striking now as they were when they happened. I share them to hold up a mirror to your face. Perhaps you'll see yourself in these pages. I pray that you don't, but if you do, then I share my bruised feelings with you in order to provoke you to gentleness and respect.

Let's call him Pete. He had, to say the least, an explosive temper. Anything, it seemed, could set him off. Although there were no assigned parking spaces in the company lot, if someone parked in the space he wanted, watch out! Parking in *his* space could lead to a volcanic tantrum, dripping with intentionally intimidating profanity. One who received such a tirade did not quickly recover.

Pete did not lead his staff, but bullied us into submission. There was no "give and take" with him. On one occasion, an employee came to him with a legitimate concern. I was nearby and overheard the employee's presentation—it was delivered respectfully and without threat. But Pete erupted at the man and ordered him out of his office—and if that weren't caustic enough, upon the man's hasty departure, Pete slammed his fist through his office door. The message was obvious, "Don't ever, *ever* mess with me!"

If Pete's managerial problems were limited to his temper, I suppose I might have been able to avoid him enough to carry on with good work. But to make the business successful, teamwork was required and that meant we had to work with him on certain projects and accounts. Not only did Pete take credit for everything that went well, he blamed everyone but himself when something went wrong. Any encounter with Pete was a no-win situation.

For example, on one occasion Pete was in my office, along with the company president. The three of us were discussing markets, strategy, and other pertinent topics. Gradually, the conversation shifted to specific problems in Pete's area of responsibility. Through a series of probing questions, the president inquired about some errors he was surprised had not already been corrected. I was interested to see how Pete would react to this confrontation. Surely he wouldn't explode at the company president, would he?

No. Instead, Pete looked for the nearest underling—me. I just about had a coronary when, in response to a question, Pete lightly shrugged his shoulders and said, "I told Jim to take care of that three weeks ago. I don't know why he hasn't done it." Moments later, he pawned another failed assignment onto me. I was rocked. I could not believe what I was hearing. I couldn't remember him—at any time—asking me to deal with the problems being discussed. All of the blame now sat squarely on *my* shoulders. When the president turned his gaze in my direction, I was almost speechless. I stammered for a moment, and then simply replied, "I'll take care of it right away."

Later, alone in my office, I pulled out old "to-do-lists," memos, notes from conversations—anything—to see whether I had been given an assignment that had fallen off my radar screen. Finally, convinced that I had not dropped the ball, I dropped in for an unscheduled meeting with Pete.

As I entered his office, it was obvious he knew why I was there. At first, he was vague and he feigned confusion about the project assignments in question. When I respectfully but firmly asked him to tell me when or how he had given me the projects, and when he saw he would not be able to sidestep the issue, he powered up and went on the offensive. Rising from his chair, he embarked on a fiery lecture about my lack of follow-through. In unmistakable, four and twelve-letter terms, Professor Pete told me that if it weren't for him, I wouldn't even have a job. After reminding me repeatedly how fortunate I was to work for him, he pointed his finger in my direction and said, "That's the way it is. If you don't like it, hit the (expletive deleted) road!"

And I did. At least for the rest of that day. Later that evening, still quaking with anger and fear, I shared the ugly incident with Linda. As a result, we prayerfully decided to seek other employment and just "gut it out" in the meantime. But oh, how I dreaded going to work! I enjoyed the tasks of my job, and certainly the fruit of it, but my blood ran cold whenever I came face-to-face with Pete.

Fortunately, I didn't have to endure the situation for long. Pete soon left the company. Not surprisingly, he went to work for one of our chief competitors. With him gone, Linda and I stopped praying for other employment.

Pete's legacy at the company? Few, if any, were sorry to see him go. A dark, angry cloud was lifted from the atmosphere of corporate life at his leaving. He was a volatile bully who left behind a horrible reputation, an assortment of broken relationships, and countless emotional abuses.

Why include Pete in this book? You may think, *Okay, Pete was a monster. We've all had bosses like that, and they clearly have no regard for God or others. If you're writing to Christian businessmen, though, you're probably not going to find many Petes among your readership.*

And I would agree with you, except—as shocking as it may seem— Pete claimed to have a personal relationship with Jesus Christ! He spoke often of his church, his pastor, and his own personal faith. By his own self-evaluation, Pete *was* a Christian businessman. Sadly, I never saw evidence of the fruit of the Spirit in his life.

Thomas Jefferson said, before his departure from the office of president, "Never did a prisoner released from his chains feel such relief as I shall on shaking off the shackles of power."[2] Power can be quite intoxicating! Some people handle it well, but others don't. In the marketplace, most of you will eventually become a manager of at least a few people if you are not already. You will move up from salesman to sales manager, or perhaps, from staff engineer to project manager. You will receive power and authority. A group of individuals will become your direct reports. At the same time, unless you own the company, you will always have individuals who exercise power and authority over you. How you exercise power over those you manage, and how you submit to those who have power over you, will greatly influence your career success, your Christian testimony, and whether you live a life that is pleasing to God.

Exercising Power through a Biblical Grid

In my business career, there were times when I managed as many as thirty or forty people. In my ministry career, I have had the responsibility of managing many associate pastors who served on my staff. At the same time, in both business and ministry, I have always had individuals or boards who held authority over me. When my work life comes to an end, how I handled power, and how I submitted to it, will have a tremendous impact upon how I am remembered by my colleagues. I take that extremely seriously, so I would like to share, in the remainder of this chapter, three dimensions of a grid through which each of us should exercise power and authority.

The Source Of Power and Authority

To understand the basis of power, we must first consider Psalm 24:
1, which says, "The earth is the LORD's, and everything in it. The world and all its people belong to him" (NLT). Used in the previous chapter, this verse clearly applies here as well.

God is the creator of the visible and the invisible. When we think of God as the creator, we tend to think of His creating rocks, trees, people, and mountains. But God is also the creator of what we can't touch: ethics, truth, reality, and power. To have a proper understanding of power, we must first acknowledge that power is a creation of God. Its proper use or abuse is *our* creation.

For example, let's consider King Solomon. After his father David died, Solomon was next in line to become the king of Israel. God met Solomon and told him to ask for anything he wanted. Here is Solomon's response. See if you can detect his thoughts about power.

> *O LORD my God, now* you have made me king *instead of my father, David, but I am like a little child who doesn't know his way around. And here I am among your own chosen people, a nation so great they are too numerous to count! Give me an understanding mind* so that I can govern your people well *and know the difference between right and wrong. For who by himself is able to govern this great nation of yours?* (1 Kings 3:7-9, NLT, emphasis added).

In his prayer, Solomon acknowledges three things about his newfound power: 1) His responsibility as king was given to him by God, from the wisdom of God. 2) It was Solomon's responsibility to govern the people—to use his power—well. 3) He would not be able to fulfill his God-given responsibilities, nor use his power well, if God did not help him. For Solomon (and for us), God was the giver of power and authority. That power and authority was to be used for the good of the people; and that power and authority could be used well only with God's help. The subsequent verses show that God was pleased with Solomon's request.

Have you ever considered that power is simply too alluring to be managed on our own? The *Star Wars* movies play endlessly upon this theme. As Luke Skywalker trains to become a Jedi knight, he learns how his newly-acquired powers can be used for good. But under the wary and watchful eye of Ben-Kenobi, and then Yoda, he also learns that that same power (The Force) can easily and quickly be taken over by the Dark Side. In fact, that's exactly what happened to Luke's father and adversary, Darth Vader.

As Malcolm Forbes said, "Those carried away by power are soon carried away."[3] There is truth to that, because we were never meant to exercise authority in our own power. Because God is the source and

41

creator of power, we are to rely on Him to help us use it wisely for the good of others.

Solomon forgot this later in his reign. First Kings 11 details how Solomon allowed his heart to be led away from God by foreign wives. He worshiped other gods, even the god Molech—a god associated with child sacrifice. He drove the workers of Israel like slaves, unconcerned for their well-being. In His grace, God did not take the kingdom away from Solomon, but He did take it away from his son, Rehoboam (see 1 Kings 12). Where was the young ruler who was in over his head and desperate for God to grant him the wisdom to govern the people well? He was gone, his heart no longer dependent upon God.

God is the source of power and authority and He gives that responsibility as He sees fit. Romans 13:1-2 bears this out in terms of government officials: "Obey the government, *for God is the one who put it there*. All governments have been placed in power *by God*. So those who refuse to obey the laws of the land are refusing to obey God, and punishment will follow" (NLT; emphasis added). So if you find yourself in a position of power, you have been placed there by God, *for God*. The power you have is not your own, nor is it for your benefit only. It is to be used for the good of others. Solomon knew this early in his rule, but forgot it later. Perhaps we would all be better stewards of the power given to us if we were overwhelmed and over our heads like Solomon was early in his life. It was when he lost this dependency that he began to abuse his power.

We see this clearly in the New Testament as well—and with another king. King Herod Agrippa, however, never did fear God. In fact, Acts 12:1-4 records several acts of persecution against the church that were instigated by Herod. Using his power, Herod:

- Persecuted some of the believers in the church (v.1).
- Had James, one of Jesus' "inner three" during His earthly ministry, killed with a sword (v.2).
- Boosted his approval rating by having Peter arrested and held for trial (v.3-4).

So Herod did not have any regard for God and did not see Him as the source of his power as king. In the account of Peter's escape, we note how flippantly he regarded people even within his own service. Acts 12:3 tells us that Herod's primary motivation for arresting Peter was because James' death greatly pleased the Jewish leaders. He had nothing against Peter personally. Rather, Peter was a political pawn to be used for Herod's advantage.

That's why Herod was enraged when Peter escaped.

Acts 12:6-17 details Peter's miraculous escape from prison by the mercy of God and the aid of an angel of the Lord. It was an incredible blessing of God that took everyone by surprise—Peter (12:11), the believers who were praying for him (12:14-17), and, of course, Herod. When morning came and Peter was curiously missing, Herod looked for someone to blame: "At dawn, there was a great commotion among the soldiers about what had happened to Peter. Herod Agrippa ordered a thorough search for him. When he couldn't be found, Herod interrogated the guards and sentenced them to death" (Acts 12:18-19a, NLT).

My former boss, Pete, never executed a staff member. But I think you can see in him how unchecked power can lessen one's regard for the dignity of another person (which is the subject of the next section). Herod's political toy was missing; someone was going to pay with his life.

And because Herod never saw his power as a God-given responsibility, his blindness ultimately became his undoing. Acts 12:20-22 gives the background of the events that led to Herod's demise:

> *Now Herod was very angry with the people of Tyre and Sidon. So they sent a delegation to make peace with him because their cities were dependent upon Herod's country for their food. They made friends with Blastus, Herod's personal assistant, and an appointment with Herod was granted. When the day arrived, Herod put on his royal robes, sat on his throne, and made a speech to them. The people gave him a great ovation, shouting, "It is the voice of a god, not of a man!"* (NLT).

The people of Tyre and Sidon were dependent upon Rome for their food and supplies, so Herod essentially had control over whether these people lived or died. Why he was angry with them in the first place isn't revealed to us, but we do know that Herod had the power to forgive them or to punish them by starvation.

Now, the people of Tyre and Sidon were pretty smart. Appealing to his pride instead of reasoning their case, they showered him with compliments, even comparing his voice to that of a god. He liked that!

In his mind, with his power, influence, authority, and control, he was as close to a god as one could get.

God did not share Herod's opinion: "Instantly, an angel of the Lord struck Herod with a sickness, because he accepted the people's worship instead of giving the glory to God. So he was consumed with worms and died" (12:23, NLT).

King Herod Agrippa was a man with more power than a human being should ever have. But rather than recognizing his charge and responsibility from God to rule wisely and for the good of the people, he abused it and viewed himself as self-sufficient. His fate is a reminder to us who have been given power by Almighty God that wise stewardship of power comes from a humble dependence upon God. We are not irreplaceable and we are not creating kingdoms for ourselves. "The earth is the LORD's and everything in it." We would be wise to exercise our stewardship of power through this filter.

The Dignity of the Individual

When power is abused, most often, people are abused. Some might say that corporate abuses such as inflating expense accounts, "borrowing" from the cash register, or giving oneself perks above and beyond anyone else's benefits don't really harm anyone. But even those abuses trickle down within the organization and hurt the people who make up the organization. Inflated expense accounts can lead to budget shortfalls, which can lead to downsizing—which seriously affects people.

But most abuses of power have to do with individual people suffering in some way at the hands of their boss. We think of mandatory overtime or being called in on Sunday. We think of ridicule and rejection. We think of being threatened with employment termination. We think of being forced to accept blame for something we did not do. We think of anything that, in some way, bruises our dignity as people.

And yet the Bible teaches that none of us has permission to damage another human being in these ways. Perhaps the best example comes from Job 31. We're told at the beginning of the book that Job was quite wealthy (before Satan took it all away). Being wealthy, Job had male and female servants attending to him and his household. Now, servants in antiquity did not have the benefits employees have today. There were no "Open Door" policies, no grievance forms, no union representatives. Servants were primarily dependent upon the graciousness of their masters.

Which is why Job's words in chapter 31 are especially striking: "If I have been unfair to my male or female servants, if I have refused to hear their complaints, how could I face God? What could I say when he questioned me about it? *For God created both me and my servants. He created us both*" (31:13-15, NLT, emphasis added).

While Job did have power and authority over his servants (they were in his employ), he did not believe that gave him permission to ignore their requests. To be unfair to them would be an affront to God. Why? Because God created them both. Job recognized the dignity of the individual because every individual has been hand-knit in the womb by God.

Let's bring this to your organization or company. You do not come in contact with anyone in the course of your day who was not created by God. Your secretary was created by God. So were your vice-president, custodian, best customer, worst supplier, and the office jester. They were all created by God and they all matter to Him, just as you are His creation and you matter to Him. Therefore, any abuse of power that strikes at the dignity of one of these God-creations is an attack on someone whom God formed. On a wide scope, this also applies to our families, civic groups, and recreational leagues (how many overzealous baseball coaches have you seen insult the dignity of a nine-year-old who missed a steal-sign?). Depending on God to help us wisely steward the power He's given to us, we must use our power in ways that uphold the dignity of the individual.

That doesn't mean you should never rebuke or confront a direct report. That doesn't even mean you can never fire someone. But it does mean that *all* interactions and hard conversations must be done in a way that retains the dignity of the individual as a God-creation.

Let's look at a few ways this principle can be implemented in your workplace:

- Don't terminate uncomfortable conversations just because you can. Give employees, especially trusted employees, opportunity to share their feelings. They will respect you for listening, and who knows: they might be right! Listening to their opinions shows you value them as human beings.
- Don't take credit for every success and blame others when things go wrong. You might feel like you're getting away with it, but I guarantee you will lose good employees. Not only does this publicly proclaim that you are more interested in yourself than

in others, it demeans those who work hard for the success of the organization.

- Don't make employees work an unreasonable number of hours while not "paying the price" yourself. You might get them to do it because you have the power; however, anger and resentment will grow quickly. Respecting their dignity means recognizing that they have lives outside the office. Honor their time with family and friends.

- When doing performance reviews, give employees ample time to push back or disagree with you. Your review of their job performance has a tremendous influence on their future. Let them vent without becoming defensive. This is another way of showing you respect their point of view.

- Never get out the bazooka if a pop gun will do. Confront individuals in a godly manner. Turn up the heat gradually. Give them ample time to perform or improve. It is true that when an employee is a poor fit, or not performing up to reasonable expectations, a change may be needed. But never threaten employees with their jobs simply to get what you want from them. Avoiding this technique allows you to do what you would want them to do to you. You're not positively motivated by threats and neither are those who report directly to you. Max De Pree said, "Authority truly motivates almost no one these days. It's really more accurate to view employees as volunteers."[4]

- Watch your mouth. Lowbrow jokes and innuendo may get nervous laughs from your reports, but such inappropriate remarks can insult their dignity, too. A secretary may put up with your crude humor because she's afraid to leave, but you're wielding a weapon against her heart. "Those who control their tongue will have a long life; a quick retort can ruin everything" (Proverbs 13:3, NLT).

This also applies to the way you treat your superiors. Just as you should preserve the dignity of the people who report to you, you also need to respect the dignity of your boss(es)—not because they can fire you, but because they, too, have been formed by God. That means:

- Don't manipulate. The people of Tyre and Sidon were smart to butter up Herod, but that doesn't mean you should offer empty compliments to your boss. If you have a request, be straightforward and respectful. By doing so you will keep his or her dignity intact. Andy Stanley writes, "When we ask, we underscore our supervisor's authority. When we demand, we undermine his or her authority."[5]

- Don't demean the boss when he or she is not around. Like you, that person was formed in the womb by God and matters to Him. Therefore, your comments, jokes, impersonations, or putdowns—even in your boss's absence—are counted as sin in God's sight.

Only God can create people. And though it may be hard for us to understand, He creates us in *His* image. Therefore, every human being has unbelievable worth that cannot be measured by spreadsheets, organizational flow charts, or performance assessments. Use your God-given power to affirm the dignity of the people who report to you. It pleases God and builds up the people He loves.

The Credibility of Your Witness

The term "Christian businessperson" offers a definition of *who you are* and *what you do*. As a Christian, you are a creation of God who has been redeemed from sin and eternal separation from God by the death and resurrection of Jesus Christ. That, fundamentally, is who you *are*. "Therefore, if anyone is in Christ, he is a new creation; the old has gone, the new has come!" (2 Corinthians 5:17).

But you also have a role to play in the world in which you live—a role through which you are to glorify God and serve others. That role is as a businessperson. Your hours on the job are not hours apart from God; rather, you are where you are so you can glorify God *there*. "So, dear brothers and sisters, whatever situation you were in when you became a believer, *stay there* in your new relationship *with God*" (1 Corinthians 7:24, NLT, emphasis added).

As a Christian businessperson, you are a follower of Jesus Christ honoring and glorifying Him, as well as serving others in the marketplace. That means your Christian witness to the non-believing world will not be based on what you say, what you profess, or what church you belong to. The credibility of your witness will be based on whether or not Christ is reflected in your life as you manage power.

In my story about Pete, I mentioned that he was a professing believer in Jesus Christ. But if you had videotaped one of his tirades and shown it to someone who did not know him and asked, "Would you characterize this man as a Christian?" they would have laughed. His behavior did not match his professed beliefs. Thus, his credibility as a Christian witness was a joke.

Pete was an extreme example, but how about you? Do people observe Christ's tenderness and compassion in you as you perform your responsibilities? Do your direct reports see the integrity, honesty, generosity, and humility that would brand you as a disciple of Jesus? When you use your authority, do you do so in a way that might cause others to say, "Now there is a man who bows to a higher authority"?

Paul writes in Colossians 4:5, "Live wisely among those who are not Christians, and make the most of every opportunity" (NLT). I am not advocating that you begin your budget meetings with prayer and Bible study. But I am challenging you to add the dimension of your Christian witness to the grid through which you filter your power and authority (along with remembering the source of your power and the dignity of the individual). You can also make the most of your evangelistic opportunities by administering your power and authority wisely and graciously.

You can be a tyrant and get good business results. But you cannot be a tyrant and give a convincing Christian witness. It is entirely possible that God may put someone under your charge just so that person can see the Christian life lived with integrity and humility in you. Your life, lived in a way that honors God, may be one link in the chain God uses to bring that individual to Himself. If that happens, you do not want to blow the opportunity by shortchanging employees, angrily assigning blame, or running your organization like a little Herod. Your words matter. Your interactions matter. Your stewardship of power matters.

Eternally.

Gary Thomas summed up the godly use of power well when he wrote, "When we have power over another and we use that power responsibly, appropriately, and benevolently, we grow in Christ, we become more like God, and we reflect the fact that we were made to love God by serving others."[6] It is possible to use power responsibly and appropriately. I hope you will, and be a blessing to others. To do so...

- Remember who has given you that power, and why.
- Preserve the dignity of your fellow created human beings.

- Remember that someone is always watching you, and your credibility as a Christian has everything to do with what people see.

Notes:

[1] Jessica Allen, *Quotable Men of the Twentieth Century* (New York: William Morrow and Company Inc., 1999), p. 183.

[2] Robert G. Torricelli; *Quotations for Public Speakers: A Historical, Literary, and Political Anthology* (New Brunswick, NJ: Rutgers University Press, 2001), p. 159.

[3] Jessica Allen, *Quotable Men.*

[4] Max De Pree, *Leadership Jazz* (New York: Doubleday, 1992), p. 194.

[5] Andy Stanley, *Choosing to Cheat: Who Wins When Family and Work Collide?* (Sisters, OR: Multnomah, 2003), p. 108.

[6] Gary Thomas, *Sacred Marriage: What If God Designed Marriage to Make Us Holy More Than to Make Us Happy?* (Grand Rapids: Zondervan, 2002), p. 195.

Chapter 5

The Minefield of Sexual Temptation

I thought to myself, *This can't be happening! Why this? Why now?*

It had been a banner day in my business career! Along with Mike—a fellow salesman from my company—I had spent several profitable hours with my best customer, a guy named Ted. Everything had clicked; from the tour of the plant to the working lunch to the exquisite entrees at dinner, our relational momentum was hurtling toward contracts, signatures, pats-on-the-back, and a fat bonus. Somewhere between the appetizers and polite refusal of dessert we had reached an agreement in principle. All that remained was finishing the deal back at the hotel.

I couldn't wait to call my wife. I was gleeful about the deal, but it was another night away from home and I needed the emotional connection. Ted, Mike, and I agreed to part ways for about 15 minutes, and then meet in the lobby to summarize the deal and make plans for the next morning. Calling home would have to wait until later.

I grabbed a few papers from my room, and considered any possible last-minute sticking points in the deal. I couldn't think of any; the deal was win/win all around. I smiled to myself; there really wasn't anything that could tank this deal.

I was gone only about ten minutes, but when I got back to the lobby, I quickly discovered that Ted and Mike were no longer interested in talking business. They had moved from the lobby to the hotel bar. In most situations, that wouldn't have bothered me too much. It meant putting up with some cigar smoke and off-color jokes, but those were small sacrifices within the big picture. I'd done it many times before, and was prepared to do it again.

But this particular situation was different. Ted and Mike had gotten a table and invited three women to join our "party." I got the sinking feeling that none of them was really interested in talking about scrap iron. I looked at Ted and Mike. Neither displayed the posture or demeanor of married men simply engaging in polite conversation with strangers. They were looking for more than light banter and "Tell me about your job" small talk. It didn't take a crime novelist to realize they were looking to forge a sexual encounter. And I had been invited to come along.

Nausea seized me. I thought to myself, *This can't be happening! Why this? Why now?* This was my largest account. And despite our well-manicured relationship; despite the win/win dimension of our business deal; and despite the obvious wrongness of Ted's intentions, I intuitively knew that if I didn't join the party, I might break the deal. Goodbye, end-of-the-year bonus! Goodbye, revenue-producing customer! And... goodbye, job?

I ducked out of view, but peered back into the languid scene at the bar. As I took it in, I was flooded with snapshots from home. I knew that by now, Linda would have our wonderful son tucked into bed. I saw her sitting in the living room, reading a newspaper or magazine, eagerly awaiting my call. It was a comforting picture. It was a picture of a life God had given me by His grace—a life I had always wanted. It was a picture that gave definition to my course of action. I made eye contact with my sales colleague and motioned for him to talk with me privately. Out in the lobby I told him I was going to head up to my room and call it a night.

"Oh, come on!" he responded. "Everything's all set.

Everything's all set? What's all set? The deal? This "no-tell" party? What's set?

"Mike," I responded, "I don't cheat on my wife. What you do is up to you, but count me out." Over Mike's shoulder I saw Ted and the three women observing our conversation.

Mike upped the ante. "Hey," he said, "just because you don't play around, don't mess things up for us. Who knows, you might even mess up the *deal*."

Well, there it was. Mentioning the deal confirmed that I wasn't the only one doing a cost/benefit analysis. But my analysis came out different from Mike's.

"I'll see you tomorrow." With that, I turned and headed for the elevator. It was out of my hands and in God's hands. Back in my room, I called my wife and told her everything. After hanging up, I prayed, caught the highlights of the night's basketball action, and then nodded off to sleep. At peace.

The next morning, I met Ted for breakfast. Our conversation was uncomfortable, stilted, and awkward, but thankfully we stuck to talking about the contract. And apparently my decision to be a party pooper didn't affect the deal. I had purchase orders in hand before the end of the morning. In the months that followed, we continued to do business, but it soon became evident that I was no longer a part of his "in-crowd." My orders gradually became smaller. I was invited to socialize with him less. Eventually, I began to search for another "best customer."

Was I tempted to have a sexual encounter with one of the ladies at Mike and Ted's "party"? In this case, not really. In fact, twenty years later I don't remember what the women looked like. But *could* I have been tempted? Of course. I would be a fool to think I couldn't be. Sexual temptation is a near-constant in the lives of most men. Because of the sexualized nature of our culture, sexually provoking images and thoughts are like mosquitoes in July. You can avoid the bites, but it's hard to avoid the bugs themselves.

While sexual temptation seems to be a part of everyday living, these hazards, when placed in a business travel context, are extremely dangerous. If you regularly travel on business, I'm sure you know what I'm talking about. You make eye contact with an attractive female in a restaurant. You're thinking about whether the mahi mahi is fresh and suddenly BAM! A woman sitting by herself is gazing in your direction. Or you turn on the television in your hotel room at night to catch the Big Ten basketball scores and the very first channel that pops up is an advertisement for a pornographic movie. All you have to do is enter a code. Or you dart into an airport bookstore to find *Fast Company* magazine and have to sift through rows of *Penthouse* and *Hustler* before you find what you wanted. Or your friends from work—good guys, guys you like—want to celebrate the sales presentation by hitting a place called "Centerfold" and you're pretty sure it's not for the half-price nachos.

The difference between Christian businessmen and non-Christian businessmen who travel is that non-Christian businessmen often have no qualms with the barrage of sexual messages and images. Most either ignore them as much as possible or view them as an acceptable form of entertainment. Christians, however, are called to a life of purity. Paul set the bar when he said, "…among you there must *not be even a hint* of sexual immorality, or of any kind of impurity…" (Ephesians 5:3, emphasis added). No fifteen-second glimpses in *Playboy* while the aisle is clear. No accompanying your friends to the strip club "just to be the designated driver." And no "harmless drinks" with the attractive flight attendant on a layover. Not a hint.

Yet a Christian businessman can barely go an hour without receiving some kind of visual suggestion that he should be engaging in sexual activity. His normal sexual appetite (and please read this chapter with the overall view that sex between a husband and wife is a gift of God and not just normal, but beautiful and God-pleasing) is suddenly thrown into overdrive. He doesn't want to offend his Lord or his wife and kids, so he is constantly aware of forces around him that tempt him. How are Christian businessmen (or anyone who travels) to gain safe passage through the minefield of sexual temptation?

If you're a businessman, you're probably familiar with the author of *The Seven Habits of Highly Effective People*, Stephen Covey. If so, you've likely heard of his principle "Begin With the End in Mind"—painting a picture of the future. In fact, you probably do it for your business all the time. Well, let's begin with the end in mind, considering what happens when you surrender yourself to sexual pleasure in the hopes you'll never get caught. Hundreds of thousands of men do it; let's see where that path leads.

"Like An Ox Going To the Slaughter"

If you are prone to "fooling around" on the road, or giving in to sexual temptation on a regular basis, the candor of Proverbs 5-7 may be just the wake-up call you need to change paths. While the path you're going on is masked with excitement and allure, it leads to destruction nonetheless. But I'm getting ahead of myself.

Proverbs 5-7 is filled with warnings about sexual immorality. Yes, I know it sounds weird coming from Solomon, who had 1,000 wives and concubines, but stay with me. Perhaps a helpful way to interpret the warnings in chapters 5-7 is by reading them within the framework of Proverbs 4.

> *Above all else, guard your heart, for it affects everything you do* (v. 23, NLT).

> *Look straight ahead, and fix your eyes on what lies before you. Mark out a straight path for your feet; then stick to the path and stay safe. Don't get sidetracked; keep your feet from following evil* (v. 25, NLT).

Are you on board?

Solomon gives explicit instructions to all of us who seek to walk with God. He advises us to *guard our hearts* and *mark out our paths*. In light of these verses, then, chapters 5-7 take an in-depth and painful look at what happens when we choose not to guard our hearts or mark out our paths.

> *Run from her! Don't go near the door of her house! If you do, you will lose your honor and hand over to merciless people everything you have achieved in life. Strangers will obtain your wealth, and someone else will enjoy the fruit of your labor. Afterward you will groan in anguish when disease consumes your body, and you will say, "How I hated discipline! If only I had not demanded my own way! Oh, why didn't I listen to my teachers? Why didn't I pay attention to those who gave me instruction? I have come to the brink of utter ruin, and now I must face public disgrace"* (Proverbs 5:8-14, NLT).

> *For a prostitute will bring you to poverty, and sleeping with another man's wife may cost you your very life. Can a man scoop fire into his lap and not be burned? Can he walk on hot coals and not blister his feet? So it is with the man who sleeps with another man's wife. He who embraces her will not go unpunished* (Proverbs 6:26-29, NLT).

> *But the man who commits adultery is an utter fool, for he destroys his own soul. Wounds and constant disgrace are his lot. His shame will never be erased. For the woman's*

husband will be furious in his jealousy, and he will have no mercy in his day of vengeance. There is no compensation or bribe that will satisfy him (Proverbs 6:32-35, NLT).

Then, in a move that I consider sheer brilliance, the writer takes all of his warnings and plants them into a real-life story that he witnessed. Solomon's pleas and urgings are far from theoretical; he writes as someone who saw folly and poor self-control undo men on a daily basis. Pay close attention to the details in his story. It's a little long, but it's a scary picture of who you or I could become if we fail to make it through this minefield.

I was looking out the window of my house one day and saw a simpleminded young man who lacked common sense. He was crossing the street near the house of an immoral woman. He was strolling down the path by her house at twilight, as the day was fading, as the dark of night set in. The woman approached him, dressed seductively and sly of heart. She was the brash, rebellious type who never stays at home. She is often seen in the streets and markets, soliciting at every corner.

She threw her arms around him and kissed him, and with a brazen look she said, "I've offered my sacrifices and just finished my vows. It's you I was looking for! I came out to find you, and here you are! My bed is spread with colored sheets of finest linen imported from Egypt. I've perfumed my bed with myrrh, aloes, and cinnamon. Come, let's drink our fill of love until morning. Let's enjoy each other's caresses, for my husband is not home. He's away on a long trip. He has taken a wallet full of money with him, and he won't return until later in the month."

So she seduced him with her pretty speech. With her flattery she enticed him. He followed her at once, like an ox going to the slaughter or like a trapped stag, awaiting the arrow that would pierce its heart. He was like a bird flying into a snare, little knowing it would cost him his life.

Listen to me, my sons, and pay attention to my words. Don't let your hearts stray away toward her. Don't wander down her wayward path. For she has been the ruin of

56

many; numerous men have been her victims. Her house is the road to the grave. Her bedroom is the den of death (Proverbs 7:6-27, NLT).

What do all those Scriptures have in common? They all demonstrate that the end result of fooling around with sexual immorality is the complete disintegration of one's life—a life filled with pain, misery, regrets, and enduring consequences. And that is why we're beginning with the end in mind: at the end of the path of sexual immorality is a life of shame.

"Yeah, But..."

Let me address your unspoken objection. You might be saying, "But Jim, I don't cheat on my wife. I would never solicit a prostitute or hook up with a woman on the road. True, I occasionally watch in-room movies, and I have a hidden stash of magazines in the basement, but I don't consider that to be adultery. Adultery is having sex with someone else's wife or having sex with someone else while you're married. It's not going to seedy places on the Internet."

There are two comments I'd like to make about that response. The first is that sexual temptation in biblical times is not the same as sexual temptation today. There were no pornographic magazines, Internet, or in-room movies. Pornography as we understand it didn't really exist. But first-century Christians, especially those in places like Ephesus and Corinth, were constantly surrounded by prostitutes and were often encouraged by the prevailing cultural norms to experience many forms of sexual pleasure. Gene Getz writes:

> *In the New Testament culture, it was common for affluent men particularly to have at least three women in their lives, including their wives. One woman might be a slave girl who lived in the same house or compound who was always available to her master for sexual pleasure. Another woman might be a prostitute down at the pagan temple, which was considered a religious rite in the various pagan religions. The other woman would be the man's wife, the one who would help carry on the family name by giving birth to children and taking primary responsibility for rearing them. ...Many of these New Testament men had the same*

> *problems and temptations in their lives as men who come to Christ in similar cultures today. Although these men hear and understand Christ's message of living morally, changes often come slowly. The power of sexual addiction often controls them, even after they have become believers.*[1]

Can you see why sexual temptation in the Bible mainly centers on actual, physical sexual encounters? That was the *cultural* norm for sexual relations. Our cultural norm today is one that mainly is gratified through pornography. *Time* magazine reported that in July of 2003, there were 260 million pages of pornography online, an increase of 1,800 percent since 1998.[2] For many men who would never think of having an actual affair, pornography has paved the way for men to experiment sexually without ever involving another human being. So they think.

Jesus refused to accept the argument that one could fantasize sexually about another person without being an adulterer. Read His familiar words closely:

> *...I say, anyone who even looks at a woman with lust in his eye has already committed adultery with her in his heart* (Matthew 5:28, NLT).

Adultery is not only an affair of the body. It is also an affair of the eyes and the heart. According to Jesus' definition of adultery, viewing pornography—whether magazines, in-room movies, strip clubs, or on the Internet—is adultery. It is lusting with our eyes and hearts. It is saying to ourselves, "If I could do whatever I want with that woman on the screen/page/stage, and I knew that I would never get caught and never lose sleep over it—if she were here right now and willing—I'd certainly do it!" That's why Jesus says lustful looks qualify as adultery; He's merely playing out the intentions of our fallen hearts, which He knows intimately.

And that's why the argument doesn't wash. You may define adultery one way, but ultimately your definition—and the definitions established by cultural norms—will always sit in subordination to the words of Jesus.

Planning For Purity

If you are a Christian businessman, and you have ensnared yourself in one of the ways I've mentioned, odds are you didn't deliberately set out to fall into sin. Many godly men have triggered the landmine of sexual temptation—even while they were hoping and praying to avoid it.

The problem is, hoping and praying involves little personal contribution. I agree with author Rick Page, who wrote a book entitled, *Hope Is Not a Strategy*.[3] Indeed, merely hoping to avoid sin will not result in purity. Preparing is essential. Proverbs 3:21-22 advises:

> *My child, don't lose sight of good planning and insight. Hang on to them, for they fill you with life and bring you honor and respect* (NLT).

Prayer and planning go a long way toward purity. In prayer, you are asking God to break through the thorns and briars that trip you up and hold you back. In planning, you are using your resources and connections to create regular, predictable routines. God moves in your interior world as you make adjustments in your exterior world. Kenny Luck writes, "As I speak to men, I tell them point blank: *There is no such thing as an irresistible temptation.* The reality is that most men who fail do so because they construct scenarios in their minds long before actually acting on one of them"[4] (author's emphasis). They begin with a heart already open to the idea of giving in. If that's the case for you—you know you shouldn't, but before you've even left the airport you're running scenarios in your mind—there's very little that prayer and hope can do for you. You've already rejected the warning in Proverbs 4:23; you're not guarding your heart.

I was eating dinner one night at a hotel restaurant in Columbus, Ohio. I was about sixty miles from home. I had early business appointments the next morning and then would be heading south to Cincinnati. As I munched on dessert, I squinted to catch as much of the Indiana game as I could on the tiny TV screen in the bar. As I paid my bill, I turned to take one last look at the score before heading to my room. Instead, my eyes happened to land on John, one of the men from my Rotary club back home. I was stunned by what I saw.

John was sitting in a booth with an arm around a young woman who was not his wife. He was visibly inebriated, and ordering another round of drinks. She flirted. He laughed. The arm on her shoulder pulled her closer. He drank. She flirted. He pulled tighter. I watched with disappointment. Not judgment—the same depravity that exists in John exists in me—but disappointment! John was a respected businessman in our city and had built a solid reputation. I had never met his wife, but he had always spoken highly of her. Before we began eating at Rotary, John was sometimes called upon to give the invocation. He and his wife had teenage girls, and he was entering a dangerous dance with a woman who couldn't have been more than a few years older than his daughters.

It seems to me that John was living by something that I called "The 50-mile rule."[5] It's been my experience, as I've observed the behavior of many traveling salesmen, that people change when they are away from home. Men who seem on the surface to live good, wholesome lives at home, often display a Dr.Jekyll/Mr. Hyde personality while on the road.

- It's the father who speaks out against pornography in his men's group, yet orders in-room "adult entertainment" when in a different time zone.
- It's the married man with Christian books on his shelves for friends to admire who visits nightclubs in hopes of finding a woman sitting alone at the bar.
- It's the executive who's regarded as a "pillar of society," a symbol of consistency, who's standing in line at the ATM to pull out more money for lap dances.

Call it the 50-mile rule, the 100-mile rule, or even the 1,000-mile rule—there is something about being in a different city, different time zone, different country where no one knows you. You'd never visit a strip club at home in Teaneck, New Jersey, because people would recognize you and you would bring shame to your family and business. But here in Los Angeles, California, no one knows who you are. No one is going to call you out. No one will check up on you at your hotel room. And over and over, the devil whispers, "No one will ever have to know."

How do you defeat that? How do you overcome sexual temptation with constraints? Let's bring back to the forefront of our minds, Proverbs 4:25-27.

> *Look straight ahead, and fix your eyes on what lies before you. Mark out a straight path for your feet; then stick to the path and stay safe. Don't get sidetracked; keep your feet from following evil* (NLT).

To follow Christ on the path to purity, you must reconfigure your ideas about spiritual living. Many Christians mistakenly confine their walk with God to designated times and places. Consequently, if they miss a worship service or small group meeting, they're inclined to think, "Well, now my faith is going to dip for sure."

In the account of Jesus and the woman at the well, the woman began protesting the *official* location of worship. Jesus replied:

> *It's who you are and the way you live that count before God. Your worship must engage your spirit in the pursuit of truth. That's the kind of people the Father is out looking for: those who are simply and honestly themselves before him in their worship. God is sheer being itself—Spirit. Those who worship him must do it out of their very being, their spirits, their true selves, in adoration* (John 4:23-24, MSG.).

In other words, Jesus says, "Forget the *where* of worship, and focus on the *who*." Worship is not a matter of showing up on Sunday—there are people who sit in pews every Sunday without fail, who haven't genuinely worshiped God in years. Just because you'll be in a different city when 9:00 a.m. rolls around next Sunday doesn't mean you can't have a walk with God. God is more interested in your heart for Him and how you are relating to Him than whether or not you've spoken the liturgy and taken notes on the preacher's message.

So the main idea for staying on the path of purity that gives shape and form to all the other practical measures is this: God is walking with me *wherever* I go. Not only does this remind you that your spiritual life is not confined to a location, it also reminds you that you're not alone when you go where you shouldn't.

So with this idea in mind, let me give you some thoughts on how to stay on the path of purity and avoid the minefield of sexual temptation.

Schedule Yourself Out of Temptation

If you spend the majority of your week in the world of business, I assume you conduct business according to certain priorities. In other words, your hours and days are designed to bring about certain desired outcomes—profit, market share, flexibility, setting standards, leadership, and so on. You know the difference between a high priority item (marketing a new product) and a low priority item (transcribing your own correspondence).

Unfortunately, what is so innately obvious in the business world often does not translate into one's walk with God. Instead of setting priorities and scheduling to fulfill them in their spiritual lives, I see many men who simply assume they will maintain a close walk with God when they travel. Then, when they stumble, they think, "Where was God?" They failed to plan ahead for purity. Practically speaking, this means setting appointments, ordering your workload, and maintaining your contacts with as much vigilance as you would for your business.

Appointments. When you travel, you schedule appointments with certain people you need to see. Schedule life-giving, purity-preserving appointments right alongside your other appointments. Schedule a phone call with your wife. Make sure you pray with her over the phone. Schedule a call with a member of your small group. Coach them beforehand to ask how you're doing when you call. This creates an outlet for you to share any temptations that have surfaced. Schedule time to meditate on Scripture and talk with God. Fill your appointment book with unbreakable commitments that work *for* your desire to stay pure, instead of against it. When your friends from work, who are observing their version of the 50-mile rule, cajole you to go with them to a bar to look for female company, wouldn't you like to glance at your PDA and say, "Sorry, I've got calls to make from the hotel room?" Scheduling yourself away from sexual temptation is a way of putting your priority of purity into concrete action. And be assured: If overcoming sexual temptation is not a personal priority of yours, no amount of scheduling will keep you from it.

Workload. What is a workload? It's where you focus your attention and energy as you seek to succeed each day at effectively fulfilling your responsibilities. At any given time your workload may involve preparing a big presentation, conceiving a marketing plan for a new product, coming up with a clever scheme to break into a new account, or any number of other tasks the company has chosen to put on your plate. You invest a great deal of time and energy in dealing with your workload. If you don't, you probably will find yourself looking for a job very quickly.

When you travel, you must bring a workload—and I'm not talking about work related to your business. If you make time in your travel itinerary to frequent strip clubs, view pornography, or chat up a single woman dining alone, then you have time for other, more significant heart-priorities. You need to bring another workload.

Send an e-mail to your spouse, or plan to make cell phone calls to her throughout the day. Staying connected to people who are important to you and who support your devotion to Jesus are lifelines when you travel.

Along with reading the Bible consistently, have an ongoing study. Read about and study topics or people in the Bible that God is putting in your heart. You may be excited about the Kingdom of God, Moses, or eternal security. Take books and notepads with you and make expanding your knowledge and worship of God a significant part of your non-work workload.[6]

Stay at hotels that offer exercise equipment. Maintaining your health is an important aspect of a quality workload. Put it in your appointment book and keep the appointment.

Through these examples, you've seen a workload that covers your physical, relational, spiritual, and mental priorities. If you think about what's really important to you, and if you design creative assignments for yourself to complete while you're away, then you will remove yourself further and further from temptation.

Contacts. Accountability is a common word in churches and small groups these days, and its familiarity has caused some men to dismiss it as the church acting as Big Brother. Accountability does have its limitations. Pastor Rick Warren once quipped in an interview, "Accountability is overrated. It works only if you want it to. If I don't really want you to know the truth, you're not going to know the truth."[7] It's hard to argue with him. 1 Corinthians 2:11 says:

> *No one can know what anyone else is really thinking except that person alone...* (NLT).

Accountability is never foolproof. Michael Brown and Kelly Hahn write, "Accountability is not an impersonal idea or abstract principle. It is not a law that 'works' when you apply it. Accountability is a relationship between two people that creates an environment in which both can work toward becoming who God created them to be."[8] This is much more personal and energizing than simply working through a list of questions once a week. Accountability celebrates, encourages, and points its participants toward the cross.

Having an accountability partner, or even simply several friends to call you while you're traveling, is the equivalent of having business contacts. If you're in a small group, ask at least one of the guys to give you a call at 10:00 p.m. It's not having someone check up on you; it's keeping your life-giving contacts in the mainstream of your life. Talk about sports, or the weather, or the killer stiff neck you got on the plane.

If you have regular accountability sessions with your friend, be honest about your temptations and struggles. Let him know about the Enemy's attacks; it will help him pray for you more intelligently.

There's nothing airtight about scheduling your way out of temptation—it's improbable that you can completely schedule yourself out of every danger zone. But scheduling appointments, creating a workload based on your priorities, and maintaining your life-giving contacts are habits based on the life you're already accustomed to, and opportunities to place yourself before God instead of sexual temptation.

Don't Touch That Dial!

I found it ironic as I began writing this book that some of my stories involved my watching TV in my room as I weighed certain dilemmas. However, the TV of the 1980's is much different from today's TV. Beer commercials feature cheerleaders in little more than bikinis; Network TV shows have become more and more sexualized; hotels offer HBO, Cinemax, and/or Showtime—all of which feature shows with nudity and sexual scenes.

In fact, the moment you turn on the television in most hotels, an in-room movie screen appears. Normally, the channel offers the latest Hollywood films first. Then, if you hang around long enough, you will be offered something from their adult entertainment library. A friend of mine staying at an expensive hotel in Dallas turned on his TV, and the very first movie on the screen was pornographic. A child could have turned on the TV and seen the advertisement!

The bottom line is that with your sexual antenna already dodging bombardments of sexual images and innuendo, the last thing you need is to be blindsided by seemingly innocuous outlets. Don't turn on the TV. I know this sounds a bit extreme, however, it is possible. Want to find out who won Monday Night Football? Turn on *SportsCenter* in the morning as you're dressing and much less on edge. Afraid you'll be bored? That's what your non-work workload is for. Feel it's unfair not to be able to turn on your TV and watch your shows? Consider Paul's words in 1 Corinthians 6:12:

> You may say, "I am allowed to do anything." But I reply, "Not everything is good for you." And even though "I am allowed to do anything," I must not become a slave to anything (NLT).

Are you allowed to watch regular TV? Sure. Does God allow you to watch Oklahoma vs. Texas Tech on Big Monday? Of course. Should you do it if it's going to tempt you to act out sexually? No. If anything is going to tempt you to sin, you need to limit your liberty. Swim in the hotel pool. Exercise in the weight room. Make the TV the one amenity you don't use. I know it sounds like the equivalent of recommending you have elective surgery, but if you struggle with sexual temptation, such a fight demands sacrifice.

Joe Stowell says, "Purity simply means that in all matters of life we are not perfect, but we keep ourselves clean."[9] In crossing through the minefield of sexual temptation, that's what you're trying to achieve—cleanliness of body, mind, and soul. I pray for you. I know the battle is fierce and, at times, overwhelming. But victory is not impossible. Jesus broke the power of sin when He took sin upon Himself on the cross and rose again. Trust Him to join you in the battle and fight on your behalf. No matter how many times you have to go into the minefield, He'll always know the way through.

Notes:

[1] Gene Getz, *The Measure of a Man: Twenty Attributes of a Godly Man* (Ventura, CA: Regal Books, 1974), pp. 44-45.

[2] Pamela Paul, "The Porn Factor." *Time*, January 19, 2004.

[3] Rick Page, *Hope Is Not a Strategy, The Six Keys to Winning the Complex Sale* (New York: McGraw-Hill; Reprint Edition, 2003).

[4] Stephen Arterburn and Kenny Luck with Mike Yorkey, *Every Man God's Man: Every Man's Guide to...Courageous Faith and Daily Integrity* (Colorado Springs: Waterbrook Press, 2003), p. 133.

[5] I have heard other teachers use the term "The Fifty-Mile Rule" or a variation of it. Because of its familiarity to me, I do not know its source.

[6] For an excellent guide to beginning such studies, see Rick Warren, *Personal Bible Study Methods* (Lake Forest, CA: Pastors.com, 1997).

[7] Comprehensive Health Plan: To Lead a Healthy Church Takes More Than Technique: An Interview with Rick Warren." *Leadership Journal*, Summer 1997, p. 28.

[8] Michael Brown and Kelly Hahn "Men's Accountability Starter Kit" (unpublished).

[9] Joseph M. Stowell, *Shepherding the Church Into the 21st Century: Effective Spiritual Leadership in a Changing Culture* (Wheaton: Victor Books, 1994), p. 96.

Chapter 6

The Minefield of
Neglected Relationships

If you must work long hours and nights for six weeks, it may mean some unusual business project came up. Everyone can understand that. But if you work long hours and nights for six months, then you've made a crucial decision about what you value most in life.
— Steve Arterburn and Fred Stoeker[1]

Unless the LORD builds a house,
*   the work of the builders is useless.*
Unless the LORD protects a city,
*   guarding it with sentries will do no good.*
It is useless for you to work so hard
*   from early morning until late at night,*
*   anxiously working for food to eat;*
*   for God gives rest to his loved ones.*
Children are a gift from the LORD;
*   they are a reward from him.*
Children born to a young man
*   are like sharp arrows in a warrior's hands.*

67

> *How happy is the man*
> *whose quiver is full of them!*
> *He will not be put to shame*
> *when he confronts his accusers at the city gates.*
> — Psalm 127 (NLT)

Driven!

I love what I do!

Ministry turns my crank. I love preaching and teaching. I love watching people come to Christ and then grow to spiritual maturity. I love leading a visionary staff that seeks to cultivate a ministry environment where lives are changed, eternal destinies are redirected, and the power of God is loosed. Let me say it again: ministry turns my crank.

However, because I love what I do, and because I tend to be a goal-oriented person with a Type A personality, I have found that I must be very, very careful about something very important.

In 1992, I was called to my first senior pastorate. Bethel Evangelical Free Church in Fargo, North Dakota, was a medium-sized church poised to be used by God in a significant way. It had a growing congregation, a positive reputation in the community, property in a major growth area of the city, excellent lay leadership, and a plan to build a new church campus. Apart from the weather, which can be extremely harsh in that part of the country, it was a new pastor's dream. I hit the ground running, and as I look back, it was quite a ride. During my five years in Fargo, God blessed in a remarkable way.

When I arrived at my new ministry challenge, I quickly immersed myself in all there was to do. I found my work absolutely exhilarating. We embarked on a capital campaign to fund our new construction, attempted to sell our existing facility, rented space for our expanding program, and excitedly looked to the future. Just prior to moving to our new location, we were somehow cramming more than 600 people into our building on Sunday mornings—and the parking lot held only forty cars! People parked on the street and often walked a few blocks to services. What makes that incredible is that the winter temperature was often ten to twenty degrees *below zero*. Wind chills could reach an incredible sixty to seventy degrees below. One Sunday, I received a call from the pastor of a church located near ours. He was calling to complain that my congregation was taking all of the spaces in *his* church's parking lot. Ouch! If this all sounds thrilling, it was.

One Monday morning I got up and started getting ready to go to work. Linda busied herself getting the boys ready for school. After the bus picked them up, she asked me to sit down for a cup of coffee. She obviously had something on her mind.

Looking me straight in the eye, she asked, "Jim, didn't we agree that you would try to take Mondays off?" I immediately knew where this conversation was heading. I squirmed.

"And Jim," she continued, "do you know that this will be the ninth or tenth Monday in a row that you have worked? For the last two or three months you have been working seven days a week. And even when you're home, you're not really home. Your mind is always somewhere else. Jim, what are we going to do about this?"

Linda was right. I had fallen victim to the minefield of neglected relationships. A devoted wife and two great young boys were being shortchanged. In my zeal to do God's work, I was neglecting my three most important earthly relationships. I offered a couple of meager excuses; however, I knew I was guilty as charged.

The minefield of neglected relationships can destroy your marriage and drive a wedge between you and your children. I was failing in my all-important role of husband, father, and spiritual leader. Unfortunately, many men get caught in this minefield.

It's not that I ever consciously decided to neglect those important relationships. No man who truly loves his family ever would. However, it happens all the time.

Now, I am not a workaholic. However, I know that the tendency toward workaholism is lurking inside of me. I have a racehorse temperament. Disengaging and putting it in neutral is very hard for me. I am goal-oriented. Achievement is important to me. I will openly confess: *I am a driven person.*

Being driven was essential to success in my business career. In the arena of sales and marketing, individuals who were lazy didn't last long. It was a dog-eat-dog environment. One needed a lot of drive and chutzpah just to survive. My normal work week consisted of five ten-hour days and a half-day on Saturday. In addition, it was not unusual to receive phone calls at home on Sunday. Often, the calls were long, taking me away from my wife and kids. I hate to admit it, but I often used my time at church on Sunday to write out "to do" lists rather than worship God. I had very little margin in my life. Stress was my constant companion.

Now, you are probably already feeling some tension. I understand completely. After all, how do you pursue a career, your family relationships, and God all at the same time? I openly admit I don't have all the answers. When it comes to balancing life, I am a fellow struggler. However, if we are going to avoid the minefield of neglected relationships, we need to challenge our beliefs about work and family.

Before I give some prescriptive wisdom on how to avoid the minefield of neglected relationships, let me first make four observations about your role as a husband and/or father in your home. If you are not yet a husband or a father—perhaps just getting started in your enthralling business career—please etch these lessons on your conscience to avoid future disaster!

The Role of Husband and Father

Raising Children: It's For Dads, Too!

I will never forget one old scrap iron dealer whom I used to visit on a regular basis. He sold a lot of raw material to my company. He had been in business for decades and had made a ton of money. Though I wouldn't call him arrogant, he certainly thought he knew just about everything about everything. When I visited him, it wasn't much of a two-way conversation. Basically, he held court. What I got was the world according to Dave. He could pontificate for hours on just about anything, and he often did.

On one occasion, the conversation got around to marriage and family. In his usual "know it all" style, he proceeded to rationalize the life he had lived. He boasted about his seventy-hour work weeks. Rarely had he taken a vacation with his family, and when he had, he usually flew back early to tend to his business. On most workdays he would leave before his children got up and come home after they were in bed. He routinely missed their school activities, ball games—even their birthday parties.

At one point in his monologue, he turned to me and said, "Raising the children was my wife's job. My job was to make money. Jim, that's the way it's supposed to be. Men work, women raise kids." I left that day thankful he wasn't my father.

Now, I am going to assume that most men reading this book would strongly disagree with his attitude (or at least wouldn't be so brazen about it). Most would say that his perspective is seriously flawed. However, if you are driven to achieve, the workaholic tendency can, and will, rear its ugly head if you are not careful. Had my wife not confronted me that morning in Fargo, I might still be working seven days a week and justifying it by pointing to all of the kingdom business needing to be done. Then again, if I had stayed on that course, my marriage would be seriously diseased—maybe even dead. That's because we're to love our wives according to God's plan, not our preconceived ideas about marriage.

In Ephesians 5, Paul makes a few assertions that are convicting to many Christian husbands. In verse 25, he writes, "Husbands love your wives, just as Christ also loved the church and gave himself up for her...." Paul is saying that just as Christ's love for the church is sacrificial, so a husband's love for his wife is to be sacrificial. We are always to be showing a love to our wife that is giving, caring, gentle, and sacrificial. In the verses that follow, Paul calls for men to cherish and invest in their wives.

Loving, cherishing, and investing in your wife will require that you spend a great deal of time working at being the husband she deserves. So put in the time! To neglect your relationship with your wife is to be disobedient to God's plan for the family. Love her in a sacrificial way.

When it comes to your relationship with your children, Scripture is equally clear. Proverbs 22:6 reads, "Train a child in the way he should go, and when he is old he will not depart from it." That statement, contrary to the views of the scrap iron dealer mentioned earlier, is not just directed to mothers. A mother and a father are partners in "training" their children. Neglecting your relationship with your children is not an option for a father who wishes to please God.

Are there going to be situations that come up that pull you away for a period of time? Of course. Project deadlines, reports, sudden road trips to visit an angry customer, and a variety of other circumstance may come between you and your family at times. But if this happens regularly, your family will stop being understanding. They'll begin to see themselves as less important than that angry client.

And friend, it's just not worth it. I remember a month during my last year of seminary when I felt as if I was never home. Research projects, along with studying Greek and Hebrew dominated my life. I remember feeling so guilty over my absence from home that I broke down and sobbed one night in my office. It was awful.

Life Is a Stewardship

As we noted in the chapter on materialism, God is the Creator of everything. There is nothing we have invented that did not come from material He had previously created. Therefore, everything we have—right down to the air we breathe and the lungs with which we breathe it—comes from God. It is all a gracious gift from His hand.

This means that when God gives us families that we neither earn nor deserve, we are expected to treat these gifts of grace as a *stewardship*. Most of the time, we think of the word stewardship in terms of financial giving ("It's time again for the annual stewardship drive!"). But stewardship basically means taking care of what has been entrusted to us. In reference to the minefield of neglected relationships, then, being a steward of the gracious gift called your family means seeing your role as father and husband as a holy trust.

Whatever position you have at your company, you are a steward. If you are a CEO, your responsibility is to steward the short and long-term direction of the company that hired you. If you are a financial officer, you are a steward of the financial solvency of the organization. Even if you are an entry-level gofer, you are a steward of certain responsibilities. So while you may not have seriously thought about your role in the home as being that of a steward, you probably innately understand this principle of stewardship.

"So I should steward my home just as I steward my responsibilities at the office, right?" you may be asking. Wrong. In fact, this is where it becomes fun!

First of all, at home you are a steward for free. There are no extrinsic incentives.

Second, the goals are different. Instead of increasing market share, developing new products, or meeting stock performance expectations, your stewardship of your family has no bottom line. There are no quarterly reviews, no strategic plans and no daily stock watches pertaining to your fatherhood (though, that would be amusing. You can almost hear the evening news anchor reporting, "In the Family Market today, Bill Tapscott backed over his daughter's bicycle in the driveway. His stock has fallen five points."). Rather, you are slowly, consistently, and patiently influencing your family to follow Jesus and to be salt and light in the world.

Third, when your direct report at the office makes a mistake, you frame your remarks within the lingo of accountability, execution, follow-through, and contingency plans. When your four-year-old smears peanut butter all over her face because she saw her mom wearing a mud mask, such lingo is ineffective.

So, stewarding your job and stewarding your home involve different sets of responsibilities and objectives. Likewise, they demand different mindsets and different expectations.

First, being a faithful steward of your family requires a different mindset because the spatial relationships are different from those within your company. On a heart level, you are far more connected to your family members than to those with whom you work. To your peer, you are Dave, vice president of marketing. You are a sublime, but funny guy who takes his work seriously. When you say, "I expected better work on the Jones account," your peers are wounded, but they get over it. Five years after you've left the company, you're a fuzzy memory—mostly reduced to your idiosyncrasies and signature moments in the office.

To your five-year-old, eleven-year-old, or even eighteen-year-old, you are "Dad." You have always been, and continue to be, a powerful shaping force in their lives. When you say, "Why did you get a B? I always got A's in English," it registers on a level that few people in their lives will ever be able to touch. Five years after they've left home, they may still remember it, because you are as close to them as their own hearts.

Therefore, your interaction with them is far more important than your interaction with your peers. Empathy, creative communication, teamwork, and shared goals may help you bring a new product to market, but love, patience, and grace will have a much deeper impact on your home, the lives of your children, and all the lives they touch now and throughout their lifetimes.

I hope you see that your stewardship as a husband and father is exceedingly more important than your stewardship at the office. Your family is a gift from God and they should be treated better than you treat your best client.

Influence is a Product of Nurture

In 1 Timothy 3:1-7, Paul lays out for Timothy the character qualities that were to qualify a man for eldership in the church. For the most part, an elder in the early church functioned in many of the same ways as today's pastors—they preached, taught, and oversaw the general direction and health of the church. Many of the qualities are to be expected—faithful to one wife, self-controlled, able to teach, and so on. But 1 Timothy 3:4-5 reveals a point of qualification that may seem unusual:

> *He must manage his own family well, with children who respect and obey him. For if a man cannot manage his own household, how can he take care of God's church?* (NLT).

For a man to be an elder, his children have to respect and obey him. To you, that may seem unfair. After all, children have a will of their own. Why should one be held accountable for the actions of his children?

I think this qualification shows the principle of influence. As a parent, you have authority over your children. You're bigger, stronger, and older then they are. You pay the mortgage—they contribute next to nothing to the survival of the family. So, in the end, you have the final say.

But how you get to the end makes all the difference. In a situation where your child is pushing the boundaries, you can do one of two things: You can exert your authority through physical force or intimidation and end the mutiny. Or you can exert your authority in ways that reveal care, understanding, respect, and integrity. The answer is still "no," but the interaction and communication allow you to have a greater amount of positive influence in his or her life.

As an elder (or a pastor), an individual has authority over those within the church. But people can be divisive. In Paul's letters to Timothy, he names certain individuals who caused so much trouble in the church, they had to be removed from the fellowship. The question for an elder was: "When people create rifts in the church, how are you going to respond?" Rather than ask the individual a canned question like that, Paul recommended that Timothy observe how the man's children behave. If they are respectful and obedient to him, Timothy could know that the man probably handled his children in a firm, but respectful way. If the children were rebellious and problematic, then the man was probably unable to confront or confront well.

Erwin McManus writes: "I am convinced that great parenting is all about influence. It is more about shaping values than it is about setting boundaries."[2] Influence is a product of nurture. Nurture is a product of time. Influence happens only in relationships where time is made available.

If you make the commitment to invest ample time in your children, you and they will reap the rewards later—when they reach that chaotic season of life known as adolescence. Steve Farrar aptly quips, "Something happens when a kid hits adolescence. When kids are small, they tend to think their dad hung the moon. When kids hit adolescence sometimes they begin to think their dad should go to the moon."[3]

There's no question that the parent/child relationship is stretched during adolescence. But the enduring quality of that relationship has a lot to do with what is invested on the front end—during those impressionable, formative years. Nurture your children. Discuss misbehavior with them. Don't lay down the law, leaving them to nurse their hurt feelings. Walk them through their poor choice, firmly but lovingly. Extend the grace given you through Jesus to them. They need to know what they did was wrong. They may even need to experience consequences as a result. But they will always need to experience grace, and no child can be positively influenced by a father when grace is denied.

Things Don't Settle Down

In the Summer 1996 issue of *Leadership Journal*, author and youth ministries expert Mike Yaconelli wrote an article entitled, "I Don't Have Any Friends." It was a disclosing look at his chronic busyness, hectic travel schedule, and the repercussions he was feeling as a result. Here are some of the more gripping sections of that article. See if you find yourself identifying with Yaconelli anywhere.

> *I came to a startling revelation a few months ago. I don't have any friends. I don't. I have a lot of acquaintances but, other than my wife, I really have no close friends. I've had some friends in the past, but not many. Eventually something happened—nothing sinister, just something like moving, having a baby, changing jobs, building a home, going back to school, changing churches. Nothing bad or wrong, just something that happened—and the next thing I knew, another friendship had slowly eroded...*
>
> *I am too busy. I am gone too much, travel too much, speak too much, and work too much. I have done an excellent job of convincing the people around me that I am too busy—too busy doing the important work I am doing—to have any time for friendships...*

If we are too busy to have friends, we are much too busy. If we are too busy to have time for our families, kids, or neighbors, we are much too busy. Most of us in the ministry are isolated, separated by our giftedness.

Toward the end of the article, Yaconelli makes a resolution to himself that any driven person knows will take the grace of God and unflagging determination to achieve:

I have decided to make some friends.
It will mean I have to stay home. It will mean I have to spend time with someone doing absolutely nothing. It will mean I have to work at something that is not easy for me.
Instead of building a ministry to thousands, maybe we ought to build a friendship with one. Instead of speaking 200 times a year, maybe we should be known as someone who knows how to have friends. [4]

Mike Yaconelli died in October, 2003, in a tragic truck accident. He was helping his father move from Oregon when he inexplicably veered off the road and crashed.[5] His wife and father were in a vehicle a few miles behind him. There was no warning, no opportunity to say good-bye, no chance to look back.

Do you need to make a resolution similar to the one made by Mike Yaconelli? If so, do it right away! Don't wait one more day! Don't tell yourself that you will do it as soon as things settle down. And, I would suggest that you write your resolution down and commit it to God in prayer. Your family will greatly benefit from your changed priorities. And your wife would probably enjoy helping you periodically measure your progress.

Whenever I'm talking with someone and they're attempting to explain why they haven't followed through on something important, but not urgent, I often hear them say, "I'll do it when things settle down." But if we are absolutely honest with ourselves, we will admit that things never settle down. Life is filled with activity, and when one season of furious activity ends, another begins. On and on it goes, most of it good, fruitful activity.

John Ortberg says, "When will things settle down? When you die. Then your life will slow waaaaay down. In fact, you'll be surprised at how much the pace of your life is going to slow when you die. But not until then."[6]

So if things are never going to settle down, and your most important relationships are being neglected, what's the answer? Make a mid-course correction.

You make your schedule. The way you spend your hours and days is yours to choose freely. Now it's true that there may be consequences if you work less and spend more time with your family than at work; but that's still a choice you freely make. Just because there are consequences doesn't mean the choice isn't free. The days of slavery are long over. You choose the quality of life you live.

Robert Greenleaf, noted authority and author on servant leadership, wrote: "Life should be leisurely, not to allow time for loafing or for slowness of pace, but to allow for organization of the optimum life; whenever one finds he or she cannot do the things that are most important for want of time, something is basically wrong with the structure."[7]

Are you shaping the structure of your life, or are you just letting it shape itself? Many people live life as though it just happens to them. They have no regard for their own responsibility to live life intelligently. As a businessperson, you are probably not this kind of person. More than likely, you have focus, direction, and drive. Well…put that to use! Put it to use in the reclamation of your role as father, husband, and spiritual leader! It's not too late. Mike Yaconelli felt he could make a change despite having lived for years on the road and speaking 200 times a year. You can make needed changes too.

Wayne Muller writes in his book *Sabbath*: "Whatever we hold as our own, however briefly, we consecrate with our very life. This alone should give us pause before we invite anything or anyone new into our already crowded and hurried lives."[8] Decide what stays and what goes in your life. Become as passionate about your family as you are about your work. The gains aren't as obvious and productivity sometimes seems elusive, but in God's economy, the results are worth more than the NASDAQ, Dow Jones, and S&P combined.

Be a Real Man!

I despise flavored coffee! My wife loves it. A few years ago she made a pot of coffee while I was still sleeping. When I got up I poured a cup, thinking it was the usual Folgers or Maxwell House. A few moments later, I was pouring it in the sink. I then told my wife in no uncertain terms, "Don't ever do that again! Real men don't drink flavored coffee!"

Well, real men may not drink flavored coffee, but let me give you a few things real men DO if they want to avoid the minefield of neglected relationships.

Prioritize

I already took you to task on this one. Don't put it off. The time gap between conviction and status quo isn't very long. Max De Pree said, "[Setting priorities] comes down to dealing with the substantive before the superficial, of dealing with the strategic before the stressful, of leaving a legacy instead of accumulated assets, of being able to find a balance in life that gives equal footing to family and service."[9] Moses said, "…teach us to number our days that we may get a heart of wisdom" (Psalm 90:12, ESV). The quality of your life and relationships in the future will depend, to a great extent, on the choices and changes you make today.

Study

Real men discipline themselves to be in God's Word regularly. The Bible has a lot to say about relationships. The mantra of our American culture is "It's all about me." However, God's Word calls upon us to be different. Scripture tells us to be other-centered rather than self-centered. The more this perspective from God's Word fills your heart and mind, the more it will shine forth in your life.

Set Goals

The book of James speaks of a man who sees himself in the mirror and then walks away, forgetting what he looks like. Real men look into the mirror of God's Word and then determine to do what needs to be done. They don't walk away and forget. When you see that God's Word is speaking to you about relationships, stop and write down the important points. Formulate a measurable goal ("I will take my wife on a date once a week"). Go back in a few weeks and reread your goal. Take time to measure your progress or lack of progress.

Pray

Ask God to make you more sensitive (and responsive) to your family's needs and desires. Real men pray for compassion, gentleness, and love toward their family. God will gladly answer your prayer.

Seek Accountability

Once you have studied, prayed, and set some goals, find another man who will hold you accountable. Real men are willing to be vulnerable. Meet with him regularly, and be honest with him about your struggles.

Communicate

Let your wife and children know that you are determined to be the best husband and father you can be. Let them know how important they are. Real men talk! Ask your wife to give you feedback on how you are doing. And don't become defensive. Take it like a real man.

Andy Stanley painted the ultimate picture of what stepping on this landmine looks like when he wrote: "One day you will come home from the office for the last time. Nobody retires from his or her family to spend his or her final days in the office. Your last day may be at sixty-five when you retire or at thirty-five when you are laid off. Either way, you are coming home. What and who you come home to will be determined by what and who you choose to cheat between now and then."[10]

In another place, he adds, "I have seen too many men and women cheat their family only to find that the companies they worked for were not nearly as loyal to them as they were to their companies."[11]

I have a long way to go. You probably do as well. We are a work in progress. May God give us grace and perseverance as we prioritize our lives and reinvest in any neglected relationships!

Notes:

[1] Stephen Arterburn and Fred Stoeker with Mike Yorkey, *Every Woman's Desire: Every Man's Guide to...Winning the Heart of a Woman* (Colorado Springs: Waterbrook Press, 2001), p. 153.

[2] Erwin Raphael McManus, *Seizing Your Divine Moment: Dare to Live a Life of Adventure* (Nashville: Thomas Nelson, 2002), p. 120.

[3] Steve Farrar, *Standing Tall: How a Man Can Protect His Family* (Sisters, OR: Multnomah, 1994), p. 190.

[4] Mike Yaconelli, "I Don't Have Any Friends: And I Think I Have Discovered the Reasons" *Leadership Journal*, Summer, 1996, pp. 41-42.

[5] Additional information on Yaconelli's life and death can be found in, "Mike Yaconelli Dies In Truck Accident," *Christianity Today*. http://www.christianitytoday.com/ct/2003/143/51.0.htm.

[6] John Ortberg, "It All Goes Back in the Box." Sermon given at Willow Creek Community Church, September, 2000.

[7] *Seeker and Servant: Reflection on Religious Leadership,* Anne T. Frank & Larry C. Spears, eds. (San Francisco: Jossey Bass, 1996), p. 1.

[8] Wayne Muller, *Sabbath: Finding Rest, Renewal, and Delight in Our Busy Lives* (New York: Bantam Books, 1999), p. 206.

[9] Max De Pree, *Leadership Jazz* (New York: Doubleday, 1992), pp. 181-182.

[10] Andy Stanley, *Choosing To Cheat: Who Wins When Family and Work Collide?* (Sisters, OR: Multnomah, 2003), p. 123.

[11] *Ibid,* p. 123.

Chapter 7

The Minefield of Spiritual Stagnation

I know that the most captivating, staggering, extravagant fact in all time and space—that God came down, became one of us, died by us and died for us, did it to make us His children and bride, and now walks every moment with us in love and companionship—that this amazing truth I can treat as no more important than, and forget as easily as, my yearly car insurance renewal. It can become dull routine, one more thing to know, do, and worry about. One more thing to try to remember.

Such a God doing such a thing surpasses all things in greatness and marvel. Nothing even remotely, even vaguely, compares with it. Yet the Sunday flyers, with yet another 40 percent off sale on kitchenware at Wal-Mart, or the pages with reviews of the latest batch of books or movies, can distract me from it. A simple backache can ruin my joy in it. An unexpected car expense can steal away my thankfulness for it.

I need a steady vigilance in holy things.

– Mark Buchanan[1]

A life of turbulence and noise may seem
  To him that leads it wise and to be praised.
But wisdom is a pearl with most success
  Sought in still waters.
  — William Cowper (from *The Task, book 3*)

Let me ask you this one question: Did you receive the Holy Spirit by keeping the law? Of course not, for the Holy Spirit came upon you only after you believed the message you heard about Christ. Have you lost your senses? After starting your Christian lives in the Spirit, why are you now trying to become perfect by your own human effort?
  — Galatians 3:2-3, NLT

Don't Skip This Chapter!

I see you. Yes, you!

I see you flipping to the back cover, checking how many pages are left before you can say you've completed this book. And I know what you might be thinking: *Only two chapters to go. This one is about spiritual stagnation, eh? Probably another challenge to read my Bible and pray. I can safely skip this one.*

Don't do it! I promise you up front that this is not another chapter on implementing and maintaining spiritual disciplines. Surprisingly, spiritual disciplines are not the antidote to spiritual stagnation (although they play a role). It is possible to read your Bible and pray every day and yet remain spiritually stagnant. So I'm telling you right now that if you continue reading this chapter, you will not be disappointed. This chapter is perhaps the most important chapter in the entire book because spiritual stagnation blinds you to the presence of the other five minefields.

I say this emphatically because many Christians become spiritually stagnant at some point in their lives. They read the Word and are unmoved. They pray and feel they might as well be talking with the cat. They sing in church, but the words have no power and impact. They feel defeated, discouraged, and distanced from God. When they wonder why, or seek to reverse this spiritual blandness, they feel guilty that they're not doing more.

Have you ever been there? If so, let me tell you about one of my favorite singers and how her life—and death—have a lot to teach us about spiritual stagnation.

Soul Starvation

I love music! I grew up in the 1960s, so when I think of the classic voices of that decade, I think of Brian Wilson, Frankie Valli, Del Shannon, Gene Pitney, and of course Paul McCartney and John Lennon. And though I can't remember all the lead singers, I loved the blends of The Temptations, Four Tops, and a variety of other Motown groups.

But my all-time favorite voice of the sixties belonged to Karen Carpenter. I still listen to her, thanks to today's wonderful technology. The CD cover says all the songs have been "digitally remastered for maximum quality." I don't know what that means, but I'm sure it has to be good—and I'm sure it accounts for the $18.99 retail price. Whatever it means, when I'm driving around town listening and singing along to "I'm On Top of the World Looking Down on Creation," I can feel the energy of her powerful, yet smooth voice (sorry for the visual; hope we don't run into each other at a stoplight).

One quick memory shows how my appreciation of Karen Carpenter hasn't always been shared by others. Years ago, I picked up my oldest son and one of his friends from Little League practice. As we drove home I felt like listening to some driving music. I popped Karen Carpenter into the CD player. After about fifteen seconds of "Close To You," my son's friend said to him, "What is your dad listening to?"

My son replied, "Karen Carpenter. He listens to her all the time."

The friend leaned over, "I can't believe *anybody* could *ever* have liked *that* song!" (I want you to know that he didn't hurt my feelings one bit. I trust that now that he has grown into adulthood, he has learned to appreciate real music and loves Karen Carpenter).

Karen Carpenter died way too young. She was only thirty-two when she died from complications related to anorexia nervosa. Basically, she avoided food and starved herself for years. She ate only a fraction of what her body needed to sustain its health. One day her heart simply gave out. That was the tragic end to the greatest female voice I've ever heard.

So why do I risk boring you with my reverie about music from the 1960s and Karen Carpenter? Because the struggles of Karen Carpenter remind me of the struggles I see many Christian businessmen experience.

Karen deprived herself of food and it led to her physical downfall. Many busy Christian businessmen deprive themselves of spiritual food and it leads to their spiritual downfall. Avoiding the spiritual nourishment and refreshment you need leads to spiritual anorexia.

One of my favorite authors, Steve Farrar, talks about this in his excellent book *Point Man*. He also draws the comparison between Karen Carpenter's struggle with anorexia nervosa and the "spiritual anorexia" that plagues many Christian men. Steve writes: "We have all seen tragic pictures of starving children in Ethiopia. Many of them are so weak they cannot stand up. Anorexic men are just as weak spiritually as those children are physically. Why? They both lack nutritious food."[2]

If you are a spiritual anorexic, your spiritual life is malnourished— and probably going nowhere. You are caught in the minefield of spiritual stagnation. What are the symptoms of spiritual stagnation? Here are a few.

When You're Spiritually Stagnant . . .

The Christian Life Seems Empty

Sometimes promises are made for the Christian life that Jesus never intended. I'm not saying that being a Christian is boring or unexciting; but I am saying that Christianity is not necessarily the thrill-a-minute, nonstop adventure some claim it to be. In one popular church growth book, the author reflects on his discipleship by saying, "I learned that there was nothing more exciting, more challenging, and more adventure-packed than living as a devoted follower of Jesus Christ. What I found out is that there's a big difference between *thrills* and *thrills that fulfill*" (author's emphasis).[3]

The problem with such a statement is that while this experience may have been true for the author, it's not necessarily a common denominator for all Christians. The early church was persecuted. Christians were being killed in public for entertainment. Our brothers and sisters face intense persecution in other countries today. I doubt they would characterize the Christian life as adventure-packed.

And when the thrills stop coming, spiritual stagnation is inevitable. So you might think, "I'll go on a mission trip, or I'll go to a conference. I'll do something that will jump start my spiritual life." But mission trips and conferences end. If the Christian life is lived from "high" to "high," you'll find you ultimately spend more time in the valleys than on the peaks. Then what?

"So are you saying that as a Christian, I shouldn't expect much?" you may be asking. No, I'm not saying that. I am saying that while the Christian life isn't like living *Lord of the Rings*, as a redeemed child of God, there is a new *quality* of life available to you. Jesus referred to it as "living water": "…the water I give…takes away thirst altogether. It becomes a perpetual spring within…giving…eternal life" (John 4:14, NLT).

Eternal life is a different quality of life than natural life. Theologian D. A. Carson notes, "The language of inner satisfaction and transformation calls to mind a string of prophecies anticipating new hearts, the exchange of failed formalism in religion for a heart that knows and experiences God, and that hungers to do his will."[4]

The picture drawn is that followers of Christ have a different quality of life within them that replenishes itself like a spring. Because of Jesus' death and resurrection, you and I—if we trust in His death for the forgiveness of sins—have the Holy Spirit within us, transforming our hearts and minds. When living water flows within us like a perpetual spring, there is no such thing as spiritual stagnation because the Spirit is always seeking to move us *forward*.

But so few of us ever live this kind of life—and it's not because we don't read our Bible or pray enough. It's because we lose sight of the big picture and settle into a false reality.

The Temporal Trumps the Eternal

When I say "false reality," I mean that so often we live each moment of each day as if it were a moment or a day without a context. We become so focused on the immediate we forget that each moment, day, month, and year is part of a larger context—eternity. Men are particularly challenged here. Because of our brain wiring, we tend to analyze events, tasks, and situations single-mindedly, without attaching them to other concurrent events, tasks, and people. We attend meetings and give no thought as to how this particular meeting may be a place where God is shaping us for His purposes. We decide to skip morning worship and never realize how that decision impacts the other facets of our lives.

What does my four-hour budget meeting have to do with my spiritual life? you may be thinking. Everything! Because the same wholly integrated person who attends that business meeting is the same wholly integrated person who is being formed by God. There is no "Harry the Accounts Manager" and "Harry the Churchgoer." They are the same integrated person.

But we botch this up quite often when it comes to living life. By living our lives in separated pieces, we tend to neglect what isn't immediately in front of us. Now guess who doesn't walk up and knock you in the head with a Bible? Jesus. Rather, the Bible shows that Jesus is more inclined to knock at the door of your heart, instead of forcing His way in: "Here I am! I stand at the door and knock. If anyone hears my voice and opens the door, I will come in and eat with him, and he with me" (Revelation 3:20).

We can't have the quality of eternal life—life emanating from a new, transformed heart—if we're not living with eternity in mind. When the temporal world encases us to the point where there is nothing beyond this minute, this day, this month, this year...we can expect spiritual stagnation to settle in.

In the previous chapter, I shared with you that I am a goal-oriented person with a Type-A personality. When you factor in a touch of Attention Deficit Disorder, it will not surprise you that sustained periods of reflection, silence, and quiet worship of God are not easy for me. In fact, to be brutally honest: Quieting my spirit, coming into God's presence, and listening for His voice is perhaps my greatest spiritual challenge. I am able to do it only when the house is quiet early in the morning and I can shut out the world. If I don't do it then, opportunities for ever doing it during the day are slim and none. Once I hit my office at the church, and the hustle and bustle of the day begin, I quickly move into high gear. Soon I'm navigating the seas of meetings, preparation, counseling, and so on. And my world begins to shrink ever so slightly into the temporal.

That is why my morning discipline is so important. The first thing I do is seek to have my world reoriented to the eternal, because the eternal—God's time and God's purposes—is ultimate reality. My call to ministry is rooted in eternity. My family life and physical health are rooted in eternity. That's why regular increments of time in the morning are crucial to my having the kind of mindset in which God can lead me.

I love the words of David in Psalm 23: "He makes me lie down in green pastures, he leads me beside quiet waters, he restores my soul."

David is referring to wonderful times of spiritual rest, nourishment, and blessing. He is describing sweet times of fellowship and interaction with his heavenly father. Most Christians know this beloved psalm. Yet very few followers of Christ—the Good Shepherd—ever experience this type of life. That's why so many Christians are spiritual anorexics. They are too busy—too caught up in the cares of this world.

"But wait a minute, Jim!" you may be saying. "I can't help it! I have a demanding job and Little League games and chores at home, as well as a variety of other demands on my time. That type of spiritual life isn't possible for me. Sure, I'd love to put it in park by a lake and let God restore my soul, but it's just not doable for me."

This is where an eternal mindset is so crucial. I'm not telling you to give up your job and family so you can live in the forests. As mentioned before, your job is a stewardship and so is your family. But you do have to remember that those stewardships have been given to you by God, and thus they have their roots *in eternity.* They are temporal in nature, but they have eternal origins. So if you fill your life completely with temporal concerns and forget about their eternal origins, *you will have a faulty frame of reference for interpreting your entire life.*

Your temporal responsibilities and stewardships must be shaped by an eternal perspective. And you can gain an eternal perspective only by spending time with God, an eternal being. When you do, you will begin to see how your parenting, account managing, neighboring, and worshiping, are not fractured pieces super-glued onto your human frame. You'll see that they are all ways in which God is shaping your life for His eternal purposes.

So what happens when you're buried in a temporal perspective, yet still feel the need to read your Bible and pray? You develop two symptoms of spiritual stagnation: legalism and consumerism.

Legalism and Consumerism Emerge

Letting an eternal perspective shape your temporal responsibilities is exceedingly important for thinking about spiritual disciplines. If I were to ask you, "Why should you read your Bible and pray?" you would possibly answer something like, "Because I'm a Christian and that's how you get close to God. When you read your Bible and pray consistently, your relationship with God grows."

What is implied here is that if, for some reason, I cannot read my Bible or pray, I will begin to grow farther from God. The equation presented is that my spatial relationship with God depends upon my faithfulness to certain spiritual disciplines. Spiritual disciplines become like a treadmill—keep walking and you're in good shape; slow down or stop and you fall on your face.

But this is inaccurate. Spiritual distance is an idea created by our achievement-oriented selves. The truth is that you are no closer to nor further away from God because of Bible reading or prayer. If you are saved by Christ, your salvation is a reality in heaven—no matter how vigilant you are about Bible reading and prayer. It is "...an inheritance that can never perish, spoil or fade—kept in heaven for you..."(1 Peter 1:4).

Of course, your level of intimacy with God is another story. How close you are to God or how far you are from Him in this sense has to do with your openness and responsiveness to Him. If you aren't able to present yourself to God in Scripture reading or prayer because you woke up late, or Tommy spilled juice on Greg's school clothes, or you realized you left your briefcase on the subway, don't think that you will be moved back two spiritual notches because you missed a day. Disciplines are great, but they become the death of us when we have more faith in them than we do in God. When this happens, they turn into "soul-killing laws."[5]

Likewise, it is entirely possible to read your Bible for 30 minutes a day and pray for an hour a day, and still have a heart that is closed off to God. It's a shame, but it's true. Have you ever read from Scripture, or spent time in prayer, and felt prompted to do something you didn't want to do; perhaps apologize to an enemy, make a costly financial contribution—something sacrificial? What did you do? If you said to yourself, "No thanks. I'm not ready for that," then you quenched the Holy Spirit, who is trying to form you to be like Jesus. In that case, it doesn't really matter that you read your Bible at all because you ignored what God was saying to you through it.

When this happens, we shift the disciplines of reading Scripture and prayer from opportunities to be shaped by God to works we accomplish to earn God's favor. If we're not reading the Word or communing with God to be formed by Him, why are we doing it? Usually, it's to make us feel like we're going somewhere on our spiritual journey. But the truth is we're only deluding ourselves if we don't put the Word into practice. That's why James wrote, "Do not merely listen to the word, and so deceive yourselves. Do what it says" (James 1:22).

So why do we often experience stress if we can't spend some uninterrupted time in Scripture? Because we think we're shirking God and we don't trust God to know our minds and hearts. So we either experience guilt and shame, or we go to great lengths to complete our disciplines—a checklist mentality that works great in the office but poorly in spiritual life. We want to congratulate ourselves on being dedicated to God. This is very close to legalism—"seeking to achieve forgiveness from God and acceptance by God through obedience to God."[6]

Legalism doesn't trust the fact that the spatial gap between us and God, caused by our sin, was closed for good by Jesus' death and resurrection. As C. J. Mahaney puts it, "Legalism claims that the death of Jesus on the cross was either unnecessary or insufficient. It essentially says to God, 'Your plan didn't work. The cross wasn't enough and I need to add my good works to it to be saved.'"[7] Can you begin to see why an eternal perspective—keeping in mind all that God has done and accomplished—is needed when it comes to our disciplines? From an eternal perspective, our Scripture reading and times of prayer are interwoven with the events in Scripture themselves and the eternal God who reigns now and forever.

The other problem with looking at our disciplines from a temporal view is that it turns us into spiritual consumers. Instead of coming to Scripture or to God in prayer to be open to Him and His purposes, we treat the Bible as a kind of cosmic Google designed to point us in the right direction to solve our problems. Got work problems? Get the answer for stress relief from Scripture. Kids running wild? Get the answer for biblical principles on parenting from Scripture so that they'll turn to God. Church lacking focus? Get the solution from Scripture so the church will turn around.

Now let me quickly say that we must have a Scriptural perspective in order to live as God's people. The problem with spiritual consumerism is that we expect God to give us what we want just because we looked for a scriptural answer. Have you ever heard anyone say, "I followed God's plan for effective parenting and my son is still on drugs. It didn't work"? Is that really any different from saying, "I tried Zantac for my heartburn, but it didn't work"? Or, is it any different from saying, "I tried Dr. Phil's methods for effective parenting, but my son is still on drugs. It didn't work"? God and His eternal Word become little more than possible remedies for our problems when we act as spiritual consumers. He becomes one choice among many other choices.

Rather than meet with God in Scripture and in prayer out of legalistic guilt or superficial manipulation, we must think of our disciplines as a time to come openly to God. We should set no agenda. Set no time limit.

Avoid any preconceived expectations. And let God lead us where He desires for us to go. If the Word is not living and active in our lives, we're missing the reason we have it: to live in harmony with the kingdom of God—reality as God sees it—until Jesus returns.

We Stop Living Out the Gospel in our Lives

God dictates what is ultimate reality. For us, reality may be the oozing traffic, the stack of memos, or the grocery list we dropped in the gutter. But not for God. God has determined what is reality, even before He created the world. Adam and Eve fell because they adopted a reality spoken by the serpent that was not reality at all. For the Israelites in the desert, reality was walking, eating manna, and complaining. But not according to God. In reality, He was shaping a people. For the Pharisees and teachers of the law, reality was that the carpenter-turned-preacher was an abomination to God. But in reality, He was God's sent One who died for the sins of the world.

So if God is the determiner of reality, what reality are we living in right now? We live in the reality of the gospel: "[Jesus] gave himself for our sins to rescue us from the present evil age, according to the will of our God and Father…" (Galatians 1:4). The Good News about Jesus Christ is the context in which we live. Therefore, as Robert Mulholland Jr. writes, "…we are to immerse ourselves completely in, totally consecrate ourselves to, and unconditionally yield ourselves to this new order of being in Christ that God offers. We are to allow our daily life to be shaped by the dynamics of that new order of being—by its values and structures, by its pervading reality of the presence, purpose, and power of God."[8]

Jesus came to earth, established the kingdom of God, died for our sins, was raised from the dead, and will come back one day to judge the world and consummate the kingdom. That is the unchangeable, overarching framework in which we live our lives. Therefore, we are to conform our lives to this reality with the help of the Holy Spirit who leads us into life in the kingdom: "So I say, live by the Spirit, and you will not gratify the desires of the sinful nature…. Since we live by the Spirit, let us keep in step with the Spirit" (Galatians 5:16, 25).

By now I hope you can see that keeping in step with the Spirit and living out the gospel require an eternal perspective—one that cannot be grasped when we are caught up in the tunnel-vision of the temporal and come to God only to get our gold star for the day or to get an answer to our problems.

So how do you keep from becoming spiritually stagnant? Well, the basics are by coming to God through His Word and in prayer.

"I knew it!" you cry. "Another arm-twist so I'll read my Bible and pray!"

But it's not. I hope I've made a compelling case that spiritual stagnation is a matter of heart distance from God, not absence from spiritual disciplines. If you rely on spiritual "highs" or become so fixated on your temporal circumstances that you close yourself off to God—even while reading and praying—and live in a way inconsistent with the gospel, you'll be spiritually stagnant. But if you come to God in faithful obedience, opening yourself to His shaping influence, taking Him and His Word on His terms, and living out the implications of the gospel each day, you'll avoid stagnation. Not completely of course; God gives us dark nights of the soul to purge us of our dependencies. But for the most part, you'll enjoy a relationship with God where He is leading you to still waters and green pastures.

I don't have all the answers. I'm a fellow struggler, and even though I am a pastor—constantly dealing with eternal things—I can still become buried by a temporal perspective. That's why when it comes to the minefield of spiritual stagnation, perspective and approach are everything.[9] When you find yourself stagnant, I hope you call to mind the words of Isaiah 66:2:

> *Has not my hand made all these things, and so they came into being?" declares the* Lord. *"This is the one I esteem: he who is humble and contrite in spirit, and trembles at my word.*

Notes:

[1] Mark Buchanan, *Your God Is Too Safe: Rediscovering the Wonder of a God You Can't Control* (Sisters, OR: Multnomah, 2001), pp. 143-144.

[2] Steve Farrar, *Point Man: How A Man Can Lead His Family* (Sisters, OR: Multnomah, 1990) p. 113.

[3] Lee Strobel, *Inside the Mind of Unchurched Harry and Mary: How To Reach Friends and Family Who Avoid God and the Church* (Grand Rapids: Zondervan, 1993), p. 124. I like the book in itself, but find the author to be overstating something not necessarily stated or implied by Scripture.

[4] D. A. Carson, *The Gospel According to John: Pillar New Testament Commentary* (Grand Rapids: Eerdmans, 1991), p. 220. Prophecies referred to are Jeremiah 31:29-34; Ezekiel 36:25-27; Joel 2: 28-32.

[5] Richard Foster, *Celebration of Discipline: The Path to Spiritual Growth* (San Francisco: HarperSanFrancisco, 1978), p. 9.

[6] C. J. Mahaney, *The Cross-Centered Life: Keeping the Gospel the Main Thing* (Sisters, OR: Multnomah, 2002), p.25.

[7] *Ibid*, p. 25.

[8] M. Robert Mulholland, Jr., *Shaped By the Word: The Power of Scripture in Spiritual Formation*, Revised Edition (Nashville: Upper Room Books, 2000), p. 77.

[9] For more on the idea of approach and spiritual disciplines, see Mulholland, Jr., *Shaped By the Word*, *Invitation to a Journey: A Road Map for Spiritual Formation* (Downers Grove, IL: InterVarsity Press, 1993).

Chapter 8

Grant, Two Months Later

It was Friday, and as afternoon blended into early evening, the thought of traffic made Grant faintly nostalgic for his old life. After all, when you left the office at 7:00 p.m. or so, traffic had thinned out considerably. Not so at 5:00 p.m., when the business workforce packed themselves "like lemmings into shiny metal boxes," according to the old Police song, and headed for wherever they were heading. This was still quite new for Grant, though 5:00 had become somewhat routine over the last few weeks. Sometimes he wouldn't make it out until 6:00, but he knew better than to leave much later than that. He strode down the office-lined hallway, catching snatches of conversations as his colleagues attempted to wrap up their days.

Grant turned the corner and joined two other employees from a different department—both waiting for the elevator. He didn't really know their names. One was Max or Mack and the other started with R. He was about to engage them in light conversation when one realized he had forgotten something in his office and started back for it. His buddy said he'd go with him—a bit reluctantly, since the elevator bell had dinged and the wait for the next one could take some time. So Grant ambled into the elevator and hit "GARAGE."

There was no distracting Muzak to occupy Grant's thoughts. He tried to think about innocuous things—thinking about life and reality seemed like too much on a Friday afternoon. It was September and the 49ers were 1-0. Grant mentally debated the merits of starting a rookie at quarterback, especially with a questionable offensive line. Maybe a veteran could handle it. "Where have you gone Joe Montana?" Grant thought. "Certainly Montana could…"

Ding! The doors opened and Grant stepped into the parking garage. He turned down an aisle of sports and luxury cars that looked depressed in a parking garage—muzzled almost. He found his own Corvette, disabled the alarm and climbed in. Reflexively, he turned on the radio, which was already on his station of preference—pure classics. Grant donned his sunglasses and, checking incoming and outgoing garage traffic, turned onto the departure ramp.

Grant handed his parking pass to the attendant, a young man who barely looked up from a textbook. Grant waited until the kid had finished his sentence, paragraph, or page. Nodding apathetically, he gave the pass back to Grant. The early evening sun was illuminating the street just beyond the garage overhang. Grant pulled forward.

This was a tricky intersection. It was always busy here, but now he faced a near blur of colors and metal as he tried to peer beyond a row of parked cars that was blocking a clear view of westbound traffic. Thankfully, it was a right turn. A left turn pretty much meant a long wait followed by a game of chicken. He was used to it.

As he was thinking about this, an impulse suddenly rose within him to turn left. *Do it*, he thought. *You know your heart is telling you to. Turn left. You know the way and where it leads. Make the left turn and forget where you're going.*

Jolted by the physical force of the impulse, Grant sat in a near stupor. He resisted turning around to see if someone was in the backseat. Lost in thought, he didn't notice the brief opening in traffic— the opportunity for an easy left or right turn. The driver behind him noticed, though, and issued a hearty honk.

That snapped Grant back to reality. He idled forward, looking left and right. The stoplight heading east turned green and a stream of cars began to eliminate any chance of an easy left turn. But he didn't want to go left, did he? He wasn't sure. He had turned right for the last few weeks at this time, but the impulse to turn left had been strong—and quite frightening. *Is that how it works?* he thought.

Will I always want to turn left when I've convinced myself I should turn right?

Eastbound and westbound traffic cruised by. Grant felt sheepish about missing his earlier opening. He was sure the guy behind him was inventing interesting names for him. Hopefully he had a right turn and could make it out quickly.

When the opening finally came, Grant shot onto Banner St. with a right turn. His momentary confusion had passed and now he was hardly aware that he had debated within himself which way to turn. The Guess Who wrapped up "Hand Me Down World," and Simon and Garfunkel began a live-performance version of "The Boxer."

Two stoplights into Banner St., Grant cut into the left lane and turned onto Garcia. He was only about four minutes away, but Garcia was a busy street. Restaurants and trinket shops lined the sidewalks. Grant sometimes ate at an Indonesian place called "Djakarta." He was especially fond of the chicken shwarmas.

Simon and Garfunkel sang on, and halfway through the song Grant noticed a verse that was not in the studio version of the song. It went like this:

> *Now the years are rolling by me*
> *They are rocking evenly*
> *And I am older than I once was*
> *Younger than I'll be*
> *But that's not unusual.*
> *No it isn't strange*
> *After changes upon changes*
> *We are more or less the same*
> *After changes we are more or less the same.*

What a great song, Grant thought. *A true classic! But is it true for me right now in my life? How can I say I'm the same person I used to be in spite of all the changes? Becoming a husband changed me. Becoming a father changed me. Lying to my boss changed me. Making money changed me. And the path I've chosen has changed me. I'm not anywhere near the same person I was two months ago, let alone years ago. Sorry Paul and Art; I like the imagery of the boxer, but I don't buy this verse.*

Garcia forked into Cassmer and Pohl. Grant, having stayed in the right lane, easily veered onto Pohl. *What's more,* he mused, *I am who I am right now in part because of changes. I would not be driving on Pohl Avenue if I had not made a decision in response to change. Why had I wanted to turn left instead of right? Had I not made a decision in response to changes a few weeks ago, I probably would have turned left. And that's the point; after changes and my responses to those changes, I am quite different. I am still Grant Roth, but a different version of Grant Roth than I was before. Even before yesterday.*

A different voice chimed in: *Do you like this version?* Grant pushed it away. Such a question could put an iceberg-shaped fissure in his soul.

Pohl intersected with Romine. There were fewer businesses here, fewer restaurants. It was still a decent part of town and the apartments that had been constructed only a few years ago still showed features of newness. Grant edged onto Romine. After two blocks, he spied an open parking space and pulled in. He paused for a moment, letting Simon and Garfunkel finish their song, then turned off the purring engine. He opened the driver's side door, stepped onto the street, and looked at the apartment building on the other side.

Against the glint of the sun reflecting off several windows, Grant saw a shade momentarily lift, then descend. She was home. He couldn't even kid himself into thinking he was in any way disappointed. He started forward.

Humming the song, but not agreeing with the words, Grant walked up the front steps as Natalie opened the door to greet him. *No,* Grant thought, *after changes we are most certainly not the same.*

After changes, we are who we decide to be.

What a Horrible Ending!

This is not the ending you would hope for. It's not a happy ending. I like happy endings. I am sure you do, too. But, real life does not always play out that way. People don't always make it safely through the minefield. Sometimes, because of bad choices, people destroy their lives. Obviously, Grant Roth had made some really bad choices. He had chosen to turn right instead of left. Over the past several years, he had made the wrong turn several times. Simon and Garfunkel were wrong. Grant Roth was definitely not "more or less the same."

But, suppose Grant Roth had made some different choices. Suppose he had handled the minefields differently. Let's rewind the tape. Let's start the chapter over. Let's consider a much happier ending—one that God would be pleased with.

Grant, Two Months Later

It was Friday, and as afternoon blended into early evening, the thought of traffic made Grant faintly nostalgic for his old life. After all, when you left the office at 7:00 p.m. or so, traffic had thinned out considerably. Not so at 5:00 p.m., when the business workforce packed themselves "like lemmings into shiny metal boxes," according to the old Police song, and headed for wherever they were heading. This was still quite new for Grant, though 5:00 had become somewhat routine over the last few weeks. Sometimes he wouldn't make it out until 6:00, but he knew better than to leave much later than that. He strode down the office-lined hallway, catching snatches of conversations as his colleagues attempted to wrap up their days.

Grant turned the corner and joined two other employees from a different department —both waiting for the elevator. He didn't really know their names. One was Max or Mack and the other started with R. He was about to engage them in light conversation when one realized he had forgotten something in his office and started back for it. His buddy said he'd go with him—a bit reluctantly, since the elevator bell had dinged and the wait for the next one could take some time. So Grant ambled into the elevator and hit "GARAGE."

There was no distracting Muzak to occupy Grant's thoughts. He tried to think about innocuous things—thinking about life and reality seemed like too much on a Friday afternoon. It was September and the 49ers were 1-0. Grant mentally debated the merits of starting a rookie at quarterback, especially with a questionable offensive line. Maybe a veteran could handle it. "Where have you gone Joe Montana?" Grant thought. "Certainly Montana could…"

Ding! The doors opened and Grant stepped into the parking garage. He turned down an aisle of sports and luxury cars that looked depressed in a parking garage—muzzled almost. He found his own Corvette, disabled the alarm and climbed in. Reflexively, he turned on the radio, which was already on his station of preference—pure classics. Grant donned his sunglasses and, checking incoming and outgoing garage traffic, turned onto the departure ramp.

Grant handed his parking pass to the attendant, a young man who barely looked up from a textbook. Grant waited until the kid had finished his sentence, paragraph, or page. Nodding apathetically, he gave the pass back to Grant. The early evening sun was illuminating the street just beyond the garage overhang. Grant pulled forward.

This was a tricky intersection. It was always busy here, but now he faced a near blur of colors and metal as he tried to peer beyond a row of parked cars that was blocking a clear view of westbound traffic. It didn't help that he needed to make a left turn. A left turn pretty much meant a long wait followed by a game of chicken. He was used to it.

As he was thinking about this, an impulse suddenly rose within him to turn right. *Do it*, he thought. *You know your heart is telling you to. Turn right. You know the way and where it leads. Make the right turn and forget where you're going.*

Jolted by the physical force of the impulse, Grant sat in a near stupor. He resisted turning around to see if someone was in the backseat. Lost in thought, he didn't notice the brief opening in traffic—the opportunity for an easy left or right turn. The driver behind him noticed, though, and issued a hearty honk.

That snapped Grant back to reality. He idled forward, looking left and right. The stoplight heading west turned green and a stream of cars began to eliminate any chance of an easy right turn. But he didn't want to go right, did he? He wasn't sure. He had turned left for the last few weeks at this time, but the impulse to turn right had been strong—and quite frightening. *Is that how it works?* he thought. *Will I always want to turn right when I've convinced myself I should turn left?*

Eastbound and westbound traffic cruised by. Grant felt sheepish about missing his earlier opening. He was sure the guy behind him was inventing interesting names for him. Hopefully he had a right turn and could make it out quickly.

When the opening finally came, Grant shot onto Banner St. with a left turn. His momentary confusion had passed and now he was hardly aware that he had debated within himself which way to turn. The Guess Who wrapped up "Hand Me Down World," and Simon and Garfunkel began a live-performance version of "The Boxer."

Three stoplights into Banner St., Grant shifted into the right lane and turned onto Palmelo. Palmelo was busy, and it being a Friday evening didn't help. Grant wished he had brought something to drink.

Simon and Garfunkel sang on, and halfway through the song Grant noticed a verse that was not in the studio version of the song. It went like this:

Now the years are rolling by me
They are rocking evenly
And I am older than I once was
Younger than I'll be
But that's not unusual.
No it isn't strange
After changes upon changes
We are more or less the same
After changes we are more or less the same.

What a great song, Grant thought. *A true classic! But is it true for me right now in my life? How can I say I'm the same person I used to be in spite of all the changes? Becoming a husband changed me. Becoming a father changed me. Lying to my boss changed me. Making money changed me. And the path I've chosen has changed me. I'm not anywhere near the same person I was two months ago, let alone years ago. Sorry Paul and Art; I like the imagery of the boxer, but I don't buy this verse.*

Palmelo turned into Avery. Traffic was picking up in spots, but more cars were entering the fray. Grant saw that the time was 5:24. *What's more,* he mused, *I am who I am right now in part because of changes. I would not be driving on Avery Avenue if I had not made a decision in response to change. Why had I wanted to turn right instead of left? Had I not made a decision in response to changes a few weeks ago, I probably would have turned right. And that's the point; after changes and my responses to those changes, I am quite different. I am still Grant Roth, but a different version of Grant Roth than I was before. Even before yesterday.*

A different voice chimed in: *Do you like this version?* Grant pushed it away.

Avery branched out into four lanes. Two were left turn lanes onto Harrison, which was a one-way street, and the other two headed toward the expressway. Cars thinned out slightly, allowing him to increase his speed. 82 South was a left turn exit so he checked his blind spot and moved over one lane. He was tired of talking to himself, debating with himself. He was even tired of Simon and Garfunkel. He was tired of a crowd yammering in his head.

Grant's Corvette funneled down the exit curve and began the tricky merge with flowing traffic. Despite the envoy of San Franciscans trying to get wherever they were going, Grant found a hole and merged safely. He would be on 82 South for about fifteen minutes, then he would need to take exit 52 to Dunham. Once on Dunham, he could take a few different ways, depending on how quickly he wanted to get where he was going.

That was home. And home was becoming a good place to be. Not overnight, of course. But in broad strokes and fine touches. Unexpected smiles or laughter. William asking Grant to tuck him in at night. Authentic prayer in the morning, resolving to avail himself of whatever God required of him. Saturday morning coffee. Gratefulness for left turns. They weren't easy turns to make, but he was finding that "easy" doesn't always mean worthwhile.

Humming the song, but not agreeing with the words, Grant accelerated as if rushing to meet the horizon. He felt like a boxer—one who fights and still remains.

No, Grant thought, *after changes we are most certainly not the same. After changes, we are who we decide to be.*

Epilogue

Nobody has a moral failure all at once. Whether the failure is ethical, sexual, or emotional, the path to moral failure is composed of choices—most of them seemingly small and innocuous. But just as Grant made several turns to get where he wanted to go, in both scenarios, our choices compound and lead us wherever we have decided to go. *Minefields in the Marketplace* was written to help you see where God is prompting you to change. The decision is yours. God is that kind of God; He lets us choose our paths. Of course, we have no control over the consequences that lie in either direction.

In my business career, I watched men—good men—make tragic choices and ultimately destroy themselves. But none of them ended up as a casualty of a given landmine all at once. It almost always happened incrementally, by degrees.

That is why I am hoping that you are reading this while you can still make changes. Maybe you've already started down some of the dangerous paths outlined in this book and illustrated in the life of Grant Roth. It's not too late to change directions. Changing directions is called repentance, and repentance leads to grace, and grace leads to change. Refusing to change directions has its own results: "God opposes the proud, but gives grace to the humble" (James 4:6). Find a few other businessmen who also need to examine themselves and can provide a network of support. With God's help, maybe you can even begin to transform the ethos of your company to one that upholds integrity, purity, charity, family, humility, and vibrant walks with God. I wrote this book so that God may be glorified by the future choices you will make, avoiding detonating the ethical landmines that lie in wait. I hope this book has been a blessing to you.

God bless you in all that you are and all that you do.

Minefields in the Marketplace

Study Guide

Chapter One: A Parable

1. In 1998, Grant Roth's mission statement was the epitome of what you would expect from a committed follower of Christ embarking on a business career. What do you think happened to Grant?

2. Though you are just beginning the book, how many "minefields" had Grant already been trapped in? Which one was he dancing dangerously close to?

3. Read through Grant's thought process one more time on pages 8 and 9. Where is his reasoning dangerously flawed?

4. Could what happened to Grant Roth happen to you? If you think it could not, reread the section on David at the end of the chapter.

5. Are you flirting with any minefields right now? Spend some time thinking about it—and be honest.

6. What is the value in having a personal mission statement? Have you ever taken the time to develop one?

7. Besides a personal mission statement, what other steps could you take now to avoid going down the same destructive path that Grant was on?

Minefields in the Marketplace
Study Guide
Chapter Two: The Minefield of Ethical Compromise

1. Contrast the words of the mythical television character J. R. Ewing with the words of Solomon in Proverbs 22:1. What do you suppose J. R. meant? What is Solomon saying about the importance of character and integrity?

2. How many different forms of ethical compromise can you think of? Which one do you believe to be the most common?

3. Why can even a seemingly harmless "fib" come back to bite you? What are some of the most common business "fibs"?

4. Reread the last paragraph on page 18. Why is it so hard to live up to the standard that is given?

5. Stealing from the company can never be an option. So, if you feel that you are being unfairly compensated, what should you do?

6. Reread the quote taken from the book by Bossidy and Charan on page 18. If you are a leader of an organization or department, how much of an impact do you have upon the ethical practices of those who work with you and for you?

7. The story of Ananias and Sapphira is tragic. Though God does not strike dead everyone who tells a lie, what does the fate of Ananias and Sapphira tell us about God's standard in regard to honesty and integrity?

Minefields in the Marketplace
Study Guide
Chapter Three: The Minefield of Materialism

1. Reread Matthew 6:24 on page 27. Why is materialism so destructive to our spiritual well-being?

2. Explain the difference between an "attitude of stewardship" and an "attitude of ownership." When it comes to your personal spending, do you seek to bring God into your decisions?

3. How does an "attitude of contentment" help us avoid the "debt trap?"

4. What would be a biblically-based perspective on personal debt?

5. Why is it that people who are overextended financially, vocationally, and recreationally are often not available to serve God? How would you rate your availability to God?

6. Reread "The Parable of the Great Banquet" on page 34. What is the lesson Jesus is teaching?

7. It has been said that materialism is the most common form of idolatry in America today. What steps are you taking to avoid this tempting minefield? Do you need a new strategy?

Minefields in the Marketplace
Study Guide
Chapter Four: The Minefield of Power

1. Numbers 12:3 in the New International Version reads "Now Moses was a very humble man, more humble than anyone else on the face of the earth." How do humility and effective leadership go together?

2. Do you agree with the author's statement that "How you exercise power over those you manage, and how you submit to those who have power over you, will greatly influence your career success, your Christian testimony, and whether you live a life that is pleasing to God"? Why, or why not?

3. As leaders and managers of people, it is very important that we remember that God is the source of power and authority. Why is it so important?

4. How is the story of Solomon a warning to those who daily exercise power and authority over others in the corporate world?

5. The Bible teaches that all individuals bear the "image" of God. How should this biblical teaching impact your use of power and authority in the workplace? Are you regularly showing dignity and respect to those God has placed under your authority?

6. Are you currently bringing glory to God as you function each day on the job? In what areas of your testimony and witness do you need to improve?

7. Do you consider the workplace to be a mission field? How will exercising power and authority in a godly way help you as you seek to evangelize co-workers?

Study Guide

Chapter Five: The Minefield of Sexual Temptation

1. Reread Proverbs 4:23 and 4:25. What did Solomon mean when he advised us to *guard our hearts and mark out our paths*?

2. Reread Proverbs 5-7. Can you list five or six words that Solomon uses to describe the person who engages in adultery? Do you agree? Why or why not?

3. What does it mean to commit adultery in one's heart? According to Jesus' definition of adultery (Matthew 5:28), is viewing pornography on the Internet a sin?

4. In your daily business life do you "plan" for purity? Why is "hope" not a strategy?

5. What does it mean to schedule yourself out of temptation?

6. When you travel out of town on business, do you take a "spiritual" workload?

7. Are you careful about what you view on television when you are alone in a motel room? Do you watch things you would be embarrassed to watch with your wife?

Study Guide

Chapter Six: The Minefield of Neglected Relationships

1. Reread the quote from Arterburn and Stoeker on the first page of the chapter. Do you agree with their premise? Under normal circumstances, what is a reasonable number of hours per week for a Christian husband and father to spend at work?

2. When you are at home, are you truly partnering with your wife in training your children? Would your wife say you are loving her in the way Scripture commands? (Ephesians 5:25)

3. Do you treat your family better than you treat your best client? If not, spend some time reflecting and praying about your priorities. Do you need to make some changes?

4. Reread the quote by Erwin McManus on page 74. Are you investing in your children the amount of time that it takes to be the "influencer" God wants you to be?

5. Why is it foolish to think that life will settle down at some point in the future? What would be a better solution to the family time "crunch"?

6. Reread the list of things that real men do to avoid the Minefield of Neglected Relationships. Set some goals and measure your progress. Are you really serious about making changes?

Study Guide

Chapter Seven: The Minefield of Spiritual Stagnation

1. How would you define "spiritual anorexia"? In short, what leads to this tragic condition?

2. Why is it dangerous to perceive of the Christian life as a series of thrilling episodes and "peak to peak" experiences?

3. What does it mean to live life with eternity in mind? How do we cultivate an eternal mindset?

4. How are you currently making yourself available to God so that He can renew your soul? Do you need to make some adjustments or changes?

5. How is it possible to pray and read your Bible regularly, and still have a heart that is closed off to God?

6. What does it mean to be a spiritual consumer? Why do you think it is so common among American Christians?

7. What does it mean to stop living out the gospel in your life? How does one avoid this dangerous trap?

8. Do you agree that "spiritual stagnation is a matter of heart distance from God, not absence from spiritual disciplines"? Explain your answer.

Minefields in the Marketplace

Study Guide

Chapter Eight: Grant, Two Months Later

A Few Final Questions and Challenges

1. Have you fallen victim to any of the minefields described in this book? If so, determine right now to seek God's mercy, forgiveness, and power. Read 1 John 1:9 and 2 Peter 1:3-4.

2. If you have not been caught in one of the minefields, is there one to which you are dancing dangerously close? Do you need a strategy for avoiding the minefield? Remember, "hope" is not a strategy.

3. As you have read the book, have you become aware of any minefields not mentioned? What would it/they be?

4. Do you recognize any of Grant Roth's struggles in your own life? If so, determine now to please God no matter what!